W9-BLB-229

The
UNIX System

INTERNATIONAL COMPUTER SCIENCE SERIES

Consulting editors   **A D McGettrick**
University of Strathclyde

J van Leeuwen
University of Utrecht

UNIX™ is a trademark of Bell Laboratories

The UNIX System

S R BOURNE (Bell Laboratories)

ADDISON-WESLEY PUBLISHING COMPANY

Wokingham, England • Reading, Massachusetts
Menlo Park, California • Don Mills, Ontario
Amsterdam • Bonn • Sydney • Singapore • Tokyo
Madrid • Bogota • Santiago • San Juan

© 1983 Bell Telephone Laboratories, Incorporated

All rights reserved. No part of this publication may be reproduced, stored in a retrieval system, or transmitted in any form or by any means, electronic, mechanical, photocopying, recording or otherwise, without prior written permission of the publisher. Printed in the United States of America. Published simultaneously in Canada.

This book was set by the author in Times Roman and Helvetica on an APS-5 photo-typesetter using output generated by the troff text-processing system.

Library of Congress Cataloging in Publication Data
Bourne, S. R., 1944–
    The UNIX system.

    (The International computer science series)
    Includes index.
    1. UNIX (Computer system)   I. Title.   II. Title:
    The U.N.I.X. system.   III. Series.
QA76.8.U65B68 1983   001.64'25   82-13888
ISBN 0-201-13791-7

British Library Cataloguing in Publication Data
Bourne, S.R.
    The UNIX system. – (International computer science
    series; 6)
    1. UNIX (Computer program)
    1. Title   II. Series
    001.64'25   QA76.6

    ISBN 0-201-13791-7

JKLM-DO—8987

To Jane, Peter, Mark, and Sarah

Preface

This book is a practical guide to the UNIX system and all users from the novice to the expert should find it useful. Many examples are used throughout the text to illustrate techniques that make the system attractive to use. By giving examples of the interactions between commands, the user is able to take full advantage of the power of the UNIX system.

The introduction reviews the historical background that led to early UNIX systems and presents the components of UNIX systems, including files and processes. The body of the book covers the major elements of the UNIX system including file management, process management, system calls, the editor, the shell, C language, troff and nroff, and the data management tools.

Chapter 2 introduces the user to the system along with some commonly used commands. The logging in procedure is explained and the available documentation is described. The two major topics introduced are the shell and the file system. All later chapters assume that this chapter has been read.

Two editors are introduced in chapter 3, ed and vi. Both programs are intended for use at a terminal and are used to create and modify files. During chapters 2 and 3 it is a good idea to have a terminal close by and to try some of the commands. If you cannot make progress ask a colleague for help. This is often the quickest way to learn how to use a system.

The shell provides the interface to the UNIX system both for interactive users and for scripts used to tailor the environment for an individual or project. Interactive use of the shell is first introduced in chapter 2. Writing shell scripts, or programs, is covered in depth in chapter 4.

The C language is introduced in chapter 5 in sufficient detail to allow reasonable sized programs to be written. Familiarity with another programming language is an advantage when reading this chapter. Managing the source for programs using make and debugging using adb are also covered here.

The next chapter describes the UNIX system interface as seen by C programmers. The emphasis is on writing programs that use the facilities provided directly by the operating system. This chapter is intended for users who write commands in C. The more advanced aspects of the file system, not described in chapter 2, are also presented.

One of the major uses of the UNIX system is text processing and document preparation. The set of programs nroff, troff, eqn, and tbl is described in chapter 7 and, together with the text editor, allow documents to be drafted and corrected with considerable ease. This chapter also contains a worked example of the formatting package used for this book.

The last chapter covers the data processing 'toolkit' consisting of programs such as awk, grep, sort, and join that provide a flexible way to manage small data bases or manipulate small quantities of data. Examples are presented of complete systems built from these parts. Each example is described in detail and the construction of new tools, not provided with the standard UNIX system, is also presented. The material from all the earlier chapters is required when reading chapter 8.

The appendices summarize the various commands used throughout the book.

This book covers many aspects of the UNIX system from the user's point of view. It assumes that the reader has some familiarity with modern computing terminology.

Acknowledgements

Many people have contributed to this book.

I am indebted to Andrew McGettrick without whose help this book would never have been finished.

I am particularly grateful to Al Aho, Doug McIlroy, and Bob Allen who read the entire book and gave detailed comments.

I would also like to thank Bob Morris, Dennis Ritchie and my other colleagues in the Computer Science Research Center for many discussions on the finer points of the UNIX system.

I would like to thank Mark Bourne, Charlie Harris, Peter Honeyman, Jim Kaiser, Mike Lesk, Dave Sincoskie, Andy Tanenbaum, Todd Tieger, and several members of Andy Hall's department at Bell Laboratories who read parts of various drafts and gave me their comments.

I am grateful to Sarah Mallen and Ann Strunk, of the Staff at Addison Wesley, and Jane Bourne for help with the final proof reading.

Marylu Buono, Geri Marki, and Sue Ward provided valuable assistance typing early drafts.

The environment provided by Bob Lucky and Hal Alles in the Computer Systems Research Laboratory is excellent and made writing this book possible.

Lastly, I would like to thank my family for their support.

Contents

Chapter 1

Introduction

UNIX describes a family of computer operating systems developed at Bell Laboratories. The UNIX system includes both the operating system and its associated commands. The operating system manages the resources of the computing environment by providing a hierarchical file system, process management and other housekeeping functions. The commands provided include basic file and data management, editors, assemblers, compilers and text formatters. A powerful command interpreter is available and this allows individual users or projects to tailor the environment to suit their own style by defining their own commands.

The background leading up to the first UNIX system is worth exploring. During the sixties the major issues being addressed by the computing science community included programming language and operating system design. In the former area such languages as PL/I, APL, SIMULA 67, ALGOL 68 and COBOL were designed and were the subject of debate, often fierce, over their relative merits. In the United Kingdom the Combined Programming Language project (CPL) was undertaken jointly by London and Cambridge Universities but failed to produce any direct results. However, it did form the basis for BCPL (Basic CPL), an ingredient of the story.

The operating systems of this period were designed for medium and large scale computers as a means of sharing the resources among users in a cost effective way. Time-sharing and interactive (as opposed to batch) use was introduced. Such questions as paging strategies, protection, activity scheduling and file system design were explored. Systems like CTSS (Crisman, 1965), Multics (Feiertag, 1969) and, in Europe, the Cambridge Multiple Access System (Hartley, 1968) were being designed and provided many of the key ideas found in the UNIX system. For example, file systems and device independent input-output, processes and command languages were all available in one form or another in these systems.

1.1 History

The story begins with Ken Thompson in 1968. Thompson had recently returned from Berkeley where Butler Lampson was working on the SDS930 operating system (Deutsch and Lampson, 1965). Dennis Ritchie joined Bell Laboratories in 1967 from Harvard where his interest was applied mathematics.

Thompson shared space with a talented group many of whom had recently abandoned Multics; a joint project between Bell Laboratories, General

1

Electric, and The Massachussets Institute of Technology. Following the with-
drawal of Bell Laboratories from Multics and the removal of the GE 645 system in March 1969, the computer science research group began looking for a
replacement computing environment. Proposals for new equipment were submitted and rejected as too expensive. Also, operating system development
was not a popular research direction after the Multics debacle.

Thompson's own interests were to build a file system rather than an
operating system. During discussions between Rudd Canaday, Thompson and
Ritchie the design was sketched out and Thompson wrote simulations of early
versions of this file system on the GECOS system.

Another thread of the story is the 'space travel' program written on the
GECOS machine by Thompson and Ritchie. This program performed poorly
on the time-shared computer and better response was needed. A cast-off
PDP 7 with a 340 display was available but the PDP 7 provided only an assembler and loader. One user at a time could use the computer, each user
having exclusive use of the machine. This environment was crude and parts
of a single user UNIX system were soon forthcoming. The space travel program was rewritten for the PDP 7 and an assembler and rudimentary operating system kernel were written and cross assembled for the PDP 7 on the
GECOS system. This early system did not provide time-sharing. Indeed,
much like the modern personal computers, the PDP 7 hardware was simple
and provided no support for such activities. An assembler and a command
interpreter were soon available. This file system provided a name structure
that was a directed graph. A single directory was used for all sub-directories
and links made through this directory.

Cross assembling meant using two computer systems and carrying paper
tapes of programs from one to the other each time a change was made. The
system was soon bootstrapped onto the PDP 7. The process creation primitive, fork, and process images were added to the system during this rewrite.
Essential utilities, such as file copy, edit, remove, and print were soon available. This system supported two people working at the same time and the
term UNIX was coined by Brian Kernighan in 1970.

The computing research group still had no computer of its own. Following a series of unsuccessful attempts a proposal was made by Joe Ossanna to
purchase a PDP 11/20 for a text preparation project. In late 1970 the PDP
11 arrived and work started to transfer the UNIX system to this more powerful machine.

The text processing project was successful and the Patent department became the first user of UNIX, sharing the facility with the research group.
This First Edition system was documented in a manual authored by Thompson and Ritchie dated November 1971. All the important ideas found in
modern UNIX systems except pipes, but including the file system, process
management, system interface, and major command utilities, were provided
with this edition.

The Second Edition appeared in June 1972 incorporating pipes at Doug
McIlroy's urging. The system and utilities were still written in assembler.
Thompson had also been working on the language B and the assembler for

this system was written in B. B was a direct descendant of BCPL, but programs were compiled in one pass to produce interpretive code.

Both B and BCPL were typeless languages, providing a single data object called the machine word making access to the PDP 11 byte handling instructions difficult. Types were therefore added to B to produce NB and an attempt to rewrite the system in NB was unsuccessful. Ritchie started work on a code generator for NB to make execution of programs faster. This language was called C although there were no structures or global variables. The language was sufficiently attractive, however, that new utilities were being written directly in C.

The year 1973 saw major progress. The system was still written in assembler but following the addition of structures to C the UNIX system was successfully rewritten in C. Thompson wrote the process management and Ritchie the input-output system.

The Sixth Edition UNIX system that became the first widely available version was issued in May 1975, and was distributed for a nominal fee.

Work continued to improve the system. A new file system allowing for larger files was written and the shell was modernized to provide better support for the many programs written in this language. The last major project undertaken by Thompson and Ritchie was to rewrite the system so that it could be transported from one computer to another. The pilot project used an Interdata 8/32, a 32-bit computer similar to the IBM 370 series, that was sufficiently different from the PDP 11 to unearth most machine dependencies. This project also generated some additions to the C language, including unions, casts, and type definitions. This work resulted in the production of the Seventh Edition UNIX system released for general use in 1979. Although the Sixth edition is still in use in some installations it has been generally superseded by the Seventh Edition system.

The UNIX system is now regarded as a standard operating system and has been implemented on many different computers ranging from micros to mainframes. The Seventh Edition system was made available for the PDP 11 16-bit computers. The first VAX 11/780 system, UNIX 32V, was bootstrapped by John Reiser and Tom London, also at Bell Laboratories. This system was further developed, and is now distributed by the University of California at Berkeley. Bell Laboratories has also continued to develop the UNIX system; UNIX System V is the version currently available for license from Western Electric Co.

Some differences exist between these versions both in the operating system and in the commands although these should cause the reader little difficulty. This text is applicable to each of these systems and features found in only one system have been avoided. The programs in this book have been compiled and run on UNIX System V from Bell Laboratories, and on the University of California, Berkeley release 4.1.

Many commands were initially written for the PDP 11 where address space was limited to 64K bytes. This constraint had a generally beneficial effect on the software. Systems are designed as a set of loosely coupled commands. Lack of address space did prevent such languages as LISP from effective implementation until the arrival of 32 bit machines.

The UNIX system is well engineered and has set a standard of simplicity for time-shared operating systems. It was one of the first operating systems to be widely available on a mini-computer, namely the PDP 11. This combination was affordable by university departments and a generation of computer scientists has been educated on UNIX systems.

The initial interface has aged well and is essentially unchanged since its original design. This stability provided the basis for the development of the user level commands. The UNIX documentation has a conciseness that is appealing although some consider it to be too brief.

The UNIX system is very successful. At the time of writing there are over 3000 UNIX systems in active use throughout the world. These can be found in universities, government laboratories, commercial organizations and many other areas of industry. At Bell Laboratories it is used by staff members both for interactive program development and as a communications and word processing system. The system is portable, easily grasped by both users and maintainers, and provides facilities not available in other, sometimes larger, systems.

1.2 The programming environment

The UNIX system is simple and elegant and provides an attractive programming environment. The facilities available include the following:

- a C compiler and debugger;
- a variety of other language processors, including APL, Basic, Fortran 77, Pascal, and Snobol;
- the text editors ed, vi, and emacs;
- text processing facilities and document preparation aids including mathematical typesetting tbl, eqn, troff, and nroff;
- compiler construction aids yacc, and lex;
- communication among users mail, and write;
- graphics and plotting; and
- applications such as circuit design packages.

These tools are made available to users via a command language that provides the interface between users and the UNIX operating system. This program is called the *shell* and programs written in this language are sometimes referred to as shell scripts.

The shell provides notation for directing input and output from commands and control flow mechanisms typical of algorithmic languages.

Techniques for effective program development have emerged in this environment and include the following:

- Arrange each program to perform a single function.
- Avoid cluttering the output of a program unnecessarily. Assume that the output from any program will be the input to another.
- Use or modify an existing tool if possible rather than rewrite a new

tool from scratch.

- Get something small working as soon as possible and then modify it incrementally until it is finished. This requires that the framework of the design should be in place before significant quantities of program are written.

1.3 UNIX system concepts

1.3.1 The file system

A file system allows users to store information by name. Protection from hardware failures can be provided and security from unauthorized access is also available. The UNIX file system is simple; there are no control blocks, devices are hidden, and there is a uniform interface for all input-output. Within the file system three types of file are distinguished.

- An ordinary file contains characters of a document or program. Executable programs (binary files) are also stored as ordinary files. No record structure is imposed on files; a file consists of a sequence of characters. A newline character may delimit records as required by applications.
- A directory holds the names of other files or directories. A user may create sub-directories to group files related to a project. Consequently, the file system is a hierarchy. A directory can be read, but not written, as if it were an ordinary file.
- Special files correspond to input or output devices. The same interface as ordinary files is available; however, information is not kept in the file system, it is provided directly by the device. The same access protection is available for special and ordinary files.

1.3.2 Processes

All user work in the UNIX system is carried out by processes. A process is a single sequence of events and consists of some computer memory and files being accessed. A process is created by a copy of the process being made. The two processes are only distinguished by the parent being able to wait for the child to finish. A process may replace itself by another program to be executed. This mechanism is both elegant and effective.

1.3.3 The shell

The shell is a command language that provides a user interface to the UNIX operating system. The shell executes commands that are read either from a terminal or from a file. Files containing commands may be created, allowing users to build their own commands. These newly defined commands have the same status as 'system' commands. In this way a new environment can be established reflecting the requirements or style of an individual or a group.

Pipes allow processes to be linked together so that the output from one process is the input to the next. The shell provides a notation enabling pipes to be used with a minimum of effort.

Chapter 2

Getting Started

2.1 Logging in

Before you can start using the system you will need a *login-name* from your system administrator. If your system uses dial-up lines you will also need the phone number of your system. In addition to your login-name you will be given a password that protects your login-name from unauthorized use.

The UNIX system supports many different terminal types ranging from simple printers to high resolution graphics terminals. Since terminals differ be sure that all the options are set appropriately. Options to check for include terminal speed, parity (even/odd), full duplex (remote), and upper/lower case; phone connections (via modems) usually operate at 300 or 1200 baud, whereas hardwired connections are more likely to operate at 1200 or 9600 baud. (300 baud is approximately 30 characters per second.)

When you first connect to the system it tries to detect the speed of your line from the first character you type, usually a **return**. If the computer prints some garbage characters try hitting **break** briefly; in some systems this signals a change of speed.

Eventually you should see

    login:

and you should now type your login-name followed by a **return**. Until you type **return** the system will normally do nothing. **login** will now ask for your password and, if possible, the terminal printing is turned off while you reply. If your login-name and password do not correspond to those known by the system

    login incorrect

is printed and you will again be prompted for your login-name. Some versions of **login** have a timeout that hangs up the line if you wait too long to type your password.

If you log in successfully a message may be printed, called the 'message-of-the-day'. This will be followed by a prompt character, usually a $ or %, from the shell. You can now start typing commands to the system.

If something goes wrong and you are unable to log in then you should get help from a local expert. There are too many potential problems to enumerate here.

2.2 Commands

A command consists of a sequence of words separated by white space (spaces or tabs). The first (and possibly the only) word is the name of the command. To illustrate,

    date

will respond with output of the form

    Wed Sep 1 12:12:19 EDT 1982

The three letters EDT denote Eastern Daylight Time.
    The command

    who

will produce a list of those users currently logged on, in order of terminal number, e.g.

    srb   tty00   May 5   11:30
    jmg   tty01   May 5   21:22
    lca   tty13   May 5   22:29
    cc   tty29   May 5   16:11
    jack   tty41   May 5   08:39

Your own login-name should appear in this list along with the time you logged in and your terminal (tty) number. The abbreviation tty is derived from Teletype, a manufacturer of terminals.
    When more than one word appears in a command the second and subsequent words are available as *arguments* to the executed command. For example, to change your password after you are logged on, type

    passwd srb

replacing srb by your own login-name. The passwd command will then prompt as follows:

    Old password:
    New password:
    Retype new password:

A password of at least six characters is recommended; some systems enforce this minimum but the practice should be observed to make password detection more difficult. Following each prompt terminal printing is turned off.
    Another example of a command with arguments is the calendar printing command. cal prints a calendar for a particular year or month. With one argument cal prints the calendar for the entire year specified by the argument. The calendar for a particular month is printed by giving the month and year as arguments. For example, cal 2000 prints a calendar for the year 2000 and

    cal 9 1982

prints

```
         September  1982
     S   M  Tu   W  Th   F   S
                  1   2   3   4
     5   6   7   8   9  10  11
    12  13  14  15  16  17  18
    19  20  21  22  23  24  25
    26  27  28  29  30
```

2.3 Terminal characteristics

Mistakes made while typing at the terminal may be corrected by *erasing* characters or by *killing* (deleting) a whole line and retyping. To erase a character a # is used. For example,

    passq#wd

is equivalent to

    passwd

To kill (or delete) a line, @ is used and the system will respond by printing a **newline**. These two characters (erase and kill) can be redefined by the user. Early UNIX systems used # and @ for character and line delete respectively and these are still the default; however, for video terminals **backspace** is a convenient erase character.

Terminals that use the ASCII character code use the character **return** on input to end a line. On output this character is printed as a **return** followed by a **linefeed** and this combination is often referred to as **newline**.

Terminal options are described to the system using the **stty** (set tty) command. These options can be expected to differ from terminal to terminal and may be altered by an individual user. For example,

    stty erase ~

alters the erase character to ~, so that, typing

    whx~o

is equivalent to **who**.

If the erase and kill characters, # or @, are needed as input, a \ is used as an escape character to prevent their interpretation as erase and kill. Then \# is equivalent to # and \@ is equivalent to @.

When a program loops, or when enough has been seen of the output of a program, it may be necessary to interrupt the activity. The **del** character or a **break** generates an interrupt signal for this purpose. Normally **del** or **break** cause the shell and other interactive programs to resume at the command level with a prompt. The character that generates the interrupt can be altered using the **stty** command; however, **break** is a signal transmitted on the serial line, and cannot, therefore, be changed.

Some terminals have a tab mechanism available that may need to be set when the terminal is switched on. The **tabs** command may be used to set the tabs for output on your terminal. Some older terminals do not interpret tabs on output and some have no **tab** key for input. On terminals that do not possess a **tab** key, the **tab** character can be entered using control-I. If your terminal does not print tabs correctly the command

    stty —tabs

can be used to instruct the system to replace tabs by a suitable number of spaces on output. An 8-space tab is assumed. The **stty** command (appendix 1) has many other options for describing terminal characteristics.

The notation used in this book for control characters such as control-I is ^I. Two other characters are available to stop and start the flow of output at a terminal. ^S will stop the flow of output to the terminal and ^Q will restart the output. Typing any other character will also restart the flow and the character will be passed on to the program. This way of controlling the flow of output is invisible to the executing program.

2.4 Documentation

A user has access to over 150 different system commands. These do not include commands written by users themselves. Complete descriptions of the system commands are available from the *UNIX Programmer's Manual*. Appendix 1 also contains summaries of the more frequently used UNIX commands.

CAL(1)   UNIX Programmer's Manual   CAL(1)

NAME
        cal — print calendar

SYNOPSIS
        cal [month] year

DESCRIPTION
        cal prints a calendar for the specified year. If a
        month is also specified, a calendar just for that month
        is printed. *year* can be between 1 and 9999. The
        month is a number between 1 and 12. The calendar
        produced is that for England and her colonies.
        Try September 1752.

BUGS The year is always considered to start in January even
        though this is historically naive. Beware that 'cal 78'
        refers to the early Christian era, not the 20th century.

Figure 2.1 The output from man cal

The documentation is also available on-line using the man command that prints sections of the user manual given a command name. For example,

man cal

will print the manual page for the cal command as shown in figure 2.1.

References to other commands take the form

command-name (section)

For example, a reference to the stty command would appear as stty (1).

A standard format is used for each of the manual entries; there are at least three sections:

NAME Gives the name of the command and a short description of its effect.

SYNOPSIS

This section summarizes the use of the command. Words appearing in bold are typed literally as they appear. Other words denote arguments to the command as described in the DESCRIPTION section. An argument beginning with a minus sign often indicates an option applicable to the command. Square brackets indicate arguments that may be omitted. Ellipses (...) indicate the possible repetition of the previous argument. For example,

stty [option ...]

is the SYNOPSIS for the stty command; the command name is stty and one or more options may follow.

DESCRIPTION

Describes the effect of the command and how its arguments are interpreted.

Other sections may also be present. A FILES section indicates files used by the command; a SEE ALSO section refers to related commands; a DIAGNOSTICS section discusses diagnostic information that may be produced; finally, a BUGS section lists known bugs and design errors in the command.

The manual is divided into eight major sections. The breakdown for each section is given below:

1   Commands available to users.
2   UNIX/C system call interface.
3   C library routines, including the standard input-output package, stdio, and the mathematical function library.
4   Special files.
5   File formats and conventions.
6   Games.
7   Word processing packages.
8   System maintenance commands and procedures.

Appendix 1 contains a brief description of the commands in this book and the Bibliography lists related documents.

Another program called learn provides computer aided instruction. Lessons are available for basic commands and file handling, the editor, advanced file handling, the eqn program for typing mathematics, the −ms package of formatting macros, and an introduction to the C programming language.

2.5 The file system

The file system provides a hierarchical naming structure. Each directory contains the names of files or further directories. There is no formatting of the file contents; each file consists simply of a sequence of characters. It is convenient to establish conventions for formatting files but this is left to individual programs. The UNIX system knows about the file format used by executable programs (a.out files).

A complete file name or *pathname* is written as a sequence of component names separated by /. The pathname

```
/usr/srb/mbox
```

starts with the directory / called the *root* that contains usr. The directory /usr contains the directory srb and within this directory is the file mbox. In this example there are three directories: /, /usr, and /usr/srb, each of which, except /, is contained in its predecessor or *parent* directory. Each / separated component of a name is limited to 14 characters. Component names may not include / and should not start with characters such as − since this can lead to confusion between command options and file names.

Directories are used to group together files related by ownership or by the purpose for which they are to be used.

Initially, each user will have a *home* directory created by the system administrator; user rhm will typically have a directory such as /usr/rhm.

Each logged in user has a *working directory*. The command

```
pwd
```

will print the complete pathname of the current (or working) directory. Immediately after logging in, the working directory is the user's home directory. (See also $HOME in the shell.)

To specify a new working directory the cd command (for change directory) is used. File names may be specified relative to the working directory. For example, after executing

```
cd /usr/srb/unix
```

the current directory will be /usr/srb/unix and the file /usr/srb/unix/ch1 can be referred to as ch1.

A user may create further subdirectories to hold files related to different projects as illustrated below.

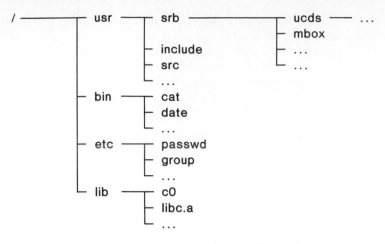

The directory /usr contains system and user directories. /etc contains control files including the password file. /bin contains executable system commands and /lib contains essential libraries including the C compiler and library. Further information about the directory structure is available in the hier section of the *UNIX Programmer's Manual*.

2.5.1 Simple file manipulation

The cat (catenate) command is one of the primitive file copying commands and copies a list of files to its standard output. The standard output is, initially, attached to the terminal although this may be changed (see below). cat is normally used to print a file at the terminal, as in,

    cat /etc/motd

that prints the file /etc/motd. (This file contains the message-of-the-day printed by login.) If no files names are given as arguments then cat reads input from the standard input. By default the standard input is also connected to the terminal.

The cat command may be used to create files by typing the contents at the terminal. For example,

    cat >newfile
    text of file
    ^D

creates the file newfile. Input is terminated by an end-of-file indication from the terminal, signaled by return followed by ^D (control-D).

This technique is of limited value. When a typing error is made only the erase and kill characters can be used. It is more convenient to use a text editor to create a file and then mistakes can be corrected as they are made. Editing files is discussed in Chapter 3.

To copy the contents of one file to another the copy command, cp, is usually used. The form of use of cp is

```
cp from to
```

where both the file names from and to are required. The two commands

```
cat file
```

and

```
cp file /dev/tty
```

are equivalent, since /dev/tty is the file name corresponding to the terminal.

If necessary cp and cat create files. Files can also be renamed and re-moved. The rm command completely removes both a file name and its con-tents. For example,

```
rm junk
```

will remove the file named junk in the current directory. If a file is removed by mistake it can sometimes be recovered by a system administrator.

The mv command moves (or renames) a file. To illustrate,

```
mv oldname newname
```

renames the file oldname as newname. The name of the file is changed, but the contents are unaltered. If the destination file, newname, exists then it is replaced by mv. If the file cannot be written the user is prompted to verify that the file should be removed. If the response is a y then the file is re-moved. Both rm and mv should be used carefully since they may destroy in-formation.

2.5.2 Manipulating directories

Files can be created, deleted, or renamed. The same operations can be ap-plied to directories. However, for directories these operations are privileged and can be performed only using the commands:

```
mkdir    Create (or make) a directory.
rmdir    Remove an empty directory.
mv       Rename a directory.
```

If the current directory is /usr/mdm,

```
mkdir tmg
```

creates the directory /usr/mdm/tmg and

```
rmdir tmg
```

removes it. rmdir only removes empty directories that are not in use as a current directory.

When a directory is created two standard entries . and .. are automati-cally created as a convenience. The name . is synonymous with the directory itself and the name .. refers to the immediate parent directory. The file

names ./mbox and ˜box are therefore equivalent. If /usr/mdm/tmg is the
current directory,

>   cd ..

will return to the parent directory, /usr/mdm, as the new current directory.
    Files may be moved or copied as a group into a directory using the mv or
cp command. Both

>   mv file₁ file₂ ... directory

and

>   cp file₁ file₂ ... directory

achieve this effect, the files having their original names in the new directory.
The first moves or renames; the latter copies, leaving the original files unchanged.
    When moving or copying files to a directory, particular care should be
taken to ensure that the destination is a directory since the mv command also
removes files. For example,

>   mv x d
>   mv y d
>   mv z d

will rename the files x, y, and z as d/x, d/y, and d/z respectively, if d is a
directory. If not, x is renamed as d, then y is renamed as d overwriting the
previous file. Finally, the file z will be renamed as d.

2.6 The shell

Simple commands are written as sequences of *words* separated by spaces.
The first word is the name of the command to be executed. Any remaining
words are passed as arguments to the invoked command. For example, the
command

>   ls −l

prints a list of file names in the current directory. The argument −l (l for
long) tells ls to print the date of last use, the size, and status information for
each file. The output is sorted alphabetically by file name.
    To execute a command, the shell normally creates a new process and
waits for it to finish. Both of these operations are primitives available in the
operating system. A command may be run without waiting for it to finish using the postfix operator &. For example,

>   print file &

calls the print command with argument file and runs it in the background.
The & is a metacharacter interpreted by the shell and is not passed as an argument to print. To help keep track of such a process the shell reports its

process number following its creation. A list of currently active processes may be obtained using the ps command.

Associated with each process, the system maintains a set of file descriptors numbered 0,1,... that are used in all input-output transactions between processes and the operating system. File descriptor 0 is termed the standard input and file descriptor 1 the standard output. Most commands produce their output on the standard output that is initially (following login) connected to a terminal. An *error output* is also provided and is conventionally used for error messages. The standard output may be redirected for the duration of a command, as in

    ls −l >file

The notation >file is interpreted by the shell and is not passed as an argument to ls. If the file does not exist, the shell creates it; otherwise, the contents of the file are replaced with the output from the command and the original file contents are lost. To append to the end of a file, the notation >> is provided, as in

    ls −l >>file

Similarly, the standard input may be taken from a file instead of the terminal, by writing

    wc <file

The wc command prints the number of characters, words, and lines contained in the standard input.

2.6.1 Pipes and filters

The standard output of one command may be connected to the standard input of another with the *pipe* operator, indicated by |, as in,

    ls −l | wc

Two commands connected in this way constitute a *pipeline,* and the effect is similar to

    ls −l >file
    wc <file

except that no file is used. Instead, the two processes are connected by a pipe that is created by an operating system call. Pipes are uni-directional; synchronization is achieved by halting wc when there is nothing to read and halting ls when the pipe is full. The synchronization is provided by the operating system, not the shell.

A *filter* is a command that reads its input, transforms it in some way, and prints the result as output. One such filter, grep, selects from its input those lines that contain some specified string. For example,

```
ls | grep old
```

prints those lines, if any, from the output of ls that contain the string old. Another useful filter is sort. For example,

```
who | sort
```

will print an alphabetically sorted list of logged in users.

A pipeline may consist of more than two commands, for example,

```
ls | grep old | wc −l
```

prints the number of file names in the current directory containing the string old.

2.6.2 File name generation

Many commands accept arguments that are file names. For example,

```
ls −l main.c
```

prints information relating to the file main.c.

The shell provides a mechanism for generating a list of file names that match a pattern. For example,

```
ls −l *.c
```

generates, as arguments to ls, all file names in the current directory that end in .c. The character * is a pattern that will match any string including the null string. In general, shell patterns are specified using the following notation.

*	Match any string of characters including the null string.
?	Match any single character.
[...]	Match any of the characters enclosed. A pair of characters separated by a minus will match any character lexically between the pair.

For example,

```
[a−z]*
```

matches all names in the current directory beginning with one letter from a through z.

```
/usr/fred/epns/?*
```

matches all names in the directory /usr/fred/epns that consist of at least one character. If no file name is found that matches the pattern then the pattern is passed, unchanged, as an argument.

This mechanism is useful both to save typing and to select names according to some pattern. It may also be used for finding files. For example,

```
echo /usr/fred/*/core
```

finds and prints the names of all core files in first-level directories of /usr/fred. (echo is a standard command that prints its arguments, separated by spaces.) This last feature can be expensive, requiring a scan of all subdirectories of /usr/fred.

There is one exception to the general rules given for patterns. The character . at the start of a file name must be explicitly matched.

    echo *

will therefore echo all file names not beginning with . in the current directory.

    echo .*

will echo all those file names that begin with . in the current directory. This avoids inadvertent matching of the names . and .. meaning 'the current directory' and 'the parent directory' respectively. (ls suppresses information for . and ...)

Care should be taken when using the rm command with generated patterns. More files could easily be removed than intended. One way to reduce the chance of error is first to echo the pattern. For example,

    echo tmp*

followed by

    rm tmp*

taking care not to introduce a space between tmp and *.

2.6.3 Quoting

Characters that have a special meaning to the shell, such as <, >, *, ?, |, and &, are called metacharacters. Any character preceded by a \ is *quoted* and loses its special meaning, if any. The \ is elided so that

    echo \?

will echo a single ?, and

    echo \\

will echo a single \. To allow long strings to be continued over more than one line a \ followed by a newline is ignored. This is sometimes called a hidden newline.

A \ is convenient for quoting single characters. When more than one character needs quoting the above mechanism is clumsy and error prone. A string of characters may be quoted by enclosing the string between single quotes. For example,

    echo '*?['

will echo

```
*?[
```

The quoted string may not contain a single quote but may contain newlines, that are preserved. This quoting mechanism is the most simple and is recommended for casual use.

A third quoting mechanism using double quotes is also available preventing interpretation of some but not all metacharacters. Discussion of the details is deferred to section 4.2.4.

Shell comments begin with # and are terminated by a newline.

2.6.4 Prompts

When the shell is used from a terminal it will issue a prompt before reading a command. By default this prompt is $. It may be changed by setting the prompt string, for example,

```
PS1=yesdear
```

that sets the prompt to be the string yesdear. If a newline is typed and further input is needed then the shell will issue the prompt > . Sometimes this can be caused by mistyping a quote mark. If the prompt is unexpected then an interrupt will return the shell to read another command. This prompt may be changed by saying, for example,

```
PS2=more
```

2.6.5 The shell and login

Following login the shell is called to read and execute commands typed at the terminal. If the user's home directory contains a file named .profile then it is executed by the shell before reading any commands from the terminal.

```
date
calendar

MAIL=/usr/spool/mail/srb
HOME=/usr/srb
PATH=.:/bin:/bin:/usr/bin:$HOME/bin
TERM=...
export MAIL HOME PATH TERM
```

Figure 2.2 A typical .profile

The profile in figure 2.2 contains typical settings of shell variables described further in section 4.1.4. This profile also prints the date and checks the calendar reminder service. The export command is described in section 4.2.1. If you always use the same terminal the TERM variable can be usefully set in the profile.

2.6.6 Review

ls	Print the names of files in the current directory.
ls >file	Put the output from ls into file.
ls | wc −l	Print the number of files in the current directory.
ls | grep old	Print those file names containing the string old.
ls | grep old | wc −l	

                             Print the number of files whose name contains the string old.

      cc pgm.c &   Run the cc command in the background.

2.7 Useful commands

2.7.1 Communication

The UNIX system is friendly, in part because it allows easy communication among users and between users and the system. The commands described in this section allow users on the same or different machines to send mail, or to write to another user. The mail command sends messages or letters to other users, whereas the write command is used to communicate interactively with a user at another terminal.

The mall command

The mail command allows messages to be received from, and sent to, other users on the system. These messages are stored in a file until the recipient reads them and removes them.

    When you log on you will be informed if there is any mail waiting for you. The shell will also let you know, before prompting, if any new mail has arrived. (See the $MAIL variable in the shell.)

    There are different versions of the mail system depending on which version of the UNIX system you have. The general behavior of these mail systems is similar although they differ in the details. The version described here is the mail command originally distributed with the Seventh Edition UNIX system.

        mail

will print the first item of mail, preceded by its post-mark. It will then prompt with a ?. This item of mail can be deleted (d), printed again (p), or the next item printed by typing a return. To save the item of mail the request

        s file

is used. The request s with no file name will save the mail item in the file mbox in the home directory. If an item is saved or deleted it is removed from the mail file on exit from mail. The q request will exit from the mail command. To exit without making any changes to the mail file the x request should be used. This is useful when mail items have been deleted in error.

    When mail is being read, typing del causes the current action (usually printing) to be terminated and a prompt is issued for the next request.

To send mail to one or more users

mail jhc ken

. . .

.

will send the text including the sender's name and a postmark. The text is terminated by an end-of-file or by a . on a line by itself. An interrupt while composing a mail message will leave the partially constructed mail in the file **dead.letter** in the home directory and exit from the **mail** command.

Mail systems provide communication between users on a single machine. Communication between users on different machines is achieved via an ad hoc network that uses the phone system to establish connections. This network originated, and is still used, to provide a machine-to-machine file copying service. Each machine in the network is named and a list is maintained on each machine of the names of other machines and their phone numbers. The mail system uses this network to deliver inter-machine mail. The mail address consists of the machine name, followed by !, followed by the user's login-name on that machine. For example,

mail research!llc

followed by the message is sufficient to send mail to **llc** on the **research** machine. Some machines are also prepared to forward mail so that

mail allegra!ucbvax!wnj

will send the message to **allegra** and then forward it to **ucbvax!wnj**. This forwarding service should be used only after agreement with the intermediate installation.

The uucp command

The **uucp** (UNIX to UNIX copy) command copies files from one machine to another. Connections between computers are either made via the phone system or, in some cases, direct high-speed links are utilized. On your system the command **uuname** will print the names of the systems that are directly accessible. This informal network of computers is in constant use and on the author's machine (allegra) over 300 machines can be called.

The synopsis is similar to the **cp** command. For example,

uucp file research!/usr/srb/ufile

will copy **file** from the local machine to **research**, the file name on that machine being /usr/srb/ufile.

In its original form **uucp** could be used to copy files from one machine to another, the only security checks applied are those provided by the file system on each machine.

The ability to copy files into and out of a computer by knowing its phone number and a relatively simple protocol presents some installations with an unacceptable security risk. Therefore uucp imposes additional restrictions over those imposed by the file system. On many systems there is a single directory used to copy files into and out of the machine called /usr/spool/uucppublic. Normally this directory is open to all users of the machine and each user will create a (sub) directory for personal use. The system administrator may also enable files to be accessed by uucp from specific directories elsewhere in the system.

The write command

In addition to mail, users can communicate directly from one terminal to another using the write command.

>   write bill

will look to see whether user bill is logged in and if so will write a message of the form

>   Message from srb on tty20 at 13:36

at his terminal. If bill is logged in more than once, write prints a message and chooses one terminal to write to. The normal protocol is for bill to reply by saying

>   write srb

that will produce a similar message at the initiator's terminal. srb would then send the first message

>   Hi, are you ready to eat lunch (o)

where (o) means over. Conversation can then continue until one or the other party decides to finish. An end-of-file, ^D, will terminate the conversation on one side and print EOF on the other terminal.

Occasionally, when a terminal is being used as a printer or when in use by a visual editor (see vi) having a message appear at random is inconvenient. Some users simply prefer not to be interrupted.

>   mesg n

denies other users write access to your terminal.

>   mesg y

will restore message permission and mesg without an argument informs you of the current state (y or n).

2.7.2 System inquiries

The ps command

A list of the active processes within the system can be obtained using the ps command (ps for process status). The options and output format for this command vary from one UNIX system to another. The a argument requests a list of all processes; otherwise, only processes for the logged in user are listed. Typical output from the command

　　ps a

is shown in figure 2.3 where the fields signify the following.

PID	The process identification number.
TT	The terminal (or tty) number.
STAT	The execution status: R for running, S for stopped briefly, and I if stopped longer than 20 seconds (idle).
TIME	How much processor time the command has used in minutes and seconds.
COMMAND	The command being executed (including arguments).

PID	TT	STAT	TIME	COMMAND
22932	00	I	0:03	ed ama.temp
22864	16	S	0:07	vi t2
22963	16	S	0:00	sh −i
22968	16	R	0:00	ps a
22967	40	S	0:00	sleep 15
27786	40	S	6:28	/bin/sh /usr/haw/bin/prints

Figure 2.3 Output from the ps command

The du command

This command determines how much disk space is being used by files in a directory and (recursively) all its sub-directories. The output from du is a list of file or directory names and the associated number of 512-character blocks used. Without an argument du lists the current directory. If arguments are specified then those files or directories are listed.

The df command

Files are stored in a *file system* that corresponds to an area of disk. The number of blocks of space available and allocated to each file system is printed by the df command. Disk space is allocated in units called blocks; a block is typically 512 or 1024 characters depending on your system. On some systems disk space is always in short supply. This command is useful if you are planning to create large files as a check to ensure that the space is available.

2.7.3 Process management

The nice, nohup, and kill commands

Whenever a command is run it competes with all other active processes in the system for processor time. The nice command informs the system that an activity is not urgent and that a lower scheduling priority is appropriate. For example, nice cp largefile newfile

runs the command

cp largefile newfile

at a lower priority. This allows other, more urgent, work to proceed.

Work is often performed by issuing commands from a terminal and waiting for them to finish. This is particularly true of file management and editing activities. If a command or set of commands is expected to take some
time to finish it is convenient to relegate the work to the background and continue working at the terminal. The shell provides the & notation for this purpose.

cp largefile newfile &

instructs the shell to run the command but not wait for it to finish. nice may
also be used with & so that,

nice cp largefile newfile &

will run the copy in the background at low priority.

If you log out and leave your terminal before the background activity
finishes the nohup (no hang up) command should also be used. This prevents
disconnecting (hanging up) the terminal from aborting the job. nohup and
nice are used in a similar way, so that,

nohup cp largefile newfile &

is typical.

When a process has been started but is no longer required it may be
killed using the kill command. kill requires a process number to be specified,
such as that produced by the ps command. Usually, kill is used for processes
that have been started in the background. However, processes that have been
started using nohup are immune to the default kill. Such processes may be
killed by specifying

kill −9 *process-id*

This form is not usually used since it does not give the receiving commands
an opportunity to clean up.

The at *command*

The at command enables a user to queue a set of activities to be executed at
some future time. Each user community adopts its own rules governing the
use of the computer resources. On heavily loaded machines, for example, it
may be unacceptable to run more than one job in the background. at may be
used to defer an unimportant job until a later time when the computer is not
so busy.

All commands described so far have been executed when they were issued. To schedule an activity for a future time at is used. For example, in

at 1600 fri runcmd

runcmd is scheduled to be executed at 4 p.m. next Friday. The command
runcmd is run exactly as if it were typed now, except that the terminal is not
available for input and output. Other arrangements must be made for the
standard input, standard output and error output.

No direct means is provided for killing an at job. The scripts are kept in
the directory /usr/spool/at and can be removed using the rm command by
the file owner.

This command is not available on some systems although an equivalent
mechanism may be available.

2.7.4 Other commands

The calendar *command*

The calendar command provides a reminder service for individual users. To
use the service create a file called calendar in your home directory containing
lines such as

jun 27 9 a.m. visit the dentist

Each day the system will look at the file and send, via mail, those lines that
contain today's or the next day's date. The calendar file is left unchanged,
providing a record of events.

The file *command*

The file command classifies its argument file names according to the information stored in the file. It is not foolproof, and sometimes confuses shell scripts
and C programs. Try, for example,

file /usr/lib/*

for a representative sample of output.

The find *command*

The find command scans a directory hierarchy (i.e. a directory and its sub-
directories recursively) for files with a specified property. Among others, the
name, age, owner, and mode of a file can be tested. When a suitable file is
found a command can be executed or the file name printed. find is useful if,
for example, you cannot remember the directory a file is stored in but can
remember its name.

find . —name precious —print

will look in the current directory hierarchy and, if a file named precious is
found, its complete pathname is printed starting at the current directory.

find . —name precious —exec ls —l {} \;

is similar, and will also execute the command ls —l .... The argument to ls,
represented as {}, will be replaced by the complete pathname of the file each

time ls is executed. The \; terminates the command to be executed and is quoted to prevent interpretation by the shell. The following examples illustrate other uses.

> find / —user mark—b —print
>> Look everywhere in the file system (i.e. starting at the root) for files owned by mark—b.

> find . —size 0 —print
>> Print the names of files with zero length in the current directory tree.

The grep command

grep has already been introduced in earlier examples, and selects lines containing a string from a list of files. If no files are specified the standard input is searched. The lines found are copied to the standard output. For example,

> grep Unix *

will print the lines from files in the current directory containing the string Unix. If more than one file is searched, grep will prefix each output line with the file name.

The general form for invoking grep is

> grep pattern [file ...]

The pattern is reminiscent of that used by the shell for file name generation. In the simplest case pattern is a literal string. The description of the general form of patterns is deferred until section 8.1.

Some of the frequently used grep options are as follows:

—h   Suppress printing of file name prefix on each line.
—n   Each line output is preceded by its line number in the file.
—v   Only lines not containing the string are printed.

The ls command

The ls command lists status information for files and directory contents. Without arguments ls lists the names in the current directory sorted alphabetically. The entries . and .. are not normally listed.

—d   For a directory list only the name, not the names contained.
—g   List the group name instead of the owner.
—l   List (long) the mode, number of links, owner, size, and modification time.
—r   Reverse the order of sorting.
—t   Sort by the file modified time instead of by name.
—u   Use time of last access instead of last modification.

The od command

Files that contain strange characters can be printed using the 'octal dump' command od. For example,

     od −b file

prints each byte of file as an integer to base 8 (octal). Other options for od include:

    −c   Print ASCII with non-graphic characters escaped using a \.
    −x   Print 16-bit hexadecimal.

Files containing more complicated formats may be printed using the adb command.

The pr command

Listings of one or more files are produced using the pr command. For example,

     pr *.c

will print all files with names ending in .c in the current directory. The output is separated into 66 line pages each headed by the file name, date and time, and page number. The final page is padded with blank lines to complete the 66 line page. Useful options include:

    −t   Suppress the additional lines at the top and bottom of each page.
    −n   Produce n-column output.
    −h text Use text as the heading of each page.
    −m   Merge. Print files simultaneously, one in each column.

The stty command

Terminals have widely differing characteristics that are communicated to the system via the stty (set tty) command. When called without arguments, stty reports the current settings of the most important options, such as terminal speed, parity and the erase and kill characters. If your terminal behaves strangely you should check that its configuration corresponds to the stty options. Terminal input and output is discussed further in chapter 6.

The tar command

Files may be copied to and from magnetic tape using cat or cp. However, copying single files in this way is not particularly convenient. The tar (tape archive) command copies a directory hierarchy, usually from tape to disk or from disk to disk. For example,

     tar rc .

reads all files and (recursively) directories from the current directory, ., and writes them onto tape. The r option reads the directory and c creates a new tape archive. The tape is a special file, like /dev/tty, whose name depends on your system. The name of the special file need not be specified since it is built in to the tar command.

To list the names of files on a tape the command

    tar t

is used. The t option stands for titles. Files are extracted from the tape and written to disk by the command

    tar x

The disk files written have the same names as those listed by tar t.

The names given to tar should be expressed relative to the current directory so that files can be extracted in other parts of the file system conveniently. Saying, for example,

    tar rc /usr/srb

should be avoided in favor of

    cd /usr/srb
    tar rc .

2.7.5 Review

The following commands allow a user to log in to the computer and get started using the terminal.

login	Read the login-name and password.
mail	Send and receive mail between users.
man	Print a section from the user manual.
stty	Set terminal options.
who	List users who are logged in.

The following important file manipulation commands have also been introduced.

cat	Concatenate and print files.
cp	Copy files.
ls	List the entries in a directory.
mkdir	Make a directory.
mv	Move (or rename) a file or directory.
rmdir	Remove a directory.
rm	Remove (or delete) a file.
pr	Format and print a file.

Chapter 3

Editing Files

Files such as programs or text for inclusion in a document may be created and modified from a terminal using a text editor. The editors are interactive allowing a dialogue to take place between the user and the system.

There are two commonly available editors: ed and vi. Of these, ed is the more widely available and uses only the basic facilities available on any terminal. Another editor, vi, is a screen editor that takes full advantage of video terminals. This chapter describes the features of both editors.

3.1 The editor ed

The editor ed is invoked by the command

    ed

No prompt will appear and the editor will wait for an editing *request* to be typed. The term *request* is used for the instructions given to commands to distinguish them from the commands themselves.

ed keeps text in a storage area called a *buffer* and provides requests to append to, delete, or modify this text. All requests are introduced by a single letter and requests may not, except where noted, be on the same line. If something goes wrong, ed will print a **?** and wait for another request to be typed.

3.1.1 Creating files

Initially, the ed buffer is empty. To place information in the buffer, the append request, abbreviated to a is used:

    a
    text to be placed in the buffer

    .

While text is being appended, the editor is in *append mode*. To get out of append mode and to terminate the text a . is required at the start of a line followed by a return.

The contents of the buffer are written to the file draft.1 using the write request

    w draft.1

The character w is separated from the file name by a space. The editor responds with the number of the characters placed in the file and the contents

28

of the buffer are unaltered by the request. After writing the buffer to the file, the quit, q, request may be used to exit from the editor. An end-of-file, ^D, will also exit from the editor. If the buffer has been changed and not written back to a file the editor will respond to w or q with a ?. This is the only message normally received from ed and can be unhelpful to the new user. Typical ed errors include:

- An unknown ed request.
- An error in the form of the request.
- A file does not exist, or cannot be read or written.

Although the process described above illustrates how to create a file, it does not indicate how to edit the contents of a file that already exists. Just as

```
w draft.ch1
```

writes the contents of the buffer to a file

```
e draft.ch1
```

reads the contents of draft.ch1 into the buffer and destroys any information that was already in the buffer. One way to invoke ed is as follows:

```
ed
e filename
[editing requests to alter buffer contents]
w filename
q
```

An equivalent effect is achieved by

```
ed filename
[editing requests to alter buffer contents]
w
q
```

When ed is given a filename as an argument the e request is not needed. Further, there is no need to remember the filename for later use by the w request, as in the second example above. The remembered file name can be printed using the f request and is set by the e and w requests.

3.1.2 Line editing

The text in the buffer is divided into lines and some requests operate with entire lines of text. The general form of requests is

```
starting-line, finishing-line request
```

The request is then applied to each line of the buffer from the starting-line to the finishing-line inclusive. Lines may be addressed numerically, starting with line 1. If the starting-line and finishing-line are the same line the general form may be abbreviated as:

```
particular-line request
```

The following examples introduce some commonly used requests.

1,4p	Print lines numbered 1 to 4 inclusive.
1,4n	Print lines 1 to 4 inclusive; each line is prefixed by its number.
10,15d	Delete lines 10 through 15 inclusive.
4,14w part1	Write out lines 4 to 14 inclusive to a file called part1. If no starting and finishing lines are given the entire buffer is written.
4r new.part	Read the contents of the file new.part and insert it immediately after line 4; when no line number is specified the contents are appended to the end of the current buffer.
4,14m 21	Move lines 4 to 14 inclusive and place them after line 21 (and before line 22).
1t2	Place a copy of line 1 after line 2. The r, m, and t requests place information *after* a particular line.

The last line of the buffer is represented by a $. Thus,

> 1,$d

deletes from the buffer everything from line 1 to the end, inclusive. This should only be used if it is intended to remove all the lines from the buffer. Similarly,

> 1,$p

prints the entire contents of the buffer.

Current line

The current line is the particular line under scrutiny and is like a finger pointing into the buffer. It is referred to as *dot* and is usually the last line edited. After an a request it is the last line appended, and after m it is the last line moved. The d request is exceptional since the last line edited no longer exists; the current line is the first line that has not been deleted. When in doubt the current line can be printed using the p request. Further, the current line number can be found by typing

> .=

To change *dot* to a particular line, without doing any editing, type the line number. Thus

> 4

prints line 4 and sets *dot* to 4. Generally, whenever a new current line is established and a new request is needed, the current line is printed.

Line addressing

Lines may be addressed in ed using a numeric line index, the current line *dot*, or as the last line of the document $. Addresses may also be formed by adding or subtracting a number from one of the above, although adding to

the last line of the document will always be an error. An address that begins
with a + or − is taken relative to the current line. A + or − on its own is
used to step forwards or backwards a line at a time.

The following editing requests illustrate some typical line addresses.

+	Advance to the next line and print it.
−	Go back one line and print it.
.,$d	Delete everything from the current line to the end of the buffer.
.−1,.+1p	Print the previous line, the current line and the next line.
.+2,$−1p	Print everything from two lines beyond the current line up to but excluding the last line of the buffer.

In all cases *dot,* the current line, is changed.

Adding and removing material

The append request is the general facility for adding information to a buffer.
The request

    10a
    text to be included between lines 10 and 11

    .

will append information immediately after line 10 of the buffer.

Two other requests are similar to the a request. Lines may be changed
using the c request that combines the effect of deleting and inserting material. For example,

    4,27c
    text to replace lines removed

    .

replaces lines 4 to 27 inclusive with the specified text. As might be supposed

    4c
    text to be added

    .

replaces line 4. In both cases a . on a line by itself terminates the input.

The insert request, i, is similar in form to the a request except that information is inserted before, rather than after, the stated line. Thus

    1i
    .ce 2
    Chapter One
    .sp 2
    Fundamentals
    .sp 2

    .

adds information at the start of a buffer and is equivalent to

    0a

    ...

    .

If no line numbers are specified, the a, c, d, i, and p requests use the current line number as default so that

    a
    text to be included

    .

is equivalent to

    .a
    text to be included

    .

Furthermore,

    d

deletes the current line and a subsequent

    p

request prints the new current line, i.e., the next line in the buffer. This can be written on a single line as

    dp

After each of the a, c, i, and m requests the current line becomes the last line appended, changed, inserted or moved respectively.

3.1.3 Context searching

Referring to lines only by number is inconvenient unless a listing is available. Simple insertions or deletions cause line numbers to alter. It is more convenient to look for a string of characters using the editor and decide if it is right, then edit it, then look again.

    The request

    /Fotran/

for example, will look through the contents of the buffer for the *next* line containing the characters delimited by / and /. The line of text found is displayed so that it can be checked to see if the intended line has been reached. In performing the search, the editor looks through successive lines of text starting at the line after the current line. If it reaches the end of the buffer without finding the line, the editor will then proceed from the start of the buffer until the entire contents have been searched back to the current line. If the line is not present, perhaps because of a mistake in the request, a ? is printed.

    A search, such as /Fotran/, is another way of addressing a particular line. Just as line numbers were used earlier, search patterns of the kind described here can also be used. A request such as

/switch/,/case/d

deletes everything between the next line containing **switch** and the next line containing **case**. It is assumed that the line containing **case** is the same as, or follows, the line containing **switch**.

If the last line of the buffer is reached without finding the search pattern, **ed** wraps around, starting again at the first line. Searching stops when the current line is reached or when the pattern is found.

A search pattern may be used as part of an address. For example,

/main/−1

will position the current line one line before the next line containing /main/.

Use of semicolon

The request

/begin/,/end/d

begins the search for **end** at the same point as it begins the search for **begin**, namely the current line. To start the search for **end** after **begin** has been found, a ; rather than a , is used as separator, as in,

/begin/;/end/d

Backward searching

Context searches using /.../ scan forward through the text. Backward scans are also possible using ?...?. When performing the backward search wrap around occurs; on reaching line 1 of the buffer the editor will jump to the end of the buffer and search backwards from there until the entire buffer has been searched.

3.1.4 Context editing

Editing a document line-by-line is slow and can be error prone. Making changes within a line is known as context editing.

Part of a line may be modified using the substitute request, **s**. The effect of

s/Fotran/Fortran/

is to replace, on the current line, the first occurrence of **Fotran** by **Fortran**. Examples illustrate some of the possibilities.

s/Fotran//
>   Replace **Fotran** by the empty string, i.e. delete it.

s/Fotran/Fortran/p
>   Replace the first occurrence of **Fotran** by **Fortran** and print the edited line for review.

.,.+1s/Fotran/Fortran/
>   Replace the first occurrence of **Fotran** by **Fortran** on the current line and the next line.

The substitute request has the same general format as the requests previously encountered, allowing

starting-line, finishing-line s/old text/new text/

or

particular-line s/old text/new text/

When line numbers are omitted the current line is assumed.

In context searches the string searched for is often the subject of the substitute request. This can happen with spelling or typing errors. The request

/Fotran/

followed by

s/Fotran/Fortran/

can be abbreviated to

/Fotran/
editor responds with the line found
s//Fortran/

The editor remembers the previous search or substitute pattern. When used after an s request,

//

searches again for the next occurrence of the previous pattern. If the wrong line appears, // may be used again to find the next line with the same pattern.

Global substitution

A simple application of the substitute request, such as

s/Fotran/Fortran/

will replace only the first occurrence of Fotran by Fortran on the current line.

s/Fotran/Fortran/g

replaces all occurrences in the current line. The g modifier indicates global replacement throughout the line.

The p modifier may also be used.

s/Fotran/Fortran/gp

causes global replacement and prints the edited line;

1,$s/Fotran/Fortran/g

causes every occurrence of Fotran in the buffer to be replaced by Fortran. When looking for strings it sometimes helps to be able to specify that a particular string occurs at the start or end of a line. The start and end of line are denoted within patterns by ⌃ and $, respectively. To illustrate:

/⌃At/	Find the next line that starts with At.
/};$/	Find the next line that ends with };.
/⌃$/	Find the next empty line.
/⌃Unix$/	Find a line that contains only Unix.

These same patterns may be used in the first substitute string.

s/⌃/The /p Place The before the first character of the current line and print the line.

4s/$/;/   Add a ; to the end of line 4.

/⌃UNIX$/s//Unix/

Find the next line containing only UNIX and replace these four characters by Unix.

The undo request

If a substitute request is executed in error the undo request,

u

will restore the line to its original form. This request only applies to the most recently executed substitution.

3.1.5 Pattern matching

Within a search or substitution string certain characters have a special meaning as described below.

The dot character

A . matches any character, so that,

/x.y/

will find the first line that contains strings like x+y, x−y, x=y.

The asterisk character

An * denotes repetition and finds zero or more occurrences of a character. The pattern

/.*;/

matches everything on one line up to and including the last ;. The longest possible match is used so that if a ; appears more than once on the line, all will be matched. For example,

s/.*;//

removes everything up to and including the last ; on the line. The request

s/(.*)//

removes from the first (to the last) and everything between them. The parentheses matched are not necessarily balanced.

This use of the * character should be distinguished from its use in the shell. In the shell * is similar to .* in the editor.

As another example,

    /a.*b/

will search for a line containing both a and b in that order, possibly separated by other characters.

The bracket characters

Square brackets denote character classes as illustrated in the following examples. As in the shell, one character from the specified class is matched.

[;:,]	Match any of the characters ;, : or ,.
[a−z]	Match any lower case character a through z.
[A−H]	Match any upper case character between A and H inclusive.
[0−9]	Match any digit.
[^0−9]	^ denotes the complement when it appears as the first character after [. This example matches any character except a digit.
[.\$*^[]]	Match any of the special characters. Only the characters ^ and] are treated specially in character classes. To include] itself in a character class it should be listed as the first character. A ^ is included when listed as anything other than the first character in the class.

The following examples illustrate the use of patterns within a substitute request.

1,$s/^[0−9]*//	Remove all digits from the start of each line.
1,$s/[0−9]*$//	Remove all trailing digits from the end of each line.
s/[.\$*^[]]//	Remove the first occurrence of any special character from the current line.
s/, e\.g\..*/./	Replace everything from the string , e.g. to the end of the line with a ..

Naming

Part of a pattern matched by a search or substitute request may be named by enclosing the pattern between \(and \). For example,

    /\(.*\)⊤\(.*\)/

will search for a line containing a tab (represented here by ⊤). The two strings enclosed between \(...\) may be used in the replacement string of a substitute request, as in,

    s//\2⊤\1/

\1 and \2 refer to the first and second parenthesised patterns. In this example, the two fields are interchanged. If more than one tab occurs within the line the right-most one is matched.

Quoting

Within a search string the following characters are treated specially:

      ^   . $ [*   \   /

To be used in their own right, as normal characters, it is necessary to *escape* them with a \. Thus

    /\./

looks for the next line containing a ., whereas

    /./

looks for the next line that contains any character (i.e. the next non-empty line).

Recall that the same quoting convention is used for the erase and kill characters, # and @. Even within the editor these characters have a special meaning when input from a terminal and must be typed as \# or \@, respectively.

To look for a line containing a / a \ is also required. Thus

    s/\//*/p

will replace / with an * on the current line and then print out the modified line.

3.1.6 Global editing

The *global request* selects lines that match a pattern and executes another request for each line found. This may be used, for example, if a word is consistently spelled wrongly or whenever a change to the whole file is required. The g request takes the form

    g/pattern/requests

For example,

    g/^{/.−1p

finds all lines starting with a { and prints the preceding line.

As with other requests the g request may be limited to a range of lines. Thus

    1,20g/^chapter/s/c/C/

executes the request s/c/C/ on all lines starting with chapter in the first 20 lines of the buffer. When several requests are to be executed then each new-line must be *escaped* with a \. For example,

    g/^chapter/s/c/C/\
    i\
    .ul1\
    .

changes every occurrence of **chapter** at the start of a line to **Chapter** and a
line containing only .ul1 is inserted immediately before it. All lines except
the last must end with a \. The requests executed by a **g** request may not include another **g** request.

The **v** request is similar to the **g** request except that it finds lines that do
not match the pattern. For example,

>   v/^\./d

deletes all lines that do not begin with a ..

3.1.7 Miscellaneous

Interrupt and hangup

An interrupt, generated by typing **del**, will cause the editor to abandon its
current activity and return to read the next request. This is useful for inter-
rupting a print request such as

>   g/.../p

If the terminal hangs up while a file is being edited, the buffer is saved
in the file called **ed.hup** in the current directory. The **diff** command may be
used to compare **ed.hup** with the original file being edited and either the **cp**
or **mv** command may be used to restore the partially edited **ed.hup** to its original name.

Delimiters

A context search is specified using /.../. A / is frequently used for delimit-
ing the string in a substitute request. However, any other character, such as
a :, can be used provided that all occurrences within the one request are consistent, as in,

>   s:Fotran:Fortran:

The delimiter may be quoted using \ if it is needed as part of the pattern.

Executing a command

To execute a command from within the editor the ! request is used. For example,

>   !mail honey
>   please call me on x7419
>
>   .

will send a message to user **honey** and return to **ed**. No changes are made to
the buffer or the file being edited.

Abbreviations

Certain abbreviations are permitted in line addresses.

- + can be omitted so that, for example, .+4 and .4 have identical
  meanings. +4 is also an abbreviation for .+4.

- — by itself moves back a line; ――― moves back three lines and is equivalent to .−3.
- /.../− is equivalent to /.../−1.

Use of ampersand

Having performed a search for a string in a substitute request, as in

    s/abc/.../

an & can be used in the replacement string to denote the first string that is found. Thus

    s/x+y/(&)/

inserts parentheses around x+y.

Non-printing characters

The l request is similar to the p request except that non-printing characters, such as tab and backspace, are replaced by printing characters as shown below. (The representations below vary with different versions of ed.)

tab	\t
backspace	\b
backslash	\\
bell	\07
formfeed	\14

If there are spaces at the end of the line they are printed followed by \n, as in,

    ... \n

Joining and breaking lines

Consider a line of text such as

    ...abc...

To insert a newline between a and b, the substitute request is used with an escaped newline. For example,

    s/ab/a\
    b/

inserts a newline between the characters a and b. The single request is typed on two lines. Conversely, two lines such as

    if x==y
       && y==z

can be formed into a single line. With the first of these lines as the current line

    j

will join them together leaving the result as the current line. In general a range of lines can be joined, as in

    1,4jp

that joins together lines 1 through 4 inclusive and prints the result.

Marking lines

The request

    line-number k*x*

marks the addressed line (by default the current line) with the name *x*. Any lower case letter may be used to mark lines. Such lines may be addressed using a single quote followed by *x*, as in,

    '*x*

E, Q, and W requests

The requests e and q will print ? to warn that the results of editing have not been written to a file and will not complete the requested action. These safeguards are suppressed if E or Q is used. These requests should be used with care since an entire editing session may be lost.

The w request writes the buffer to a file, destroying any previous file contents. Information may be appended to a file using the W request.

3.2 **The editor** vi

Once **ed** has been learned its limitations soon become apparent. It was designed in the days of slow mechanical terminals such as the Teletype model 33 and model 37 teleprinters. Video terminals have space on the screen for at least 24 lines of 80 characters each and vi is an editor developed to take advantage of such devices. For best effect these terminals should be operated at 9600 baud but can also be used reasonably at 1200 baud. Below 1200 baud **ed** is the best choice.

vi needs to know the terminal type before it can be used. The terminal type is specified by setting the environment variable TERM. In the shell this is written, for example,

    TERM=2621 export TERM

The string assigned to TERM depends on the terminal, in this example a Hewlett Packard 2621.

If the correct name for the terminal is unknown, the TERM variable can be set to **dumb** and vi will work on any terminal although it will not use the visual features that make it attractive.

The command

    vi pgm.c

will display the first few lines of pgm.c on the screen and editing requests may be issued to vi. If there are unexpected characters on the screen, then the terminal type (TERM) is probably incorrect or has not been exported from the shell. The request

> :q

terminated by a return will exit from the editor. The request

> :q!

corresponds to the Q request of ed and forces vi to exit even if the current buffer has not been written to a file.

Requests to vi consist of one or more characters, another difference from ed and some requests require a terminating return or esc.

Once the terminal type is set correctly immediate differences from ed can be seen. Some requests take effect immediately and are not printed on the screen. Others are printed on the screen and appear on a line near the bottom. Error messages from vi are explicit, as opposed to the ? from ed and also appear on the line near the bottom of the screen.

3.2.1 Window control

The philosophy of this editor is that what you see on the screen is part of the buffer. The screen acts as a *window* on the buffer. To move this window forward through the buffer the following requests are available:

> ^F

to move a full screen and

> ^D

to scroll half a screen. The notation ^F means control-F and is explained in chapter 2.

To move backwards through the buffer

> ^B

is used for a full page and

> ^U

scrolls half a page backwards. When the end of the buffer is reached vi will display non-existent lines as a ~.

You will now be able to observe the *cursor;* on some terminals it blinks; on others it is displayed as inverse video. The cursor marks the current position within the buffer.

3.2.2 Cursor control

The cursor can be positioned on the screen in preparation for editing requests. The line containing the cursor is the current line and the cursor position is also used by vi requests. The requests providing fine cursor control are:

space	Move one character to the right.
backspace	Move one character to the left.
return	Move to the start of the next line.

+   The same as a **newline**.
−   Move to the start of the previous line.
$ Move to the end of this line.

Other requests are available to move the cursor. If necessary these requests will also move the window on the buffer.

/pattern/

will search forward and leave the cursor pointing at the next occurrence of **pattern** in the buffer. Like **ed**, ?...? searches backwards.

Coarse cursor movement is available using the G request that moves to a specified line of the buffer. A number followed by the G request will position the cursor at that line within the buffer. By default the last line of the buffer is used, so that,

G

will position the cursor at the end of the buffer.

The cursor can also be moved forwards or backwards a whole word at a time; if there are no words remaining on the current line the cursor will be moved to the next or previous line respectively.

w   Move the cursor forward to the beginning of the next word.
b   Move the cursor back to the start of the previous word.
e   Move the cursor forward to the end of the current word.

In these requests a word is considered to consist of alphanumeric characters and _. The capital letter versions W, B, and E treat any non-blank character as part of the word allowing the cursor to be moved over punctuation and other non-alphanumeric characters. (A non-blank character is any character other than a space or a tab.) These requests may be preceded by a count, so that,

3w

moves forwards 3 words.

3.2.3 Additions and deletions

Characters can be inserted or removed at the position marked by the cursor. To remove a single character type

x

and to remove the next 3 characters at the cursor type

3x

Characters are inserted using the i or **a** request. For example, an insert request, i, is written

i...esc

where ... represents inserted material and **esc** is the **escape** key on your terminal. Inserted material is placed immediately before the cursor and may contain as many lines as needed. Insertion continues until the **esc** is typed.

The append request starts inserting after the cursor rather than before it and has the form

> a...esc

Before describing further vi requests it is worth noting that any ed request can be used from within vi by typing a : followed by the ed request. For example, to quit from vi type

> :q

and to write the buffer back to the file and quit type

> :wq

Once changes have been made you cannot exit from vi using :q unless you have written the buffer to the file.

If a file does not have write permission vi will display a message and refuse to write the file.

3.2.4 Line editing

Material may be appended within a line using the i or a requests. Line by line additions are more readily achieved using the open request

> o
>
> ...
>
> esc

that takes the material ... and appends it, line by line, after the current line. The O request has a similar effect but inserts material before the current line.

To remove material from a document, various requests are provided:

x	Delete the current character.
dd	Delete the line containing the cursor.
dw	Delete the current word.
D	Delete the remainder of the current line.
r c	Replace the current character with c.

Most requests may be preceded by a repetition count.

> 3dd

will delete 3 lines starting with the current line.

3.2.5 Moving material

Material may be moved from one place to another using a delete request followed by the p request that puts the deleted material after the cursor position. If whole lines have been removed then whole lines will be inserted; whereas, if characters within a line were removed then characters will be inserted after the cursor. A typical sequence would be as follows:

/main/	Look for the string main.
4dd	Delete 4 lines.
3+	Move forward 3 lines.
p	Put the 4 deleted lines after this line.

When characters have been deleted using the x request, the p request will put them back after the cursor, so that for example,

> xp

will exchange the cursor character with the one following it. Deleted material may be put back before the current line or before the cursor using P.

When mistakes are made they can be undone using the u request that reverses the last change. All changes made to the current line may be undone using the U request. However, this does not work if you move to another line and move back even though no editing occurs.

Material that has been deleted can be recovered using the p or P requests. Up to the last 9 items deleted may also be recovered. For example,

> "5p

will put back the 5th most recently deleted item.

The . request repeats the last editing change.

> dd . . .

will, therefore, remove 4 lines.

Lines may be copied using the yank request Y. For example,

> Yp

will yank (copy) the current line into a hidden buffer, and p will place the copy after the current line.

3.2.6 Review

To summarize, the following requests are sufficient to get started with vi, allowing material to be added and removed, the result to be written to a file and to quit. These should be mastered before moving on the the next section.

^D	Scroll the window forwards.
^U	Scroll the window backwards.
^F	Move forward a page.
^B	Move backward a page.
return	Move the cursor down.
—	Move the cursor up.
space	Move the cursor right.
backspace	Move the cursor left.
dd	Delete the current line.
i	Insert text before the current character.
o	Insert text after the current line.
p	Put back deleted or yanked text.
x	Delete the current character.
Y	Yank lines into a buffer.
:w *file*	Write out the changes to *file*.
:q	Quit. :q! bypasses checking.
del	Abandon the current request.

3.2.7 More advanced features

The requests described so far can be learned with a few sessions at a terminal. This section describes features that are useful if the editor is used frequently.

Screen and cursor control

H	Move cursor to the home (first) line of the screen.
L	Move cursor to the last line of the screen.
M	Move cursor to the middle of the screen.
hjkl	Move the cursor left, down, up or right respectively.
wbe	Move the cursor forward, back, or to the end of a word.
/.../	Search forwards for the pattern ....
?...?	Search backwards for the pattern ....
z.	Center the screen at the current line.
z cr	Redraw the screen at the current line; cr denotes **return**.
z n.	Use an *n* line window centered on the screen.
%	Move to the next or previous balanced (,), {, or }.
^E	Display one more line at the bottom of the screen.
^L	Redraw the screen.
^Y	Display one more line at the top of the screen.
0	Move the cursor to the start of the line.

Editing requests

A...	Append to the end of the current line (ends with **esc**).
C...	Change the rest of the line (ends with **esc**).
D	Delete the rest of the line.
I...	Insert at the beginning of the current line (ends with **esc**).
J	Join the current line and the next line.
X	Delete the character before the cursor.
cw...	Change the current word (ends with **esc**).
rx	Replace the current character with *x*.
~	Change the case (upper/lower) of the current character.
&	Repeat the last :s request.

Using ed requests

ed requests may be used from vi by preceding them with a :. The following are the commonly used requests.

:sh	Execute a shell.
:!cmd	Execute cmd and return to vi.
:r *file*	Read *file*.
:s...	Substitute one string for another.
:g...	Globally search for a string.

Objects

Some requests, such as d take as an argument an *object* specifying what to delete. When the request letter is doubled, as in dd, the request applies to the current line.

Examples of object specifications have already been used, as in dw and cw, where w denotes a word. Objects are specified as follows:

c	A single character.
w	The next alphanumeric word.
W	The next non-blank word.
H	The home line (top) of the screen. 3H is 3 lines from the top of the screen.
L	The last line on the screen. 3L is 3 lines from the bottom of the screen.
/.../	The next line containing the pattern ....
)	The end of the current sentence. A sentence ends with a blank line, or one of the characters . ! ? followed by a blank line or two spaces.
(	The start of the current sentence.
}	The end of the current paragraph. A paragraph is defined as ending with a blank line or one of the nroff requests .bp, .IP, .LP, .PP, .QP, .LI, or .P.
{	The start of the current paragraph.
]]	The end of the current section; defined as ending with one of the nroff macros .NH, .SH, .HU, or .H
[[	The start of the current section.

The following requests take one of the objects listed above:

cx...	Change up to and including *x* with material terminated by an esc.
dx	Delete up to and including *x*.
yx	Yank the object *x* for use by a subsequent p or P request.
>x	Indent by 8 spaces up to and including the line containing *x*.
<x	Remove an indent of 8 spaces up to and including the line containing *x*.
!x cmd	The text of the object specified is passed as the standard input to cmd. The command is executed and its standard output replaces the object text.

For example,

> !!date

replaces the current line with the output from the date command.

> !}sort

will call sort with its standard input as the next paragraph and replace the paragraph with the sorted output.

Counts

A number preceding a request is a repeat count with the following exceptions.

new window size	[[	]]	:	/	?	
scroll amount	^D	^U				
line or column number	z	G	|			

Editing multiple files

vi can be used to edit a list of files. When invoked as

> vi file ...

the first file in the list is displayed for editing. When the first file has been edited the :n request will read the next file in the list into the buffer. If the buffer has not been written back to the file, an error message is printed and no action taken. Also, the quit request, :q, will display a message and refuse to exit unless all files in the list have been edited. The autowrite option of :set (see below) can be used to change this behavior.

Crash recovery

A system crash happens when the hardware or the system fails and has to be restarted. Although this should be infrequent, vi protects the user from loss of editing time by saving a copy of the buffer in a file. This saved copy is also available if your terminal line hangs up. In either case vi will try to leave mail for you, giving the name of the file being edited and how it can be recovered. The file can be recovered using the −r option when vi is invoked. For example, if the file being edited was named precious, then

> vi −r precious

will restart the editor from where you left off using the saved copy of the buffer. The last editing operation may have been lost depending on the time of the crash.

Setting options

vi has many options for controlling its behavior. To print the current settings the request

> :set all

is used. Each option has a name and is set by one of the forms

> :set *option-name*
> :set *option-name*=*value*

and is unset by

> :set no *option-name*

The options are described below with the abbreviation, if any, in parentheses.

autoindent(ai)	Supply program indentation automatically.
autowrite(aw)	Automatic write before :n and !.

ignorecase(ic)	Ignore upper/lower case when searching.
list	Tabs print as ^I.
number(nu)	Lines are displayed prefixed by numbers.
paragraphs(para)	The names of nroff macros that start paragraphs for the } and { requests. Initially set to IPLPPPQPbpP LI.
redraw(re)	Simulate a smart terminal.
sections(sect)	The name of macros that start sections for the [[and]] requests. Initially set to NHSHH HU.
term	The name of the terminal type being used.

These options may also be set in the shell variable EXINIT. For example,

```
EXINIT='set ai aw'
export EXINIT
```

arranges for autoindent and autowrite to be set, by default, on entry to vi.

Defining new requests

A definition mechanism is provided in vi allowing a single character to replace a sequence of requests. For example,

```
:map = :.=^VCR
```

defines = to be equivalent to :.= where the ^V escapes the return (CR) at the end of the request. In this request two return characters are required, one for the definition itself and one to terminate the :map request.

As another example,

```
:map ; eas^Vesc
```

defines ; to add the letter s at the end of the current word. Again, ^V escapes the character esc in the definition.

The following characters have no associated action in vi and are candidates for definition using the map request.

```
K   V   g   q   v   ,   ;   _   *   =
```

Chapter 4

The Shell

The shell is both a programming language and a command language and is often referred to as the command interpreter of the UNIX system. Similarities exist with the command interpreters of the Cambridge Multiple Access System and of CTSS. The notation for simple commands and for parameter passing and substitution is similar in these languages.

As a command language the shell provides a user interface to the UNIX operating system. The shell executes commands that are read either from a terminal or from a file. Files containing commands may be created, allowing users to build their own commands. These newly defined commands may be parameterized and have the same status as the system commands defined in /bin and /usr/bin. In this way a new environment can be established reflecting the requirements or style of an individual or a group.

The design of the shell, therefore, takes into account both interactive and non-interactive use. Except in some minor respects, the behavior of the shell is independent of its input source.

As a programming language the shell provides string-valued variables and control flow primitives including branching and iteration. The notation is oriented towards ease of use at a terminal so that strings are not normally quoted. The output from an arbitrary command may be used as a string, enabling arithmetic and other facilities not provided by the shell to be accessed as commands.

Commands are similar to function calls in a language such as C. The notation is different in two respects. First, although the arguments are arbitrary strings, in most cases they need not be enclosed in quotes. Second, there are no parentheses enclosing the list of arguments nor commas separating them. Command languages tend not to have the extensive expression syntax found in algorithmic languages like C. Their primary purpose is to issue commands; it is therefore important that the notation be free from superfluous characters.

4.1 Shell procedures

Interactive use of the shell was introduced in chapter 2. This chapter introduces the shell as a programming language and describes how new commands can be created.

The shell may be used to read and execute commands contained in a file. For example,

```
sh file [ args ... ]
```

calls the shell to read commands from file. Such a file is called a *command* or *shell* procedure. Arguments may be supplied with the call and are referred to in file using the positional parameters $1, $2, ... For example, if the file wg contains

```
who | grep $1
```

then

```
sh wg fred
```

is equivalent to

```
who | grep fred
```

Files have three independent attributes, *read, write* and *execute.* The command chmod may be used to make a file executable. (See section 6.3.2 for details.) For example,

```
chmod +x wg
```

will ensure that the file wg has execute status. Following this, the command

```
wg fred
```

is equivalent to

```
sh wg fred
```

This allows shell procedures and programs to be used interchangeably. In either case a new process is created to run the command.

As well as providing names for the positional parameters, the number of positional parameters in the call is available as $#. The name of the file being executed is available as $0.

A special shell parameter $* is replaced by all positional parameters except $0. A typical use of this is to provide some default arguments, as in,

```
nroff −T450 −ms $*
```

that simply prepends some arguments to those already given.

Shell procedures can be used to tailor the environment to the tastes and needs of a group or an individual. Since procedures are text files requiring no compilation, they are easy to create and maintain.

4.1.1 Control flow - for

A frequent form for shell procedures is to loop through the arguments ($1, $2, ...) executing commands once for each argument. An example of such a procedure is tel that searches the file /usr/lib/telnos containing lines of the form

```
...
fred mh0123
bert mh0789
...
```

The text of tel is

```
for i do
        grep $i /usr/lib/telnos
done
```

The command

```
tel fred
```

prints those lines in /usr/lib/telnos that contain the string fred.

```
tel fred bert
```

prints those lines containing fred followed by those for bert.

The for loop notation is recognized by the shell and has the general form

```
for name in w1 w2 ...
do command-list
done
```

A command-list is a sequence of one or more simple commands separated or
terminated by a newline or ;. Furthermore, reserved words like do and done
are normally preceded by a newline or ;. A list of reserved words is given in
appendix 6. name is a shell variable that is set to the words w1 w2 ... in
turn each time the command-list following do is executed. If in w1 w2 ... is
omitted then the loop is executed once for each positional parameter; that is,
in $* is assumed.

Another example of the use of the for loop is the create command whose
text is

```
for i do >$i; done
```

The command

```
create alpha beta
```

ensures that two empty files alpha and beta exist and are empty. The notation >file may be used on its own to create or clear the contents of a file.
Also note the ; (or newline) required before done. The notation <file may
also be used to test for the existence of a file.

4.1.2 Control flow - case

A multiple way branch is provided for by the case notation. For example,

```
case $# in
    1)      cat >>$1 ;;
    2)      cat >>$2 <$1 ;;
    *)      echo 'usage: append [ from ] to' ;;
esac
```

is an append command. When called with one argument as

```
append file
```

$# is the string 1 and the standard input is copied onto the end of file using the cat command.

> append file1 file2

appends the contents of file1 onto file2. If the number of arguments supplied to append is other than 1 or 2 then a message is printed indicating proper usage.

The general form of the case command is

> **case** word **in**
>   pattern) command-list ;;
>   ...
>
> **esac**

each branch being terminated by ;;. The ;; preceding esac is optional.

The shell attempts to match word with each pattern in the order in which the patterns appear. If a match is found the associated command-list is executed and execution of the case is complete. Since * is the pattern that matches any string it can be used for the default case.

A word of caution: no check is made to ensure that only one pattern matches the case word. The first match found defines the set of commands to be executed. In the example below the commands following the second * will never be executed.

> case $# in
>   *) ... ;;
>   *) ... ;;
> esac

Another use of the case construction is to distinguish between different forms of an argument. The following example is a fragment of a cc command.

```
for i
do      case $i in
        —[ocs]) ... ;;
        —*)     echo 'unknown flag $i' ;;
        *.c)    /lib/c0 $i ... ;;
        *)      echo 'unexpected argument $i' ;;
        esac
done
```

To allow the same commands to be associated with more than one pattern the case command provides for alternative patterns separated by a |. For example,

> case $i in
>   —x|—y) ...
> esac

is equivalent to

```
case $i in
        -[xy])   ...
esac
```

The usual quoting conventions apply so that

```
case $i in
        \?)      ...
esac
```

will match the character ?.

4.1.3 Here documents

The shell procedure tel in section 4.1.1 uses the file /usr/lib/telnos to supply
the data for grep. An alternative is to include the data within the shell procedure as a *here* document, as in,

```
for i
do      grep $i <<!
        ...
        fred mh0123
        bert mh0789
        ...
!
done
```

In this example the shell takes the lines between <<! and ! as the standard
input for grep. The string ! is arbitrary, the document being terminated by
a line that consists of the string following <<.

```
ed $3 <<%
g/$1/s//$2/g
w
%
```

Figure 4.1 The procedure edg

Parameters are substituted in a here document before it is made available to the grep command, as illustrated by the procedure edg in figure 4.1.
The call

```
edg string1 string2 file
```

is then equivalent to the command

```
ed file <<%
g/string1/s//string2/g
w
%
```

and changes all occurrences of **string1** in **file** to **string2**. No quit command is needed in **ed** if the buffer has been written to the file; an end-of-file is sufficient.

Substitution can be prevented using a \ to quote the special character $, as in,

```
ed $3 <<+
1,\$s/$1/$2/g
w
+
```

This version of **edg** is equivalent to the first except that **ed** will print a ? if there are no occurrences of the string $1. Substitution within a here document may be prevented entirely by quoting the terminating string, for example,

```
grep $i <<\:
        ...
:
```

The document is presented without modification to **grep**. If parameter substitution is not required in a here document this latter form is more efficient.

4.1.4 Shell variables
The shell provides string-valued variables. Variable names begin with a letter and consist of letters, digits and underscores. Variables may be given values by writing, for example,

```
user=fred box=m000 acct=mh0000
```

that assigns values to the variables **user**, **box** and **acct**. No space should appear around the = character. A variable may be set to the null string by saying, for example,

```
TERM=
```

The value of a variable is substituted by preceding its name with $; for example,

```
echo $user
```

will echo **fred**.

Variables may be used interactively to provide abbreviations for frequently used strings. For example,

```
b=/usr/fred/bin
mv pgm $b
```

will move the file **pgm** from the current directory to the directory /usr/fred/bin. A more general notation is available for parameter (or variable) substitution, as in,

```
echo ${user}
```

that is equivalent to

```
echo $user
```

and is used when the parameter name is followed by a letter or digit. For example,

```
tmp=/tmp/ps
ps a >${tmp}a
```

will direct the output of ps to the file /tmp/psa, whereas,

```
ps a >$tmpa
```

would cause the value of the variable tmpa to be substituted.

Special variables

Except for $? the following are set initially by the shell. $? is set after executing each command.

$?   The exit status (return code) of the last command executed as a decimal string. Most commands return a zero exit status if they complete successfully, and a non-zero exit status otherwise. Testing the value of return codes is deferred until the section on if and while commands.

$0   The name of the command procedure being executed. This variable can be used to distinguish cases when a command has more than one name. For example, the following script is called ttyhp and a link to the same file exists called ttyblit. If the file is called any other name, and executed by that name then the default case applies. The command sets terminal options using the stty command

```
case $0 in
        ttyblit)    stty erase ^H kill @ ff0 tabs ;;
        ttytek)     stty erase ^H kill @ tek −tabs ;;
        *)          stty erase ^H kill @ ;;
esac
```

$#   The number of positional parameters (in decimal). Used, for example, in the append command (section 4.1.2) to check the number of parameters. $# is also updated by the set command.

$$ The process number of this shell (in decimal). Since process numbers are unique among all existing processes, this string is frequently used to generate temporary file names. For example,

```
ps a >/tmp/ps$$
...
rm /tmp/ps$$
```

$!   The process number of the last process run in the background (in decimal).

$-   The current shell flags, such as −x and −v.

Some variables have a special meaning to the shell and should be avoided for general use. These variables are typically set in the file .profile, in the user's home directory.

$MAIL   When used interactively the shell looks at the file specified by this variable before it issues a prompt. If the specified file has been modified since it was last looked at, the shell prints the message you have mail before prompting for the next command. For example, for user fred this variable is set as

MAIL=/usr/spool/mail/fred

$HOME   The default argument for the cd command. The current directory is used to resolve file name references that do not begin with a /, and is changed using the cd command. For example,

cd /usr/fred/bin

makes the current directory /usr/fred/bin. The command cd with no argument is equivalent to

cd $HOME

$CDPATH   The list of directories that is searched by the cd command. Each directory name is separated by :. A typical setting of this variable is

CDPATH=:..:$HOME/desk

that specifies that cd should search the current directory, the parent directory, .., and lastly, $HOME/desk. For example, if the directory ../src exists and there is no src directory in the current directory,

cd src

will change directory to ../src and print this string as confirmation.

$PATH   A list of directories that contain commands (the *search path*). Each time a command is executed by the shell a list of directories is searched for an executable file. If $PATH is not set, then the current directory, /bin, and /usr/bin are searched by default. $PATH consists of directory names separated by :. For example,

PATH=.:/bin:$HOME/bin:/bin:/usr/bin

specifies that the current directory (the . before the first :),

./bin, $HOME/bin, /bin, and /usr/bin are to be searched in that order. In this way individual users can have their own commands in $HOME/bin that are accessible independently of the current directory. The directory ./bin is included to allow access to any directory named bin from the current directory. This separates commands from data files within a directory associated with some project or activity.

If the command name contains a / then the directory search is not used; a single attempt is made to execute the command. The form ./cmd may be used to bypass the search path for command in the current directory.

$PS1　　The primary shell prompt string, by default, $.

$PS2　　The shell prompts with $PS2 when further input is needed, by default, the value is > .

$IFS　　The set of characters used for blank interpretation (see section 4.2.4).

4.1.5 The test command

The test command is intended for use by shell programs. In some versions of the shell test is built-in for efficiency reasons. For example,

    test −f file

returns zero exit status if file exists and non-zero exit status otherwise. In general, test evaluates a predicate and returns the result as its exit status. Some of the more frequently used test arguments are given here.

test s　　　　　True if the argument s is not the null string.
test −f file　　True if file exists and is not a directory.
test −r file　　True if file is readable.
test −w file　　True if file is writable.
test −d file　　True if file is a directory.

Arithmetic is not provided by the shell but is available indirectly using the expr command.

4.1.6 Control flow - while and until

The actions of the for loop and the case branch are determined by data available to the shell. A while or until loop and an if then else branch are also provided and their actions are determined by the exit status returned by commands. A while loop has the general form

    while command-list₁
    do command-list₂
    done

The value tested by the while command is the exit status of the last simple command following while. Each time round the loop command-list₁ is executed; if a zero exit status is returned then command-list₂ is executed; otherwise, the loop terminates. For example,

```
while test $1
do      ...
        shift
done
```

is equivalent to

```
for i
do ...
done
```

shift is a shell command that renames the positional parameters $2, $3, ... as $1, $2, ... and loses $1.

When until is used in place of while, the loop termination condition is reversed. The following example waits until the file exists.

```
until test −f file
do sleep 300; done
commands
```

The until test succeeds if the file exists. Each time the loop is executed it waits for 5 minutes (300 seconds) before trying again. (Presumably another process will eventually create the file.)

4.1.7 Control flow - if

Also available is a general conditional branch of the form,

```
if  command-list
then    command-list
else    command-list
fi
```

that tests the value returned by the last simple command following if. The else part is optional. Since this construction is bracketted by if ... fi it may be used unambiguously anywhere that a simple command may be used. Furthermore, there is no dangling else to hinder interactive use.

The if command may be used with the test command to test for the existence of a file as in

```
if test −f file
then    # process file
else    # do something else
fi
```

A complete example of the use of if, case and for constructions is given in section 4.1.10.

A nested if command of the form

```
if ...
then     ...
else     if ...
         ...
         fi
fi
```

may be written using an extension of the if notation as,

```
if ...
then     ...
elif     ...
         ...
fi
```

The example in figure 4.2 is the dw command that recursively scans a directory tree and lists files found. The PATH variable is set to ensure that the right commands are executed. Often the command search path includes ., the current directory. By setting the path explicitly this command has guarded against the possibility of finding a command, also called dw, or test, in a sub-directory.

The for loop checks each name in the current directory. If it exists and is a file, no action is taken; if it is a directory dw is called (recursively) to list the contents in the same way.

```
PATH=/bin:/usr/bin:$HOME/bin

cd $1
ls −l

for i in *
do       if test −f $i
         then     :
         else     dw $i
         fi
done
```

Figure 4.2 The dw command

The sequence

```
if command₁
then     command₂
fi
```

may also be written

```
command₁ && command₂
```

Conversely,

command$_1$ || command$_2$

executes command$_2$ only if command$_1$ fails. In each case the value returned
is that of the last simple command executed.

4.1.8 Command grouping

Commands may be grouped in two ways,

{ command-list ; }

and

(command-list)

In the first, command-list is simply executed. The second form executes
command-list by a separate shell process. For example,

(cd x; rm junk)

executes rm junk in the directory x without changing the current directory of
the invoking shell.

The commands

cd x; rm junk

have the same effect but leave the invoking shell in the directory x.

For historical reasons the parentheses are special characters like | and ;
and will be recognized anywhere unless quoted. The braces are reserved
words and, like if and do will only be recognized following a newline or semicolon.

4.1.9 Debugging shell procedures

The shell provides two mechanisms to help when debugging shell procedures.
The first may be invoked within the procedure as

set −v

(v for verbose) and causes lines of the procedure to be printed as they are
read. It is useful to help isolate syntax errors. It may be invoked without
modifying the procedure by saying

sh −v proc ...

where proc is the name of the shell procedure. Unwanted side effects may be
avoided using the −n flag that prevents execution of commands. (set −n at a
terminal will render the terminal useless until an end-of-file is typed.)

The command

set −x

will produce an execution trace. Following parameter substitution each command is printed as it is executed.

Checking for unset shell variables is provided by the −u flag. Using this
flag, any attempt to substitute for a variable that has not been set will cause
an error message to be printed and execution will stop. (Try these at the ter-

minal to see what effect they have.) All flags may be turned off by saying

    set −

and the current setting of the shell flags is available as $−. (In some systems a different notation turns off the flags.)

4.1.10 The man command

Figure 4.3 is a version of the man command that prints sections of the *Programmer's Manual*. It is called, for example, as

    man sh
    man −t ed
    man 2 fork

The first line prints the manual section for sh. Since no section is specified, section 1 is used. The second line will typeset (−t option) the manual section for ed. The last line prints the fork manual page from section 2.

```
cd /usr/man

N=n s=1            # default is nroff ($N), section 1 ($s)

for i
do      case $i in
        [1−9]*)  s=$i ;;
        −t)      N−t ;;
        −n)      N=n ;;
        −*)      echo unknown flag \'$i\' ;;
        *)       if test −f man$s/$i.$s
                 then    ${N}roff −man man$s/$i.$s
                 else    # look through all manual sections
                         found=no
                         for j in 1 2 3 4 5 6 7 8
                         do      if test −f man$j/$i.$j
                                 then    man $j $i
                                         found=yes
                                 fi
                         done
                         case $found in
                         no) echo \'$i: manual page not found\'
                         esac
                 fi
        esac
done
```

Figure 4.3 A version of the man command

4.2 Advanced use

4.2.1 Parameter transmission

Shell variables may be given values by assignment or when a shell procedure is invoked. An argument to a shell procedure of the form name=value that precedes the command name causes value to be assigned to name before execution of the procedure begins. The value of name in the invoking shell is not affected. For example,

    user=fred command

will execute command with user set to fred. The −k flag causes arguments of the form name=value to be interpreted in this way anywhere in the argument list. Such names are sometimes called keyword parameters. If any arguments remain they are available as positional parameters $1, $2, ...

The set command may also be used to set positional parameters from within a procedure. For example,

    set − *

will set $1 to the first file name in the current directory, $2 to the next, and so on. The first argument, −, ensures correct treatment when the first file name begins with a −.

The *environment* of a process is a list of name-value pairs that is passed to an executed program in the same way as a normal argument list. The shell interacts with the environment in several ways. On invocation, the shell scans the environment and creates a variable for each name found, giving it the corresponding value. Executed commands inherit the same environment. If the user modifies the values of these variables or creates new ones, none of these affects the environment unless the export command is used to bind the shell's parameter to the environment. The environment seen by any executed command is composed of any unmodified name-value pairs originally inherited by the shell, plus any modifications or additions made to exported variables.

When a shell procedure is invoked both positional and keyword parameters may be supplied with the call. Keyword parameters are also made available implicitly to a shell procedure by specifying in advance that such parameters are to be exported. For example,

    export user box

marks the variables user and box for export. When a shell procedure is invoked copies are made of all exported variables for use within the invoked procedure. Modification of such variables within the procedure does not affect the values in the invoking shell. It is generally true of a shell procedure that it may not modify the state of its caller without explicit request by the caller. (Shared file descriptors are an exception to this rule.)

A name whose value is intended to remain constant may be declared readonly. The form of this command is the same as that of the export command, readonly name ...

Subsequent attempts to set readonly variables are rejected.

4.2.2 Parameter substitution

If a shell parameter is not set then the null string is substituted for it. For example, if the variable d is not set

    echo $d

or

    echo ${d}

will echo nothing. A default string may be given as in

    echo ${d−.}

that will echo the value of the variable d if it is set and . otherwise. The default string is evaluated using the usual quoting conventions so that

    echo ${d−'*'}

will echo * if the variable d is not set. Similarly

    echo ${d−$1}

will echo the value of d if it is set and the value (if any) of $1 otherwise. A variable may be assigned a default value using the notation

    echo ${d=.}

that substitutes the same string as

    echo ${d−.}

and if d were not previously set then it will be set to the string .. The notation ${...=...} is not available for positional parameters.

If a value must be provided and no default is available, the notation

    echo ${d?message}

may be used to echo the value of the variable d if it has one. Otherwise message is printed by the shell and execution of the shell procedure is abandoned. If message is absent then a standard message is printed. A shell procedure that requires some parameters to be set might start as follows.

    : ${user?} ${acct?} ${bin?}
    ...

: is a command that is built into the shell and does nothing once its arguments have been evaluated. If any of the variables user, acct or bin are not set then the shell will abandon execution of the procedure.

4.2.3 Command substitution

The standard output from a command can be substituted in a similar way to parameters. The command pwd prints on its standard output the name of the current directory. For example, if the current directory is /usr/fred/bin then the command

    d=`pwd`

is equivalent to

    d=/usr/fred/bin

The entire string between grave accents (`...`) is taken as the command to be executed and is replaced with the output from the command. The command is written using the usual quoting conventions except that a ` must be escaped using \. For example,

    ls `echo "$1"`

is equivalent to

    ls $1

Command substitution occurs in all contexts where parameter substitution occurs (including here documents) and the treatment of the resulting text is the same in both cases. This mechanism allows string processing commands to be used within shell procedures. An example of such a command is basename that removes a specified suffix from a string. For example,

    basename main.c .c

will print the string main. Its use is illustrated by the following fragment from a cc command:

```
case $A in
    . . .
    *.c)    B=`basename $A .c`
    . . .
esac
```

that sets B to the part of $A with the suffix .c stripped.

Here are some composite examples:

for i in `ls −t`; do ...
> The variable i is set to the names of files in time order, most recent first.

set `date`; echo $6 $2 $3, $4
> Print, e.g., 1970 Feb 3, 11:59:59. The output from date is Tue Feb 3 11:59:59 GMT 1970 and the shell breaks up this output as arguments for the set command. The result is assigned to the positional parameters.

a=`expr $a + 1`
> Increment the shell variable a by 1.

4.2.4 Evaluation and quoting

The shell is a macro processor providing parameter substitution, command substitution and file name generation for the arguments to commands. This section discusses the order in which these evaluations occur and the effects of the various quoting mechanisms.

Before a command is executed the following substitutions occur.

- *Parameter substitution*
  $user is an example of parameter substitution. Only one evaluation
  occurs and the shell does not rescan the substitution string for further substitutions. To illustrate, if the value of the variable X is the
  string $y then

      echo $X

  will echo $y.

- *Command substitution*
  `pwd` is an example of command substitution. For example, within
  a profile, the HOME variable might be set as

      HOME=`pwd`

  making the profile independent of the login directory.

- *Blank interpretation*
  Following the above substitutions the resulting characters are broken
  into non-blank words *(blank interpretation)*. For this purpose
  blanks are the characters of the string $IFS. By default, this string
  consists of space, tab and newline. The null string is not regarded
  as a word unless it is quoted. For example,

      echo ''

  will pass on the null string as the first argument to echo, whereas

      echo $null

  will call echo with no arguments if the variable null is not set or set
  to the null string.

- *File name generation*
  Each word is finally scanned for the file pattern characters *, ?, and
  [...] and an alphabetical list of file names is generated to replace the
  word. Each generated file name is a separate argument.

The evaluations described above also occur in the list of words associated
with a for loop. Only parameter and command substitution occurs in the
word used for a case branch.

As well as the quoting mechanisms described in section 2.6.3 using \ and
'...' a third quoting mechanism is provided using double quotes. Within double quotes, parameter and command substitution occurs but file name generation and the interpretation of blanks does not. The following characters have
a special meaning within double quotes but may be quoted using \.

$	Parameter substitution.
`	Command substitution.
"	End the quoted string.
\	Quote the special characters $ ` " \.

For example,

```
echo "$x"
```

will pass the value of the variable x as a single argument to echo. Similarly,

```
echo "$*"
```

will pass the positional parameters as a single argument and is equivalent to

```
echo "$1 $2 ..."
```

The notation $@ is the same as $* except when it is quoted.

```
echo "$@"
```

will pass the positional parameters, unevaluated, to echo and is equivalent to

```
echo "$1" "$2" ...
```

When no parameters are present this notation provides a null argument that is useful in the following script.

```
for i in "$@"
do cat $i
done
```

The null argument guarantees that the loop is executed once. In this example, each file is processed, and if no files are provided as arguments the standard input is copied.

Figure 4.4 gives, for each quoting mechanism, the shell metacharacters that are evaluated.

	Metacharacter					
	`'`	`"`	`` ` ``	`\`	`$`	`*`
`'`	t	n	n	n	n	n
`"`	n	t	y	y	y	n
`` ` ``	n	n	t	y	n	n

Key: t   terminator
        y   interpreted
        n   not interpreted

Figure 4.4 Shell quoting mechanisms

In cases where more than one evaluation of a string is required, the built-in command eval may be used. For example, if the variable X has the value $y, and if y has the value pqr then

```
eval echo $X
```

will echo the string pqr.

In general the eval command evaluates its arguments (as do all commands) and treats the result as input to the shell. The input is read and the resulting command(s) executed. For example, if the variable subscript has the value **user**, then

    eval echo \\$L_$subscript

is equivalent to

    echo $L_user

In this example, **eval** is required since there is no re-interpretation of the **$** character after substitution.

An **eval** may also be used when syntactic characters, such as |, are to be evaluated following substitution.

4.2.5 Error handling

The treatment of errors detected by the shell depends on the type of error and on whether the shell is being used interactively. An interactive shell is one whose input and output are connected to a terminal (as determined by the gtty system call). A shell invoked with the −i flag is also interactive.

Execution of a command (see also section 4.2.7) may fail for any of the following reasons.

- Input-output redirection may fail, for example, if a file does not exist or cannot be created.
- The command itself does not exist or cannot be executed.
- The command terminates abnormally, for example, with a bus error or a memory fault. See figure 4.5 for a list of signals of most interest to shell programs. The quit signal produces a core dump if not caught. However, the only external signal that can cause a core dump is quit and this signal is ignored by the shell.
- The command terminates normally but returns a non-zero exit status.

Signal	Description
1	hangup
2	interrupt
3	quit
9	kill (cannot be caught or ignored)
15	software termination (from the kill command)

Figure 4.5 UNIX system signals for shell programs

In all cases the shell will go on to execute the next command. Except for the last case, an error message will be printed by the shell. All remaining errors cause the shell to exit from a command procedure. An interactive shell will return to read another command from the terminal. Such errors include the following.

- Syntax errors, e.g. if ... then ... done where done should be fi.
- A signal such as interrupt. The shell waits for the current command, if any, to finish execution and then either exits or returns to

the terminal. The **trap** command is used to alter this default action on interrupt.

● Failure of any of the built-in commands such as cd.

The shell flag —e causes the shell to terminate if any error is detected.

4.2.6 Fault handling

Shell procedures normally terminate when an interrupt is received from the terminal. The **trap** command is used if some cleaning up is required, such as removing temporary files. For example,

        trap 'rm /tmp/ps$$; exit' 2

sets a trap for signal 2 (terminal interrupt), and if this signal is received will execute the commands

        rm /tmp/ps$$; exit

exit is another built-in command that terminates execution of a shell procedure. The exit is required in this example; otherwise, after the trap has been taken, the shell will resume executing the procedure at the place where it was interrupted.

Signals can be handled in one of three ways. They can be ignored, in which case the signal is never sent to the process. They can be caught, in which case the process must decide what action to take when the signal is received. Lastly, signals can be left to cause termination of the process without the process having to take any further action. If a signal is being ignored on entry to the shell procedure, for example, by invoking the procedure in the background (see section 4.2.7) then **trap** commands (and the signal) are ignored.

The use of **trap** is illustrated by the fragment of a command in figure 4.6. The cleanup action is to remove the file junk$$ and exit.

---

        trap 'rm —f junk$$; exit' 0 1 2 3 15

Figure 4.6 An example of the use of the trap command

The **trap** command should appear before the creation of the temporary file; otherwise it would be possible for the process to die without removing the file.

Signal number 0 is not used by the system and so it is assigned by the shell to indicate exit from a shell procedure.

A procedure may elect to ignore signals by specifying the null string as the argument to trap. The following fragment is taken from the **nohup** command.

        trap '' 1 2 3 15

and causes **hangup**, **interrupt**, **quit** and **kill** to be ignored both by the procedure and by invoked commands.

Traps may be reset by saying, for example,

trap 2 3

that resets the traps for signals 2 and 3 to their default values. A list of the current values of traps may be obtained by writing

trap

There is no need for a **trap** command to include an **exit**. The procedure **scan** (figure 4.7) is an example of the use of **trap** where execution resumes once the trap has been executed. **scan** takes each directory in the current directory, prompts with its name, and then executes commands typed at the terminal until an end-of-file or an interrupt is received. The : command does nothing once its arguments have been evaluated, so that

trap : 2

causes interrupts to be effectively ignored while executing **eval $x**. When waiting for input, executing the statement **read x**,

trap exit 2

is in effect.

```
d=`pwd`
for i in *
do      if test   d $d/$i
        then      cd $d/$i
                  while     echo "$i:"
                            trap exit 2
                            read x
                  do trap : 2; eval $x; done
        fi
done
```

Figure 4.7 The scan command

read x is a built-in command that reads one line from the standard input and places the result in the variable x. It returns a non-zero exit status if either an end-of-file is read or an interrupt is received.

4.2.7 Command execution

To run most commands the shell first creates a new process using the system call **fork**. Commands requiring a new process include simple commands, commands enclosed in parentheses, and shell constructs such as **while** and **for**, with input-output redirection present. No new process is created for built-in commands.

The *execution environment* for a command includes open files, the **umask** value, the current directory, and the states of signals, and is established in the child process before the command is executed. The built-in command **exec** is used when a new process is not needed and simply replaces the shell with a new command. For example, a simple version of the **nohup** command is

```
trap " 1 2 3 15
exec "${@?}"
```

The **trap** turns off the signals specified so that they are ignored by subsequently created commands and **exec** replaces the shell by the command
specified as arguments.

4.2.8 Input-output redirection

Most forms of input-output redirection have already been described. In the
following, **word** is only subject to parameter and command substitution. No
file name generation or blank interpretation takes place so that, for example,

```
echo ... >*.c
```

will write its output into a file whose name is *.c. Input-output specifications
are evaluated left to right as they appear in the command. If **word** is the
null string then no redirection occurs. For example,

```
cat <$1
```

Is the same as **cat** with no redirection if $1 is unset or the null string.

> word	The standard output (file descriptor 1) is sent to the file **word** that is created if it does not already exist.
>> word	The standard output is sent to file **word**. If the file exists then output is appended (by seeking to the end); otherwise the file is created.
< word	The standard input (file descriptor 0) is taken from the file **word**.
<< word	The standard input is taken from the lines of shell input that follow up to but not including a line consisting only of **word**. If **word** is quoted then no interpretation of the here document occurs. If **word** is not quoted then parameter and command substitution occur and \ quotes the charac-ters \, $, ` and the first character of **word**. In the latter case \newline is ignored (cf. quoted strings). If **word** is the null string then an empty line terminates input.
>& digit	The file descriptor **digit** is duplicated using the system call **dup** and the result is used as the standard output.
<& digit	The standard input is duplicated from file descriptor **digit**.
<&–	The standard input is closed.
>&–	The standard output is closed.

Any of the above may be preceded by a digit in which case the file
descriptor created is that specified by the digit instead of the default 0 or 1.
For example,

```
... 2>file
```

runs a command with error output (file descriptor 2) directed to file.

... 2>&1

runs a command with its standard output and error output merged. (Strictly speaking file descriptor 2 is created by duplicating file descriptor 1 but the effect is usually to merge the two streams.)

Within a shell procedure the standard input, output and error output may be redirected using the above forms and the **exec** command. For example,

exec >stdout 2>errout

redirects the standard output to the file **stdout** and the error output to **errout**. These are the default output for subsequently executed commands.

The environment for a command run in the background such as

list *.c | lpr &

is modified in two ways. Firstly, the default standard input for such a command is the empty file /dev/null. This prevents two processes (the shell and the command) that are running in parallel, from trying to read the same input. Chaos would ensue if this were not the case. For example,

ed file &

would allow both the editor and the shell to read from the same input at the same time.

The other modification to the environment of a background command is to turn off the quit and interrupt signals so that they are ignored by the command. This allows these signals to be used at the terminal without causing background commands to terminate. The hangup signal is not automatically ignored by background processes. The **nohup** command is provided for this purpose. Consequently, the convention for a signal is that if it is set to 1 (ignored) then it is never changed even for a short time. The shell command **trap** has no effect for an ignored signal.

4.2.9 Invoking the shell

The following flags are interpreted by the shell when it is invoked. If the first character of argument zero is −, then commands are read from the file .profile. A system profile is also executed on some systems. Shell output is written to file descriptor 2.

−c s   If the −c flag is present then commands are read from the string
       s. This form is often used by C programs that pass commands to
       the shell for execution. This is how **ed** implements the ! request.
−s   If the −s flag is present or if no arguments remain then com-
       mands are read from the standard input.
−i   If the −i flag is present or if the shell input and output are at-
       tached to a terminal (as told by **gtty**) then this shell is *interactive*.
       The terminate signal is ignored (so that **kill 0** does not kill an in-
       teractive shell) and the interrupt signal is caught and ignored (so
       that **wait** can be interrupted). The quit signal is always ignored
       by the shell.

Errors detected by the shell, such as syntax errors cause the shell to return a non-zero exit status. If the shell is being used non-interactively then execution of the shell file is abandoned. Otherwise, the shell returns the exit status of the last command executed (see also **exit**).

4.3 Built-in commands

Certain functions are built into the shell, either of necessity, or for efficiency reasons. These commands are executed in the shell process and except where specified no input-output redirection is permitted.

:
No effect; the command does nothing and returns zero exit status.

. file
Read and execute commands from file and return. The search path $PATH is used to find the directory containing file.

break [n]
Exit from the enclosing **for** or **while** loop, if any. If n is specified then break n levels.

continue [n]
Resume the next iteration of the enclosing **for** or **while** loop. If n is specified then resume at the n-th enclosing loop.

cd [arg]
Change the current directory to **arg**. The shell parameter $HOME is the default **arg**. Also, the shell variable CDPATH is used to search for directories containing **arg**. This is fully described in section 4.1.4. **chdir** is a synonym for **cd**.

eval [arg ...]
The arguments are read as input to the shell and the resulting command(s) executed.

exec [arg ...]
The command specified by the arguments is executed in place of this shell without creating a new process. Input-output arguments may appear and, if no other arguments are given, cause the shell input-output to be modified.

exit [n] Causes the shell to exit with exit status n. If n is omitted then the exit status is that of the last command executed. (An end-of-file will also exit from the shell.)

export [name ...]
The given names are marked for automatic export to the environment of subsequently executed commands. If no arguments are given then the exported variable names are listed.

login [arg ...]
Equivalent to **exec login arg** ....

newgrp [arg ...]
Equivalent to **exec newgrp arg** .... **login** and **newgrp** are only built into some versions of the shell.

read name ...
One line is read from the standard input; successive words of

the input are assigned to the variables name in order; any
remaining words are assigned to the last variable. The return
code is 0 unless an end-of-file is encountered.

readonly [name ...]

The value of the given names may not be changed by subsequent assignment. If no arguments are given then a list of all
readonly names is printed.

set [−ekntuvx [arg ...]]

  −e If non-interactive then exit immediately if a command
fails.

  −k All keyword arguments are placed in the environment for a
command, not only those that precede the command name.

  −n Read commands but do not execute them.

  −t Exit after reading and executing one command.

  −u Treat unset variables as an error when substituting.

  −v Print shell input lines as they are read.

  −x Print commands and their arguments as they are executed.

  −   Turn off the −x and −v options. The form of this request
varies from system to system.

These flags can also be used on invocation of the shell. The
setting of flags may be found in $−. Remaining arguments to
the set command are assigned, in order, to $1, $2, ... If no
arguments are given then the values of all names are printed.

shift   The positional parameters from $2 ... are renamed $1 ....

times   Print the accumulated user and system times for processes run
from the shell.

trap [arg] [n] ...

arg is a command to be read and executed when the shell receives signal(s) n. arg is evaluated once when the trap is set
and once when the trap is taken. Trap commands are executed
in order of signal number. If arg is absent then all trap(s) n
are reset to their original values. If arg is the null string then
this signal is ignored by the shell and by invoked commands. If
n is 0 then the command arg is executed on exit from the shell,
otherwise on receipt of signal numbered n. trap with no arguments prints a list of commands associated with each signal
number.

umask [ddd]

The user file creation mask is set to the octal value ddd (see
the umask system call). If ddd is omitted, the current value of
the mask is printed.

wait [n]Wait for the specified process and report its termination status.
If n is not given then all currently active child processes are
waited for. The return code from this command is that of the
process waited for.

Chapter 5
The C Programming Language

C is the programming language used to write the UNIX operating system and most of its commands. The language was developed at the same time the system was being written and has evolved to its current state over a decade. Both machine dependent and machine portable programs may be written and compilers for the language exist for many different machines although the first compiler was written for a PDP 11/45.

Historically C was influenced by BCPL, a language developed at M.I.T. and later at Cambridge University. The link between these two languages was through the language B.

BCPL is a typeless language that supports only one object, the machine word. All language operations are defined on words and storage is also allocated on this basis. The language is appealing because of its simplicity. A portable compiler was available in the late 1960s and it was used for writing operating systems.

The historical origins of C help explain some aspects of the language design. It was intended for systems programming and similarity to the machine was considered important. For example, the ++ operator has a direct equivalent in the PDP 11 instruction set. Features allowing portable programs to be written, such as unions, were added to the language in the late 1970s. Traces of the typeless origin of C can still be seen in the ease with which integers and characters, or pointers and integers, can be mixed in some implementations. Type checking is also absent when parameters are passed to functions.

C provides different basic data objects such as int, char, float and double and also has types derived by aggregation using arrays and structures. Other derived types include enumerations, pointers, unions and structures. The type structure of C is similar to languages like ALGOL 68 and Pascal. C differs in the strictness with which type mismatches are treated. Some C compilers will, for example, permit the assignment of a pointer value to an integer variable. In Pascal no semantics are defined for this operation and it is, therefore, not implemented. The permissive approach to types adopted in C allows programs such as storage allocators to be written provided some information is available about the implementation.

C provides standard control flow primitives such as if and switch for selection and while and for for iteration. In addition, functions may be defined to return values and can be called recursively. A function that returns no value may be declared void in a similar way to ALGOL 68.

This chapter introduces C as a language and also describes ways that C

programs can be organized, maintained and debugged. C is used to describe
the UNIX system calls in the next chapter.

The next section of this chapter describes briefly, and with examples, the
main elements of the C language. Since this language has evolved over many
years there are different versions of the compiler in existence. An attempt
has been made to avoid these differences but some features may be missing or
implemented differently on your own computer.

5.1 Sample C programs

5.1.1 A simple program

The following simple C program

```
main()
{
        printf("It works.\n");
}
```

will print the text

It works.

on the standard output.

The source text of the program must be placed in a file whose name ends
with .c, such as simple.c. To compile this program the C compiler is invoked
by the cc command

cc simple.c

that produces an executable program called a.out. Alternatively, using the
−o option of the cc command

cc −o simple simple.c

produces the executable program in the file simple. The executable program
can then be executed by typing the command

simple

Let us return to the original C program. All C programs, by convention,
have a function called main where execution of the program begins. In this
program it is the only function defined. The parentheses () indicate that no
parameters are used by main. The text of main is enclosed between { and }.
There is only a single statement terminated by a ; calling the function printf
to format output. Character strings are enclosed within double quotes as in
the example above. In strings, \n denotes the newline character and causes a
new line to be started on the output.

5.1.2 An octal dump

The program in figure 5.1 is a simplified version of the od command that
reads its standard input and prints each character as an octal integer (base 8)
on the standard output. After every 10 characters a new line is started.

This program illustrates several new features of C. The functions getchar and putchar are the two basic input-output routines defined in the C system library. getchar returns the integer equivalent of the next input character from the standard input. Conversely, putchar takes an integer as its argument and prints the corresponding character on the standard output.

The first line of the program is the #include statement incorporating the definitions required when using the standard input-output library. The value returned by getchar when an end-of-file is reached is denoted by the symbolic constant EOF that is defined in the *header* file <stdio.h>.

```c
#include <stdio.h>

int main()
{
        int c, n;

        n = 1;
        while ((c = getchar()) != EOF) {
                printf("%o ", c);
                if (n++ >= 10) {
                        n = 1;
                        printf("\n");
                }else{
                        printf(" ");
                }
        }
        if (n != 1) {
                /* end unfinished line */
                printf("\n");
        }
        return(0);
} /* main */
```

Figure 5.1 A simple octal dump command

The body of main consists of declarations and statements in that order. Let us examine the various parts in some detail:

main()   Declare the function main required in all C programs as the starting point of execution.

int c, n; Declare two integer variables called c and n.

n=1;   Assign 1 to n.

(c = getchar())!=EOF

The expression c=getchar() is an assignment that can also be used as part of an expression. Its value within the expression is the quantity assigned to c. The operator != tests for inequality so that (...)!=EOF returns true if the next character read is not the end-of-file.

```
while (...) {...}
```
The condition in parentheses is evaluated and, if true, the loop body enclosed in {...} is executed. This process is repeated until the condition is false. The loop body is the statement enclosed between braces.

```
printf("%o", c);
```
Print c according to the octal format %o.

```
n++
```
Add 1 to n. The value of this expression is the value of n before being incremented.

```
n++ >= 10;
```
Compare the value of n with 10 and return true or false; 1 is added to n after its value has been used in the comparison.

```
if (...) {...}
```
The condition in parentheses is evaluated and, if true, the statements enclosed between the braces are executed. Otherwise, the statement following **else** is executed.

5.1.3 Average distances

In the game Star Trek it is an advantage to know the average distance of a star base from every quadrant before starting to play. In deciding whether to play a particular game it is useful to know the average distance of any point from every other point on a grid. The program in figure 5.2 prints averages for a grid of size 9×9.

- The #include and #define statements are interpreted by the C preprocessor. #include has already been introduced in the previous example and is used here to obtain the declaration of **sqrt()** from the standard mathematical library. #define is a constant declaration. Whenever XMAX is used in the program it is replace by 9.
- The declaration

      double average();

  introduces the function and its result type **double**. This allows the function to be used before it is defined later in the program.
- The declaration

      double sum = 0.0;

  introduces the real variable **sum** and initializes its value to zero. All variables must be declared and the declaration must precede the first use.
- The for statement

      for (x=0; x<XMAX; x++) {
              statements;
      }

  is equivalent to the **while** statement

```
x=0;
while (x<XMAX) {
        statements;
        x++;
}
```

and repeatedly executes *statement* until x exceeds or equals XMAX.

```
#include <math.h>

#define XMAX 9
#define YMAX 9

double average();

int main()
{
        int x, y;
        double sum = 0.0;

        for (x=0; x<XMAX; x++) {
                printf("%d: ", x);
                for (y=0; y<YMAX; y++) {
                        double s=average(x, y);
                        sum+=s;
                        printf("%.2f ", s);
                }
                printf("\n");
        }
        printf("average=%f\n", sum/(YMAX*XMAX));
} /* main */

double average(x0, y0)
        int x0, y0;
{
        int x, y;
        double sum = 0.0;

        for (x=0; x<XMAX; x++) {
                for (y=0; y<YMAX; y++) {
                        double d = (x−x0)*(x−x0)+(y−y0)*(y−y0);
                        sum += sqrt(d);
                }
        }
        sum /= (XMAX*YMAX−1);
        return(sum);
} /* average */
```

Figure 5.2 The program average

- The output statement

      printf("%d: ", x);

  prints x as a decimal integer followed by : . The first argument to printf is a string that is printed except for embedded *formats*.
  The format determines how the remaining arguments are interpolated within the printed string. A *format* such as %d is replaced by the decimal representation of the next integer argument. Within this program the formats %f and %.2f are also used; the former prints a floating-point number using a default format, whereas in the latter case the floating-point number has two digits after the decimal point. The format %6.2f requests a field of width 6 with two places after the decimal point.

- The statement

      double s = average(x, y);

  declares the variable s and initializes it to the value returned by the function average, called with parameters x and y.

- The statement

      sum += s;

  introduces the assignment operator += and is equivalent to

      sum = sum+s;

  Similarly, in the function average

      sum /= (XMAX*YMAX−1);

  is equivalent to

      sum = sum/(XMAX*YMAX−1);

- The definition of average declares its result type as double and the two parameters required, x0 and y0. The statement

      return(sum);

  exits from the function with the resulting value sum.

The program average is compiled as

    cc −o average average.c −lm

The argument −lm instructs cc to load the mathematical subroutine library containing the definition of the sqrt function.

5.2 The language

This section presents the details of the C programming language starting with identifiers, constants, basic data types, expressions, and followed by flow of control, function declarations, arrays and pointers and finally, storage classes.

5.2.1 Lexical considerations

Comments and spaces

Comments start with the characters /* and end with the next occurrence of
/. Within a comment / is not treated specially so that nesting is not permitted. Spaces, tabs and newlines are also used to separate identifiers and
reserved words.

Identifiers

Identifiers are used for variables, labels and function names. An identifier
consists of a sequence of letters or digits starting with a letter; an _ is also
considered to be a letter; upper and lower case letters are distinct.

External identifiers (used in more than one program file) are often limited to 6, 7 or 8 characters in length and there may be no distinction between
upper and lower case letters. These details depend on the implementation.

Certain identifiers are reserved for use as language keywords and may
not be used as variable names. The list of reserved keywords is shown in figure 5.3. In some implementations **asm** and **fortran** are also reserved.

auto	else	int	typedef
break	entry	long	switch
case	enum	register	union
char	extern	return	unsigned
continue	float	short	void
default	for	sizeof	while
do	goto	static	
double	if	struct	

Figure 5.3 Reserved words in C

Basic data types

The language supports several basic data types. Briefly, the type determines
how the object in an identifier's storage is to be interpreted.

A character variable will store any object from the available character
set and its value is that of the equivalent integer (ASCII or EBCDIC) character code.

Up to three sizes of integers are available: **short int**, **int**, and **long int**.
Longer integers provide at least as much storage as shorter integers. Unsigned integers are written **unsigned short int**, **unsigned int**, or **unsigned long
int**. The int may be omitted when **unsigned** is present. Unsigned integers
obey the laws of arithmetic modulo 2^n where n depends on the implementation.

Single precision floating-point numbers have type **float** and double precision floating-point numbers have type **double**.

Figure 5.4 illustrates typical storage requirements for the basic data
types for the PDP 11/45 and VAX 11/780. On both machines ASCII is the

character code used.

Type	PDP 11/45	VAX 11/780
char	8	8
short int	16	16
int	16	32
long int	32	32
float	32	32
double	64	64

Figure 5.4 Sizes of objects in C

Constants

An integer constant is a sequence of digits. The constant is a decimal number unless the sequence of digits starts with a leading zero; then the constant is regarded as an octal number. If the string of digits is preceded by 0x or 0X (0 being the digit zero) the digits that follow are assumed to be hexadecimal where a f or A F are the digits corresponding to 10 through 15, respectively.

When an octal, decimal or hexadecimal constant exceeds the largest unsigned machine integer it is considered to be long. Long constants are written by placing an l or L immediately after the usual form. For example 0L is a long zero.

Character constants are enclosed within single quotes, thus 'c'. The value of a character constant is the numerical value in the character set of the machine. A \ is used as an escape character to introduce certain special characters as shown below:

Character	Escape
newline	\n
horizontal tab	\t
backspace	\b
carriage return	\r
formfeed	\f
backslash	\\
single quote	\'
null	\0

Any character can be written as \ddd where d is an octal digit. If a \ is followed by any other character than these mentioned above then the \ is ignored.

String constants are written as a sequence of characters enclosed between double quotes, as in "...". Within a string the same escape character conventions described for character constants apply. A digit following the null character should be written \000d where d is the digit. Additionally, \"

is used for the double quote character itself, and \newline is ignored allowing long strings to be continued over more than one line. The null character '\0' is automatically inserted at the end of string constants.

Floating-point constants contain either a decimal point or an exponent part and possibly both. The general form is

integer-part . *fractional-part* e ± *exponent*

All floating point constants are implemented as double-precision. The following are examples of floating point constants.

```
0.0
3.14159
3e10
```

5.2.2 Expressions and operators

Expressions in C are formed from constants, identifiers, subscripted variables, structure or union references, and function calls combined using both unary and binary operators.

Binary operators are left associative, unless otherwise stated, so that

```
a − b − c
```

is interpreted as

```
( a − b ) − c
```

The binary operators can be grouped under the following categories.

Arithmetic operators

The binary arithmetic operators are, +, −, *, and /, together with the modulus operator % for integers. Whenever / is used between integers, integer division takes place; the decimal point and all subsequent digits of the result are omitted. If positive integers are divided, the quotient is truncated toward zero; if either operand is negative the result is machine dependent.

Relational operators

The operators >, >=, <=, and < are the relational operators, greater-than, greater-than-or-equal-to, less-than-or-equal-to, and less-than respectively. These operators return 0 if the comparison is false and 1 if it is true.

Equality operators

The equality operator is == and the inequality operator is !=. The value returned is 0 if the result is false and 1 if it is true.

Shift operators

The two operators << and >> allow a bit pattern (the left operand) to be shifted by n places left or right, respectively; n must be non-negative and not greater than the size of the objects in bits. If the quantity is signed, either zeros or ones fill vacated positions for a right shift depending on the implementation. If the quantity being shifted is unsigned then zeros are always used to fill vacated positions.

Bitwise operators

There are three bitwise operators &, |, and ^. The & operator performs the AND operation on corresponding bits. The | operator performs the inclusive OR operation on corresponding bits. The ^ operator performs the exclusive OR on corresponding bits.

Logical operators

There are two logical operators && and ||. The logical AND operator && returns 1 if both operands are non-zero, and 0 otherwise. The && operator differs from & in that the right operand is evaluated only if the left operand is non-zero.

The logical OR operator || returns 1 if each of the operands is non-zero, and 0 otherwise. Again a left-to-right evaluation is used, the second operand is not evaluated if the first operand is non-zero.

Comma operator

    exp₁ , exp₂

exp_1 is evaluated and its result discarded; the result delivered is exp_2. The comma operator is useful when the evaluation of exp_1 can influence the result of exp_2, as in

    while (reserv++, word()!='\n') ...

but the language syntax requires a single expression. In this example, reserv is used by the function word.

Assignment operators

An assignment has the form

    lvalue = rvalue

An *lvalue* is one of the following:

    identifier
    * expression
    expression . f
    expression -> f
    expression [e expression]
    (lvalue)

and an *rvalue* is any C expression. The left hand and right hand sides of the assignment are evaluated and the rvalue is stored in the location specified by the lvalue.

When a value is assigned to a variable, truncation may occur. For example, in the context of the declaration

```
int i;
char c;
```

the assignment

```
c = i;
```

may lose some information in the value stored in c. This is sometimes called truncation. The program checker lint will detect this potential problem.

The operator += is defined so that

```
x += y
```

is equivalent to

```
x = x + y
```

The result of the operation is the value stored in the left hand variable following the assignment.

The operator += is a special case of a set of assignment operators that include =, −=, *=, /=, %=, >>=, <<=, &=, ^=, and |=. Operators of this form are defined so that

```
x op= y
```

and

```
x = x op y
```

are equivalent except that x is evaluated only once.

Conditional operator

The conditional operator ?: takes the form

$$exp \ ? \ exp_1 \ : \ exp_2$$

If exp is non-zero, the result is the value of exp_1, otherwise it is exp_2. If the types of exp_1 and exp_2 are different, conversion will occur to yield the result. Mixing arithmetic and non-arithmetic values for exp_1 and exp_2 should be avoided.

A conditional expression may not be used directly on the left hand side of an assignment since it does not deliver an lvalue.

Unary operators

The unary operators are listed below. e represents an expression; v denotes an lvalue.

Operator	Description
*e	Contents of e, for use with pointers.
&v	Address of v, for use with pointers.
−e	Unary minus.
!e	Logical (Boolean) negation.
~e	Bitwise complement of e.
++v	Equivalent to v=v+1.
−−v	Equivalent to v=v−1.
v++	Produces the value of v and then increases v by 1.
v−−	Produces the value of v and then decreases v by 1.
(type)e	Cast e to the specified type.
sizeof(e)	The number of bytes occupied by e.
sizeof(type)	The number of bytes occupied by items of this type.

Conversion of values

Conversion of values from one type to another is available explicitly using the cast operator. Conversion also occurs automatically when an expression appears as a function argument or as an operand. The rules for the conversion of arithmetic values are described below. Pointers are discussed in section 5.2.5.

- A char or a short is converted to int. A character is considered signed, and sign extension occurs during the conversion to integer. Unsigned short integers should be used where appropriate. A float is similarly converted to double.
- Then, if either operand is double the other is converted to double.
- Otherwise, if either operand is long the other is converted to long.
- Otherwise, if either operand is unsigned the other is converted to unsigned.
- Otherwise both operands are int.

When passing arguments to functions no type checking occurs. However in this context, a short or char value is always converted to an int and a float to a double. It is advisable to be sure that the necessary type conversions have been performed. For example, sin(3) is incorrect since the sin function expects a double as its argument and not an int. Correct forms for this call are sin((double)3) or sin(3.0).

Operator precedence and associativity

Figure 5.5 summarizes the operators from higher to lower precedence. Operators on the same line have the same precedence level. When several operators of the same precedence level appear together, they usually associate left-to-right. However, exceptions to this rule are listed. When in doubt, or if the expression is complicated, use parentheses.

The order of evaluation of expression operands and function arguments is not defined by C. As a result the order of side-effects when calling functions cannot be relied upon. Further, expressions involving the commutative operators

```
*       +       &       |       ^
```

may be arbitrarily rearranged by the compiler, so that

```
a + b + c
```

may be evaluated as (a+b)+c or as a+(b+c).

Operator	Associativity
() [] -> . ! ~ ++ -- - * & * / % + - << >> < <= > >= == != & ^ | && || ?: = += ... ,	right to left right to left right to left

Figure 5.5 Operator precedence in C

5.2.3 Control flow

C provides a range of control flow facilities. Normal sequencing of statements is provided by juxtaposition. Branching is provided by if and switch and iteration by for, while and do.

The conditional statement

The form of the conditional statement is

> if (expression) statement$_1$ else statement$_2$

The expression is evaluated and if it is non-zero statement$_1$ is executed; otherwise statement$_2$ is executed. Both statement$_1$ and statement$_2$ can be a block or compound statement of the form

```
{
        optional-declarations
        statements
}
```

The else statement can be omitted producing

if (expression) statement,

The statement

if (expression$_1$)
      if (expression$_2$)
           statement$_1$
      else
           statement$_2$

is potentially ambiguous since the **else** part could be associated with either the first or second **if**. C chooses to associate the **else** with the first **if**. This form should be avoided by using the compound statement, as in,

if (expression) {
    . . .
}

The switch *statement*

The switch statement provides a multi-way branch of the form

switch (expression)
    statement

The expression is evaluated to produce an integer result. The statement normally takes the form of a compound statement several of whose statements may be labeled by

case constant-expression:

The constant-expression may be an integer or character constant such as 1 or ´A´ possibly combined with the operators

```
~ − * / % + −
<< >> & ^ | ?:
< <= > >= == !=
```

The statement labeled by a **constant-expression** is executed if the integer value of the **switch** expression is equal to the **constant-expression**. If no match is found control is transferred to the **default** statement, if any. At most one statement may be labeled

default:

Execution continues from one case to the next and the break statement

break;

is required to exit from within the **switch** to the statement following the **switch**.

Iteration

The while loop has the form

> **while** (expression)
>   statement

The **expression** is evaluated and if it is non-zero, **statement** is executed. This process is repeated until a zero value is returned by **expression**. The statement of a while loop can be compound.

The general form of the for statement is convenient for loops that have an initial condition, an increment and an exit condition. Its form is

> **for** (expression$_1$; expression$_2$; expression$_3$)
>   statement

Formally, this is equivalent to

> expression$_1$;
> **while** (expression$_2$) {
>   statement;
>   expression$_3$
> }

The for and while loop statements evaluate the condition that terminates the loop at the start of the loop. The do...while form of loop tests an expression after the statement is executed. Thus,

> **do** statement
> **while** (expression);

executes the **statement** and then checks the value of **expression** before repetition.

To terminate a loop during execution the **break** statement is used. The effect of

> break;

is to terminate the innermost enclosing **for**, **while**, or do loop, or **switch** statement. The **break** statement does not permit a jump outside several nested loops. To achieve this effect the goto statement is used. Thus

> goto error;

where error is a label marking a statement, as in

> error: statement

A label has the same form as an identifier and it must be defined in the same function body as its accompanying goto. Thus jumps from one function to another are not permitted. The subroutines setjmp and longjmp described in section 5.2.9 provide for 'non-local' jumps.

Another statement that can help avoid the use of goto is

```
continue;
```

that causes the current execution of the loop body to terminate and the next iteration to begin. It is equivalent to a jump to the end of the loop body, but not out of the loop itself.

5.2.4 Functions

Functions in C are similar to routines in ALGOL 68 or to procedures in PL/I. A body of program can be named and then invoked elsewhere as many times as needed. A function may be defined, even if it is only called once, simply to identify an activity.

All functions need a definition that introduces the result type, argument types, and formal parameter names, and the body. If a function is to be used textually before it is defined a declaration may be made specifying the result type and function name, as in the example of the function **average** in section 5.1.3. Otherwise, only a definition is needed.

The general form of a definition is

```
result-type function-name ( argument-names )
        argument-declarations
{
        function-body
}
```

If there is no result, the result-type **void** is used and no value should be returned. If the result-type is omitted then **int** is assumed. Functions that are called before they are defined or declared are also assumed to return an **int** value.

The statements in the function body begin with declarations of local variables. Subsequent program statements may contain the **return** statement. If no **return** statement is present then the function will end after the last statement in its body. A return statement of the form

```
return;
```

exits from the function to the place where the call occurred but no value is returned. If the caller expects a value to be returned then the statement

```
return expression;
```

should be used.

Function calls

Functions may be called either as a statement or as part of an expression. When used as a statement any value returned is discarded. If a function is used within an expression a value should be returned.

Function arguments (or parameters) are passed by value. Each argument is evaluated and a copy made available to the called function. This allows the formal parameters of a function to be used as variables within the function body without affecting the values of variables where the function is

called. Some functions, such as, printf accept a variable number of arguments of differing types. However, printf assumes that the format string and
the number and type of the arguments is in agreement. If not, unexpected
results can occur.

No type checking is performed to ensure that the type of the formal and
actual parameters match. However, lint does perform these checks.

A single result may be returned using the return statement. Results may
also be returned through parameters using pointers.

When a function does not deliver a result it should only be called as a
statement. Functions may be recursive, even mutually recursive. However,
function definitions may not be nested.

5.2.5 Arrays and pointers

Arrays

Arrays provide a set of variables of the same kind. Thus

    int a[10];

makes available 10 integer variables a[0], a[1], ..., a[9]. The square brackets select an element of the array. Subscripted variables such as a[i] or
a[2*i+4] are lvalues and can appear in expressions, be passed to functions
and be assigned to, as in,

    a[i]=4;

In a similar way,

    char c[100];

makes available 100 character variables c[0], c[1], ..., c[99].

Multi-dimensional arrays are introduced, as in,

    int matrix[10][100];

thereby creating the elements matrix[i][j] for $0 \leqslant i \leqslant 9$, $0 \leqslant j \leqslant 99$.

The bounds of arrays are constant and fixed at compile time. The C
preprocessor is normally used to define constants for use as array bounds.

Arrays can be passed as parameters to functions. However, unlike Pascal, bounds for one-dimensional arrays may be omitted from the parameter
specifications, as in,

```
    int length(buffer, size)
          char buffer[], size;
    {
          int i=0;
          while (i<size && (buffer[i]!=' ') ) {
                i++;
          }
          return(i);
    }
```

No space is allocated for the array itself when it appears as a function parameter. When the function is called the value passed is a pointer to the first element of an array. In this example, it is assumed that the number of elements in **buffer** is passed as the separate argument **size**. One way to ensure this is to write, for example,

length(*array,* sizeof(*array*))

Only the last bound may be omitted from an array parameter, so that a two-dimensional array is declared, for example,

```
void invert(matrix)
        int matrix[10][];
  ...
```

Strings are arrays of characters. Conventionally, strings in C end with the null character '\0' (\ followed by zero). The existence of this null character makes string copying particularly simple. For example,

```
void copystr (str1, str2)
        char str1[], str2[];
{

        int i;
        for (i=0; (str2[i]=str1[i]) != '\0'; i++)
                ;

}
```

copies **str1** into **str2**. The body of the **for** loop is the null statement and the copying is performed by the assignment str2[i]=str1[i] as a side effect of evaluating the loop termination condition.

Pointers

String manipulation can be simplified using pointers. A pointer is a variable whose value is the address of another variable. If **pn** is a pointer to the variable **n** that holds the integer 3, this can be expressed pictorially as shown in figure 5.6. Each box is labeled by its lvalue; the contents being the value of the corresponding variable.

When pointers are declared the indirection operator * appears in the declaration. For example, **pn** is declared as

int *pn;

The rationale for this form of declaration is that *pn is an integral value and the notation follows the use of * for indirection.

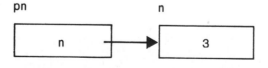

Figure 5.6 Pointers in C

The *address-of* operator & produces the address of a variable. For example,

&x

yields the address of the variable x. Both

*pn = n;

and

pn = &n;

are defined; the latter results in pn pointing to the value held by n, i.e. the original 3. However, the assignment

pn = n;

is illegal since pn is offered the integral value 3 whereas the address of an integer variable is required.

Pointers and arrays are closely related. In the context of

char *cp;
char buffer[100];

the statements

cp = &buffer[0];

and

cp = buffer;

are equivalent. The pointer addresses the zero-th element of the buffer. In a similar way

cp = &buffer[4];

and

cp = buffer+4;

assigns to cp the address of the fourth element of the array.

A string constant may be assigned to a character pointer since the value of the constant is the address of its first element. For example,

char *cp = "...";

In general, a pointer p and integer i can be added to yield the address of the i-th element beyond the array element pointed at by p. Thus, if cp points to buffer[0], then

buffer[i]

is equivalent to

*(cp+i)

The result is an lvalue.

Subtraction of an integer from a pointer is similarly defined. Further, two pointers to objects of the same type may be subtracted to yield an integer corresponding to the number of objects between them. Usually, the two pointers will be pointing to the same array.

The increment and decrement operators are defined for pointer variables. cp++ increments cp by the size of the object pointed to; the value of cp is used in the expression and then the value of cp is incremented. Similar definitions exist for cp−−, ++cp, and −−cp.

Examples

The next two examples illustrate the use of pointers. The function **swap** is defined as

```
swap(x, y)
        int *x, *y;
{
        int temp;
        temp = *x;
        *x = *y;
        *y = temp;
}
```

and is called as

```
swap(&a, &b);
```

where a and b were originally defined by

```
int a, b;
```

The effect is to interchange the values of the two integer variables.

The following example illustrates another implementation of string copying:

```
void copy(str1, str2)
        char *str1, *str2;
{
        while (*str1++ = *str2++)
                ;
}
```

This function is more efficient than that produced by our earlier string copying function. The test for '\0' has been deliberately omitted since this is the default test in a condition.

5.2.6 Structures and unions

Structures group together pieces of related information. For example, the name, age, and weight may be used to characterize a person. Thus

```
struct{
        char name[30];
        int age;
        float weight;
} someone;
```

defines **someone** to be a structure having three members (or fields), namely **name**, **age** and **weight**. To access a structure member the field selection operator . is used, so that,

    someone.age = 21;

or

    copystr("Spike", someone.name);

assigns to the individual fields **age** and **name** respectively.

To avoid repeated writing of a structure declaration an abbreviation can be used. A declaration such as

```
struct  person{
        char  name[30];
        int  age;
        float  weight;
    };
```

makes available the *structure tag* **person**, equivalent to the type **struct{...}** used previously. Using this structure tag the above declaration may be written

    struct person someone;

An alternative abbreviation introduces a name for the type using the **typedef** statement. The form of this statement is the same as a declaration except that it is preceded by the keyword **typedef**; the identifier declared is not a variable but a name for the type.

For example,

    typedef struct{...} person;

defines **person** to be equivalent to **struct{...}**. The declaration

```
struct{
        char  name[30];
        int  age;
        float  weight;
    } someone;
```

can then be replaced by

    person someone;

Besides application of the operators . and &, no other operator can be applied to structures. Some versions of C allow structures to be assigned or passed as arguments to functions; however, structures are usually manipulated by pointers. The size of the structure is automatically taken into account when structure pointers and integers are added or subtracted.

If **ptr** is a pointer to a structure, such as **person** already defined, then

    ptr −> age

is defined as

```
*( ptr . age )
```

and is an lvalue pointing to the **age** member of **person**.

Self-referential structures can be defined. For example,

```
struct node
{
        struct node *left;
        struct node *right;
        int val;
};
```

The definition of **node** makes use of **node** itself; it does not contain a member of type **node** but includes pointers **left** and **right** to objects of type **node**. Pointers to such structures are common and, for each structure defined, it is convenient to define **nodeptr** as

```
typedef struct node *nodeptr;
```

for use with the definition of **node** above.

To determine how much space is occupied by a particular structure, the **sizeof** function is used.

```
sizeof(object)
```

or

```
sizeof(type)
```

returns the number of bytes occupied by the object or an object of the specified type.

To create binary trees such as **node** defined above, storage allocation facilities are required. In C storage allocation and deallocation is the responsibility of the programmer. Two routines are provided.

```
malloc(n)
```

allocates n contiguous bytes of store and returns the address of the first of these; as, for example, in

```
struct node *ptr;
ptr = malloc(sizeof(struct node));
```

Since **malloc** guarantees that the pointer returned is non-zero the value zero is used to denote the nil pointer value, as in,

```
#define nilnode ((nodeptr)0)
```

Storage is returned to the free pool using the statement

```
free(ptr);
```

The value **ptr** must have been obtained by an earlier call of **malloc**.

The example shown below illustrates the use of structures, pointers and the storage allocator **malloc** and uses the definitions introduced so far for **node**. In this example the function **new** is defined to take an integer value and return a pointer to a newly created tree node containing that value:

```
nodeptr  new(v)
        int       v;
{
        nodeptr n = (nodeptr)malloc(sizeof(struct node));
        n->left = n->right = nilnode;
        newval = n->val = v;
        return(n);
} /* new */
```

The variable **newval** is set to the last value created and will be used shortly.
Another function required is to print a tree and this is defined as

```
void  print(n)
        nodeptr  n;
{
        if(n != nilnode) {
                print(n->left);
                printf("%d\n", n->val);
                print(n->right);
        }
} /* print */
```

The remainder of the program is shown in figure 5.7 and consists of a function called **split** that sorts a new node into the tree, given the root, and the function **main** that contains the overall organization required. **split** is unusual in that it keeps the most recently accessed nodes near the root of the tree.

Unions

Variables provide for the storage of a particular type of value. For example, a **float** cannot be assigned to (stored in) a variable i declared as an **int**. In a program that allocates a significant amount of storage it is often necessary to be able to use the same variable to store different types of value. The union type is provided for this purpose.

For example,

```
union  number {
        int  i;
        float  f;
} x;
```

declares storage for the variable x that is large enough for either an int or float value. Only one value at a time may be kept in x. If x contains an int value it can be accessed as x.i and if it is a float value it is accessed as x.f.

The language itself does not keep track of the type of the value stored in x. This is the responsibility of the user. Either an integer variable can be used for this purpose or it may be possible to deduce the type of x from other information available when writing the program.

```
int        newval;

void split(ladr, radr, tree)
        nodeptr *ladr, *radr;
        nodeptr tree;
{
        if( tree == nilnode ) {
                *ladr = *radr = nilnode;
        }
        else if(newval > tree->val) {
                *ladr = tree;
                split(&tree->right, radr, tree->right);
        }else{
                *radr = tree;
                split(ladr, &tree->left, tree->left);
        }
} /* split */

main(argc, argv)
        int argc;
        char *argv[];
{
        nodeptr root=new(0);

        while(argc-- > 1) {
                nodeptr r = new(atoi(argv[1]));
                split(&r->left, &r->right, root);
                root = r;
                argv++;
        }
        print(root);
} /* main */
```

Figure 5.7 Tree sorting program

5.2.7 The C preprocessor

The C compiler automatically invokes a preprocessor when a program is compiled. Lines beginning with the # character are interpreted by the preprocessor. Several facilities are provided.

Constant definition and macro expansion

A line of the form

        #define identifier token ...

causes identifier to be replaced throughout the remainder of the file by one or more tokens, where each token is an identifier, keyword, constant, string, operator, or punctuation such as ; . For example,

#define BUFSIZ 512

allows **BUFSIZ** to be used in the program and is replaced by 512 wherever it appears. Replacement of defined constants does not occur within string constants.

Macros may also be defined and may have parameters.

#define identifier(arg$_1$, arg$_2$, ..., arg$_n$) token-string

causes all subsequent occurrences of identifier(p$_1$, p$_2$, ..., p$_n$) to be replaced by the token-string with arg$_1$ replaced by p$_1$, arg$_2$ by p$_2$, ..., and arg$_n$ by p$_n$. The argument list can be empty, however the macro preprocessor checks that the number supplied and the number defined agree.

Macros are sometimes used to replace function definitions, usually for efficiency reasons. A macro argument, unlike a function argument, is evaluated once each time it appears in the definition, so that using the definition

#define max(a, b) ((a)>(b) ? (a) : (b))

the call

max(i++, j++)

will increment either i or j twice.

Parentheses surround the arguments in the definition to avoid possible ambiguities. Since macros are evaluated by the C preprocessor, unexpected results could occur resulting from operator precedence. For example, without any parentheses in the above definition,

max(p?q:r,s)

would expand into

p ? q : r > s ? p ? q : r : s

that is understood by C to be the same as

(p ? q : ((r>s) ? (p?q:r) : s))

File inclusion

The contents of a file (usually containing some definitions) can be included in a C program by the statement

#include "filename"

that causes the statement to be replaced by the entire contents of the file filename. The file is sought first in the directory holding the original C program; if it is not there then some standard system directories are searched.

#include <filename>

also causes the line to be replaced by the file contents; however, the filename is sought only in standard directories, *not* in the directory of the original C program.

Conditional compilation

Conditional statements allow part of a program to be compiled depending on some condition. Typically the decision depends on which machine is being used or on whether a program is at a debugging stage.

Conditional compilation is written in the form

```
#if ...
        section one
#else
        section two
#endif
```

or the form

```
#if ...
        section one
#endif
```

The test can take the following forms.

```
#if  constant-expression
```

tests the value of the constant expression (section 5.2.3) and, if zero, the text that follows is included.

```
#ifdef  identifier
```

includes the following text if **identifier** has already been defined to the preprocessor by a #define line.

```
#ifndef  identifier
```

includes text that follows if identifier is currently undefined to the preprocessor. The statement

```
#undef  identifier
```

removes **identifier** from the list of defined identifiers.

Certain identifiers are defined in some implementations and should be avoided except to determine the kind of machine you are compiling for. These are as follows:

```
gcos    ibm     interdata       mert
os      pdp11   tss     unix    vax
```

5.2.8 Language structure

C is a block structured language similar to ALGOL 60. However, it differs in one important respect; function declarations cannot be nested. In C, blocks are sequences of declarations and statements enclosed by { and }; when declarations are absent this construction is called a compound statement. Within blocks or compound statements, individual statements themselves can be blocks or compound statements.

The normal scope rules associated with block-structured languages apply. If a variable x is declared in an inner block that definition causes other outer

declarations of x to be superseded until the end of its block. In these circumstances the outer x can still be accessed indirectly, for example, by use of
a pointer.

Storage class specifiers convey information about the storage requirements and scope of variables. In C there are several such specifiers. These
include auto, static, extern, register, and typedef and they qualify declarations. Thus

```
static int a[20];
```

or

```
auto char c;
```

Of these, typedef is called a storage class specifier for convenience; no
storage is reserved. Further, a register declaration is similar to auto. It sug-
gests to the compiler that associated variables should be placed in registers
for efficiency purposes; only limited numbers of register variables are available on a given machine and then only for variables of certain types, e.g. integers or pointers.

At most one storage class specifier may accompany each declaration. If
the specifier is missing, auto is assumed inside a function and extern outside
a function.

Let us consider first external variables. If a function accesses any global
variable that variable must be an external variable. It must be defined outside the function, perhaps in another file; the definition allocates storage.
The variable may also be declared within the function, as in,

```
char line[80];
main()
{
        extern char line[];
        ...
}
```

Variables that are not external are said to be internal.

Each variable that is local to a routine is called an automatic variable,
and has storage class auto. Such variables typically are allocated space from
a stack. They are created on entry to the function and removed on exit.
Care should be taken with pointers to such variables since they have only a
limited lifetime.

Finally there is the storage class static. Static variables may be internal
or external. Internal static variables, i.e. those declared inside functions, are
like the own variables of ALGOL 60. The value of the variable persists from
one call of the function to the next, unlike an automatic variable. External
static variables are declared outside functions and are known throughout the
remainder of the file in which they are declared, but are not available in any
other file. Functions may be declared static and then are limited in scope to
the file in which the definition occurs. This is useful for restricting the avai-
lability of the function.

Declarations can contain an initialization of the variables declared.

- Static and external variables are always initialized to 0.
- All expressions that initialize static or external variables must be constant expressions or expressions that reduce to the address of a previously declared variable possibly offset by some constant amount.
- Automatic and register variables may be initialized by arbitrary expressions containing constants and previously declared variables and functions.
- Automatic arrays, structures and unions may not be initialized.

The following examples illustrate initializations:

```
int prime[ ] = {2, 3, 5, 7};
```
Since no bounds are present the size of the array is determined from the size of the aggregate thus creating prime[0], ..., prime[3].
```
char message[ ] = "You have mail.\n";
```
The string initializes the array message and provides the bounds; note that '\0' is added at the end of the array.
```
int table[4][3] = {{2, 3, 5},
                    {7, 9, 11},
                    {13, 17, 19},
                    {0, 0, 0}};
```

5.2.9 The standard C library

The standard input-output library

The functions provided in the standard input-output (stdio) library constitute an efficient user-level input-output library. The in-line macros getc and putc read and write characters quickly. The higher level routines gets, fgets, scanf, fscanf, fread, puts, fputs, printf, fprintf, fwrite can be freely intermixed with the lower level operations getc and putc.

A file with associated buffering is called a *stream,* and is declared to be a pointer to a defined type FILE. fopen creates descriptive data for a stream and returns a pointer to designate the stream in all further transactions. There are three normally open streams with constant pointers declared in the header file and associated with the standard open files:

stdin   The standard input file.
stdout   The standard output file.
stderr   The standard error output file.

The constant NULL designates no stream at all.

The integer constant EOF is returned upon end-of-file or upon error by integer functions that deal with streams and is defined in the header file <stdio.h>. Any program that uses the standard input-output package should include this header file.

For purposes of efficiency, the standard library buffers a line of output to a terminal by default and attempts to do this transparently by flushing the output whenever a **read** from the standard input is necessary. This is almost always transparent, but may cause confusion or malfunctioning of programs which use standard input-output routines but use **read** themselves to read from the standard input.

The function printf

The function **printf** formats output according to a control string and was introduced in section 5.1.2. Available formats are as follows:

%c	Character.
%d	Decimal integer.
%f	Floating-point number.
%o	Octal integer.
%s	String.
%x	Hexadecimal integer.
%%	The % character itself.

Any of the numeric formats may be preceded by the letter l to indicate **long**. A format may also include field width specifications. A − indicates a left adjusted field. A number following the % character denotes the minimum field width for the converted value. A second number may be specified separated by . from the first and indicates the maximum field width. Some examples of formats illustrate:

%2d	Print decimal, padding with spaces on the right to ensure a minimum of two characters output.
%−3d	Print in decimal with spaces on the left to ensure a minimum width of 3 characters.
%.12s	Print a string with a maximum of 12 characters printed.
%ld	Print a long integer. The l modifier applies to all the numeric formats.

The function scanf

The function corresponding to **printf** for input is called **scanf**. The format specification is similar but the remaining arguments are the addresses of variables where the converted values are to be stored. Blanks are usually ignored and any literal character in the control argument is matched with the corresponding character in the input. For example,

```
double d;
scanf("%lf", &d);
```

will read into the variable d the value of the next floating-point constant in the input.

As another example, the call

```
int i; float x; char name[50];
scanf("%d%f%s", &i, &x, name);
```

with the input line

    25   54.32E−1   thompson

will assign to i the value 25, x the value 5.432, and name will contain
thompson\0. Using the same declarations

    scanf("%2d%f%*d%[1234567890]", &i, &x, name);

with input

    56789 0123 56a72

will assign 56 to i, 789.0 to x, skip 0123, and place the string 56\0 in name.
The next call to getchar will return the character a.

The scanf function returns the number of input items read; missing or
illegal data items are not counted. If end-of-file is encountered EOF is returned.

String functions

A complete set of string copying and comparison functions is available and is
described in appendix 3.

Error recovery routines

Two standard library routines setjmp and longjmp are provided for error
recovery.

The routine setjmp is declared as

    int setjmp(where)
            jmp_buf where;

and, when called, saves the program state for use by longjmp. The value returned is 0.

The routine used to recover the saved program state is

    void longjmp(where, val)
            jmp_buf where;
            int val;

After a call to longjmp execution resumes at the original call of setjmp. The
value returned to setjmp is val. A system header file is used to declare the
data type jmp_buf.

These routines are useful for interactive programs that need to recover
from serious errors, return to a standard place in the program, and ask the
user for further instructions.

5.2.10 Postscript

The following dogma is observed by most C programs written in the standard
distributed system. Sometimes the only important attribute of a particular
rule is that many people use it. Other rules represent techniques that make
the programs easier to read or write.

- Use **typedef** and avoid complicated declarations.
- Use **#define** for constants and use upper case names. In particular, avoid integer constants in a program for buffer sizes and other quantities that can reasonably be varied.
- Avoid using macros for functions except where efficiency is important.
- Always declare the result type of functions and use an explicit return statement. Always return a value from **main** since it is the exit status of the command.
- Check the returned value from system calls for an error condition.
- Use system header files such as <math.h> and <stdio.h> in section 5.1. Do not assume the values for constants such as **EOF** or for characters in the machine's character set.
- Avoid conditional expressions where the branches have non-numeric types.
- Adopt a consistent layout style and use braces for the control flow statements. A comment at the closing brace of a function definition helps if the function body extends over more than a page.
- Use casts to convert values returned by storage allocators to the appropriate type.
- Keep header files containing structure definitions separate from the main program. Do not use more than one copy of such declarations; refer to header files using the #include statement. Keep related functions in the same file and use the **static** definition for functions local to a file.
- Use **ifdef** as little as possible. Over-use may make the program unreadable.
- Run the **lint** command and understand its output.

5.3 Program organization and management

5.3.1 Compiling programs

C programs are compiled using the cc command. Simple programs, such as those in the earlier examples, are easily maintained as a single file. For example,

```
cc average.c
```

compiles the program **average.c** leaving a corresponding executable **a.out** file.

```
cc −o average average.c
```

leaves the executable program in the file **average**. If this were part of a larger program split over two files **average.c** and **main.c**, the compilation for both files to produce an executable program is

```
cc −o average main.c average.c
```

To avoid recompiling both **main.c** and **average.c** each time a change is made, an intermediate step can be introduced. This involves keeping the *object* files main.o and average.o produced using the command

```
cc -c main.c average.c
```

The executable program average is then produced by

```
cc -o average main.o average.o
```

A program such as the shell consists of 35 files whose combined length is 4800 lines. Of these, 24 *source* files contain function definitions and the remaining files are *header* files containing definitions used by one or more of the source files. This organization is typical of UNIX programs. By splitting up the complete source into functional subsections compilation time following a change can be reduced and the use of function names can be localized to a single subsection using the **static** declaration. Reading and understanding the program may also be easier.

5.3.2 The make command

When developing a multi-file program with more than one source or header file, keeping track of which files need to be recompiled following modifications can be error prone and tedious. The make command is designed to relieve the user of this book-keeping activity and serves to document the relationships between files.

make enables dependency information between files to be specified. When invoked, make updates a *target file* if it depends on files that have been modified since the target was last modified, or if the target does not exist. With each dependency an action can be specified, such as compiling a source file to produce the corresponding object file or printing a file that has been changed since it was last printed.

The description of the dependencies and actions is kept in the *makefile* called, by default, either makefile or Makefile. For example,

```
average:    main.o average.o
            cc -o average main.o average.o
```

is the makefile for the program average defined earlier in this chapter. The makefile should be read as

average *depends on* main.o *and* average.o

and if either .o file is more recent than the file average then execute the command

```
cc -o average main.o average.o
```

make already knows enough about .c and .o files to know that cc should be used if a .c source file is more recent than the corresponding .o object file.

A refinement of this makefile is needed if a header file such as defs.h were included in main.c and average.c. Additional dependency information might be

```
main.o average.o: defs.h
```

that would cause both files to be recompiled if **defs.h** were changed.

In general, a makefile contains a sequence of entries that specify dependencies. The first line of an entry is a list of targets separated by spaces, then a colon, then a list of files. Text following a semicolon, and all following lines that begin with a tab, are shell commands to be executed to update the target.

Using **make**, program development consists of the following steps:

- Think and edit.
- Make.
- Test and repeat.

Without arguments, **make** assumes that the first dependent file in the *makefile* is the *target* file. The target can be explicitly specified, so that

    make main.o

would ensure that **main.o** is up to date.

make has some useful options. To discover those actions necessary but without executing any actions the command

    make −n

is used. Normally, **make** prints each command before it is executed. This output can be suppressed using the −s option. Occasionally, a system of files can be up to date although the dates associated with the files are inconsistent. The command

    make −t

will modify the dates of files to ensure consistency by *touching* the files concerned.

A makefile may also contain comment and string substitution requests. A comment begins with a # and ends with a newline.

Makefile entries of the form

    string1 = string2

are macro definitions and subsequent appearances of $(string1) are replaced by **string2**. If **string1** is a single character, the parentheses are optional.

make contains a list of suffixes that provide some default rules. The default list is

    .SUFFIXES:; .out .o .c .e .r .f .y .l .s .p

The rule to create a file with suffix **s2** that depends on a similarly named file with suffix **s1** is specified as an entry for the *target* **s1s2**. In such an entry, the special macro $* stands for the target name with suffix deleted, $@ for the full target name, $< for the complete list of prerequisites, and $? for the list of files that are out of date. For example, a rule for making optimized .o files from .c files is

    .c.o: ; cc −c −O −o $@ $*.c

5.3.3 The lint command

For programs longer than a few lines some additional tools are useful. The lint command has already been mentioned and is a program that is worth becoming familiar with. Although some of its messages may be irrelevant, others should be heeded as indicating questionable programming practice.

The consistency between function definitions and their calls is typically not checked by C compilers. Various other checks, often referred to as type checking, are also not performed. lint attempts to fill this gap. As well as checking for type consistency, unused variables and functions are listed, and some instances of variables used before they are set are detected.

Some constructions listed by lint as dubious are legal. For example,

```
if (1!=0)
```

reports "constant in conditional context". A more realistic example might be produced by insufficient parentheses, as in

```
if (x&1==0)
```

where

```
if ((x&1)==0)
```

was probably intended.

5.3.4 Program libraries

A program library in the C environment is stored as an *archive* file. Each member of the archive file is itself an object file, members being added, updated or removed using the ar command. By convention archive or library files have names ending with .a. For example, the library that is automatically invoked when compiling a C program using cc is kept in /lib/libc.a.

Within the distributed UNIX systems the standard libraries are documented in sections 2 and 3 of the manual. The default C library (libc) consists of the functions in section 2 (UNIX system calls), section 3 (without a suffix) and section 3S containing the standard input-output (stdio) package. If functions from 3S are used then the statement

```
#include <stdio.h>
```

should appear in the program.

Certain mathematical functions, such as sqrt(), are documented in section 3M of the manual and require

```
#include <math.h>
```

in source files. When producing an executable program that uses this mathematical library the cc command should include −lm, as in,

```
cc −o average main.o average.o −lm
```

Other libraries are used by naming the library (archive) file or using the −l... option of cc for standard libraries.

Library maintenance

A library allows a set of subroutines to be used by other programs. Libraries
are created and maintained using the ar command and are conventionally
kept in files with names ending in .a. The contents of a library are object
files, sufficient information being present to enable the subroutine to be relo-
cated and linked with the main program. The program ld is the link editor
(or loader) used by the cc command to produce executable a.out files from
object files and libraries.

A library file is only scanned once for undefined names. If the subroutines in the library itself refer to other names in the library, then these definitions must appear earlier than their corresponding definition. This imposes
an ordering constraint on library file members.

Current versions of the UNIX system provide the program ranlib that
creates a table of contents for a library archive enabling the loader ld to access its members at random. In UNIX system V these functions have been
incorporated into ar and ld. On older UNIX systems two tools lorder and
tsort are provided for this purpose. Given a set of object files, lorder generates a list of dependent name pairs, and tsort takes such a list and produces
a partial ordering of this list suitable for ld.

The archive program may also be used to consolidate any set of files.

5.3.5 Performance measurement

The time command

The overall time taken to execute a command may be determined using the
time command. Using the average program from section 5.1.3 as an example,

    time average

will first print the output of the average command, followed by

                    6.0 real   5.4 user   0.1 sys

The *real* time is the time elapsed on the clock for the entire execution. The
user time is processor time spent executing the user's part of the program,
and the *sys* time is the amount of time spent in the system executing system
calls. Programs that perform a lot of input or output may use significant
amounts of system time.

Profiling

A C program may be profiled to provide a count of function calls and how
much time is spent in each function. No changes need be made to the program but it must be compiled with the −p option of the cc command. When
the program is run the file mon.out is created containing the profile data and
the prof command is used to print the data.

As an example, the command average from section 5.1.3 was recompiled
with this option. The program was run and the output produced by

prof average

is shown in figure 5.8.

%time	cumsecs	#call	ms/call	name
62.8	3.62			_sqrt
30.4	5.37			_frexp
5.2	5.67	81	3.71	_average
0.6	5.71			__doprnt
0.3	5.72			__flsbuf
0.3	5.74			_close
0.3	5.76			_printf
0.3	5.77			_write
0.0	5.77	1	0.00	_main

Figure 5.8 The output from prof average

In this example, only the functions compiled with the −p option have been profiled.

5.3.6 Miscellaneous tools

Executable programs produced by cc contain a symbol table that can be used when debugging. Once a program is working this extra information can be removed (and file space saved) using the **strip** command, as in

strip average

To discover the program and data sizes for an executable program

size average

will print

text−size + data−size + bss−size = total−size

The **bss−size** is the length of the uninitialized data segment.
To obtain a list of all the names used by a program

nm average

is used. The output includes the name of every symbol and whether it is a data-symbol (variable) or text-symbol (program label or function name).

5.4 Debugging a C program

Most programs do not work the first time they are run. If you are fortunate you will have an idea from the program's behavior what is wrong with it. Otherwise, you are faced with a choice: think, add printf statements to print the values of key variables during execution, or use a debugger. If you choose to use a debugger, **adb** is available on PDP 11/45 or 11/70. On a VAX 11/780 **sdb** (see appendix 1) is available and provides more C oriented facilities. This section describes **adb** since it is more basic and more universally available, although the operation of **sdb** is similar.

A program can fail in the following ways:

- It can loop indefinitely.
- It can exit unexpectedly with a memory fault or other violation of the hardware.
- It runs although it has unexpected behavior and does not function properly.
- It can fail to get the resources (such as files) it needs.

A program that fails with one of the errors listed in section 6.6.1 may generate a **core** file containing the data and program from the aborted run. From a terminal generating the quit signal using a ^\ terminates a process with a core dump unless that process has made arrangements to catch the signal.

adb provides requests to look at core image files resulting from aborted programs, print variables in a variety of formats, modify binary files, and run programs interactively with embedded breakpoints. It can be used to examine any file although it is intended for a.out and core files.

5.4.1 Debugging a core image

For debugging, **adb** is invoked as

    adb objfile corefile

where objfile is an executable file and **corefile** is a core image file. Frequently,

    adb

is sufficient, the defaults being a.out and **core**, respectively. An end-of-file or the request

    $q

will exit from **adb**.

The debugging request

    $c

gives a C backtrace of the subroutines called. The request

    $C

gives a C backtrace plus an interpretation of all the local variables in each function and their values (in octal). The request

    $e

prints out the values of all external variables. A specific external variable can also be printed (in decimal) using

    name/d

5.4.2 adb **requests**

adb has requests for examining locations in either the program file or the
core file. The **?** request examines the contents of **objfile,** the **/** request examines the **corefile.** The general form of these requests is

> **address ? format**

or

> **address / format**

   adb maintains a current address, called *dot,* similar to the current line in
the editor **ed.** When an address is entered, *dot* is set to that location, so that

> **0126?i**

sets *dot* to octal **0126** and prints the instruction at that address. The request

> **. ,10/d**

prints **10** decimal numbers starting at the current address. *dot* is the address
of the last item printed. When used with the **?** or **/** requests, the current address can be advanced and the next item printed by typing return; it can be
decremented and an item printed by typing ^.
   An **adb** address is an expression made up from decimal, octal, and hexadecimal integers, and symbols from the program under test. These may be
combined with the operators:

Operator	Description
+	Addition.
−	Subtraction.
*	Multiplication.
%	Integer division.
&	Bitwise conjunction.
|	Bitwise disjunction.
#	Round up to the next multiple.
~	Bitwise negation.
*a	Contents of *a* in corefile.
@a	Contents of *a* in objfile.

Binary operators are left associative and are less binding than unary operations; there are no precedence rules and all arithmetic within **adb** is 32 bits.

5.4.3 adb **formats**

To print data, a format describes the printout. The following are the most
commonly used format letters that follow the **/** and **?** requests. Format
letters are also available for long values, for example, **D** for long decimal, and
F for double floating point. The last format is remembered so that a request
without a format prints the requested location in the previous format.

Format	Description
b	One byte in octal.
c	One byte as a character.
o	One word in octal.
d	One word in decimal.
f	Two words in floating point.
i	A machine instruction.
s	A null terminated character string.
u	One word as unsigned integer.
w	Write a word to the file.

The most general form of a request is

address, count request modifier

that sets *dot* to address and executes the request count times.
The following table illustrates the **adb** requests.

Request	Description
?	Print contents from a.out file.
/	Print contents from core file.
=	Print value of the current address.
:	Breakpoint control.
$	Miscellaneous requests.
!	Escape to the shell.
>	Assign to **adb** variable.

adb catches signals, so that the quit signal cannot be used to exit from **adb**. An interrupt causes **adb** to abandon the current request and return to read another request. The request $q ($Q, or ^D) exits from **adb**.

5.4.4 Setting breakpoints in adb

A program may be executed under the control of **adb**.

adb a.out −

prepares **a.out** for testing. To start up the program under test, the request

:r ...

is used. Following the :r request, arguments can be supplied and some simple input-output redirection is permitted Control is now handed over to the program under test and **adb** waits either for the program to terminate or for it to receive a signal. When a signal is received, such as an interrupt from the terminal, or a memory fault, **adb** will regain control and the program is suspended. The program under test may also be stopped when a specific function is executed by planting a breakpoint. Breakpoints are set by

address [, count] : b

where **address** is a C function name.

To print the location of breakpoints type

$b

The display will indicate a count field. A breakpoint is bypassed count−1 times before causing a stop.

To delete a breakpoint

address : d

is used.

Whenever adb is in control, locations can be examined, breakpoints removed, variables modified, and the process resumed.

The quit and interrupt signals act on adb itself rather than on the program being debugged. If such a signal occurs then the program being debugged is stopped and control is returned to adb. The signal is saved by adb and is passed on to the test program using

:c

This can be used to test signal handling routines. The signal is not passed on to the test program if

:c 0

is used instead.

The program being debugged can be single stepped by

:s

If necessary, this request will start up the program being debugged and stop executing after the first instruction.

5.4.5 Address mapping

The system provides several executable file formats. These are used to tell the system how to arrange the program in memory. adb interprets these file formats differently and provides access to the segments through a set of maps.

A map is created for each file examined by adb and is used to translate addresses into locations within the file. The map for the a.out file is referenced by ? whereas the map for core file is referenced by /. Furthermore, a good rule of thumb is to use ? for instructions and / for data when looking at programs. To print out these maps type

$m

Each map contains two segments consisting of a base b1, b2, an extent e1, e2, and a file offset f1, f2. Given an address A, the location in the file is calculated as follows

$$b1 \leqslant A \leqslant e1 \implies \text{file address} = (A - b1) + f1$$
$$b2 \leqslant A \leqslant e2 \implies \text{file address} = (A - b2) + f2$$

Chapter 6

UNIX System Programming

This chapter describes the C interface to the UNIX programming environment. The problems of writing programs that interface directly with the UNIX system are discussed. The topics include creating and removing files, creating processes, handling interrupts, sending signals, and the use of pipes.

6.1 Argument conventions

Most commands are written either as shell procedures or as C programs. In both cases the arguments to the command are made available as strings of characters when the command is executed. A loosely defined set of argument conventions exists that should be followed when designing new commands. Initial arguments of the form

−letter

frequently specify options. Other arguments are normally treated as file names. Consequently, it is unwise to use file names that begin with a minus-sign; they can cause considerable confusion. Commands vary in their treatment of arguments. Some check more carefully for consistency than others. Commands that do not expect arguments cannot be relied upon to check that none are supplied.

The general form of most command argument conventions is

command-name [options] [files]

An option sometimes requires two arguments, as in the −o option of the cc command; for example,

cc −o simple simple.c

There are some exceptions to the rule of treating arguments as options. The **test** command is described in chapter 4 and evaluates its arguments as an expression. Another example is the **dd** command, described in appendix 1, that converts and copies a file.

Argument handling in C programs

A C program begins execution with a call to the function main declared as

```
int main(argc, argv, arge)
        int argc;
        char *argv[];
        char *arge[];
```

argv is a pointer to a vector of arguments expected by main and argc is the number of elements in argv. Suppose the corresponding command expects three arguments p1, p2, and p3, then

```
argc      is 4,
argv[0]   is the name of the command,
argv[1]   is a pointer to p1,
argv[2], argv[3]
          are pointers to p2 and p3, respectively, and
argv[4]   is 0.
```

Each of the arguments accessed through argv[1], argv[2], and argv[3] is represented as a string of characters and is terminated by '\0'.

```
int main(argc, argv)
        int argc;
        char *argv[];
{
        while (--argc>0) {
                printf("%s%c", *++argv, (argc>1) ? ' ' : '\n');
        }
        return(0);
}
```

Figure 6.1 The echo command

arge contains information about the environment. Many programs omit the declaration of arge and use the getenv subroutine to access environment values. This topic is discussed further in section 6.5.6.

Although C compilers permit arguments to be omitted if they are unused, it is good practice to declare them anyway. The C program checker lint checks for unused arguments.

As an example of argument handling a simple echo command is given in figure 6.1. echo prints its arguments separated by spaces on the standard output.

A more complete example of handling command arguments is illustrated in the outline of the cat command shown in figure 6.2. The −u option sets a flag that is used within the function copy. If no file name arguments are given, the standard input is copied. The function copy with a nil string is assumed to copy the standard input and is shown in figure 6.3.

The loop body examines each argument of the vector argv and discriminates on the first character. If a − is present, the argument is treated as an option; otherwise it represents a file name and is copied to the standard output. Adding options is easy, since the framework for argument handling is in place.

6.2 Basic input-output

The buffered input-output package (stdio) is summarized in chapter 5 and is usually adequate for simple input-output requirements. This section describes the lowest level of input-output available in the UNIX system.

```
int  unbuff;

int  main(argc, argv)
          int  argc;
          char *argv[];
{
          char c;
          char *cp;
          int  copied = 0;

          while (argc > 1) {
                    switch (*argv[1]) {
                    case '-': /* argv[1] is the option string */
                              cp = argv[1];
                              while(c = *++cp){
                                        /* process each letter */
                                        switch(c){
                                        case 'u':          unbuff++;
                                                  break;
                                        default: /* unexpected letter */
                                                  ;
                                        }
                              }
                              break;

                    default: /* other arguments */
                              copy(argv[1]);
                              copied++;
                    }
                    argc--; argv++;
          }
          if(copied==0){
                    copy((char*)0);
          }
          return(0);
}
```

Figure 6.2 A skeleton of the cat command

Input-output operates with open files that are represented by file descriptors, each file descriptor being represented as an integer. Some file descriptors can be assumed to exist when any user program is run. These are:

0   Standard input (read only).
1   Standard output (write only).
2   Standard error output (read and write).

These are opened by login and may have been redirected by the shell. When a file has been opened or created by a program, the file descriptor will have to be remembered for use in input and output operations. File descriptors are used for both pipes and files.

A file may be opened for reading, writing or updating, i.e. both reading and writing simultaneously. Random access is available for files, but not for pipes. This topic is discussed in section 6.4.2.

Normally, input-output is sequential. If a particular byte was last written or read, the next input-output call implicitly refers to the next byte. For each open file the current position is maintained and this value is the address of the next byte to be read or written. If n bytes are read or written the current position is advanced by n bytes.

Objects other than characters may be stored in a file. For example,

```
int i;

while(...) {
        write(1, &i, sizeof(i));
}
```

will write a sequence of int values to the standard output. The same form should be used when reading the information from the file. Also, the same kind of computer should normally be used. The sequence of characters stored in the file is implementation dependent. These same constraints should be observed for any data type other than char.

To summarize: if bytes are written then bytes should be read; if integers are written, integers should be read.

6.2.1 The open system call

The open system call creates files or makes existing files available for reading or writing. It is declared as

```
int open(name, mode)
        char *name;
        int mode;
```

name is the address of a string of characters (terminated by '\0') representing the complete pathname of the file. The second argument mode indicates

0   for reading,
1   for writing, and
2   for reading and writing.

On some systems open takes a third argument. The value returned by open is the file descriptor that is used for all input-output to the file. The current reading or writing position is initially set to the beginning of the file.

If the file cannot be opened, −1 is returned. Failure can result for any of the following reasons.

- The file does not exist.
- A directory in the path name does not exist.
- Too many files are already open.
- The file is not readable or writable, as necessary.

To discover whether a file descriptor corresponds to an open file, the dup system call may be used. The call

    dup(filedescriptor)

returns a new (duplicate) file descriptor if its argument is an open file. If filedescriptor is invalid or there are too many files already open, then −1 is returned. Another way to test the status of an open file is to use the fstat system call (section 6.4.3).

6.2.2 Reading and writing files

Once a file has been opened, reading and writing can take place using the functions read and write.

The function read takes the form

    int read(filedescriptor, buffer, nbytes)
            int filedescriptor;
            char *buffer;
            int nbytes;

A call of read places nbytes characters in the location pointed to by buffer. The value returned by read is either

- the number of characters read if an end-of-file is not reached, or
- zero if the end-of-file is reached.

read may return fewer characters than requested.

The character ^D at a terminal causes any partially constructed line to be transmitted to the program waiting for a read system call. (See also section 6.4.4.) If no characters are available to be read then the call of read returns a zero. By convention, this is the end-of-file indication. Further reading may return more characters although this practice should be avoided.

The function write takes the form

    int write(filedescriptor, buffer, nbytes)
            int filedescriptor;
            char *buffer;
            int nbytes;

and outputs nbytes characters from the array buffer to the file described by filedescriptor. For efficiency, buffers of size 64 bytes or more are recommended although any length can be used within the limits of available

memory and the size of the array. If an error occurs, such as a bad file
descriptor or a bad buffer address, write returns −1. When writing robust
programs it is advisable to include checks for error conditions to take account
of events such as running out of file space.

To illustrate the use of **read** and **write** the following program copies its
standard input to its standard output a character at a time.

```
char c[1];

while (read(0, c, 1)==1) {
        write(1, c, 1);
}
```

The identifier c is declared to be a character array since this does not require
the appearance of & in the uses of c. The address of the **char** c[0] is automatically used as the argument.

The program given above is inefficient since it invokes a system call for
each character read and written. The program in figure 6.3 is considerably
more efficient since it avoids this overhead. The function **copy** defined below
is used by the **cat** command described in figure 6.2.

```
#define BUFSIZ 512

copy(s)
        char *s;
{
        char buffer[BUFSIZ];
        int length;
        int fd = 0;        /* assume standard input */
        if (s) {
                fd = open(s, 0);
        }
        do{     length = read(fd, buffer, BUFSIZ);
                write(1, buffer, length);
        } while (length > 0);

        return(0);
}
```

Figure 6.3 The copy **subroutine**

When **read** reaches the end-of-file and there is nothing more to read it
returns −1 as previously described. However, **read** may fail for other reasons
such as an interrupt being received or the file descriptor being invalid. A
complete list of errors resulting from failure of system calls is given in the
errno section of appendix 2. To use the symbolic names of these errors it is
necessary to include the file errno.h, as in,

#include <errno.h>

The system call **close** completes the introduction to system calls dealing with file descriptors.

close(filedescriptor)

ends the association between the **filedescriptor** and its associated file (or pipe). Normally all files are closed automatically when their associated process dies, but since the number of open files per process is limited it is sometimes necessary to do this by program. **close** returns 0 if successful and −1 if the file descriptor is unknown.

6.3 The file system revisited

6.3.1 File permissions

Each file has an associated set of permissions that determines who can access the file and whether the access is restricted to read **(r)**, write **(w)** or execute **(x)** or some combination. There are three classes of users that are used to decide access rights.

u   The owner or creator of the file (user).
g   The members of a group.
o   The general user population (other people).

In each class, permissions are established by the owner of the file. A complete set of current information about an individual file (or directory) may be obtained using the −l option of the **ls** command. For example,

ls −l /etc/motd

produces

rw−rw−r−−   1   adm   0   Jul 28 20:03   /etc/motd

The string rw−rw−r−− represents the *protection mode* of the file /etc/motd. The first three characters, rw−, are the access rights for the owner of the file, the next three are the group access (see below for groups) and the last three, r−−, are the access rights for all other users. In this example, the owner and group members can read and write the file and other users can only read the file. The next field is the number of links and is 1 for newly created files. **adm** is the login-name of the file owner. The next field is the number of bytes in (or the size of) the file. In this example, the file has zero length. The date is the last time the file was written or modified and the last field is the file name.

Files that are intended for execution (binary programs or shell procedures) need the execute flag to be set in the file mode. The executable program /bin/sh is listed by **ls** −l as

```
rwx--x--x    1    bin    24272   Jan 10 18:03     /bin/sh
```

indicating that it is executable for all three classes of users but is readable and writable only by the owner.

Executable programs may also have the *set-user-id* or *set-group-id* mode and this is discussed in section 6.5.4.

The access rights for the owner of a file are determined only by the owner part of the mode, even though the user may also be a group member. A file whose mode is

```
---r--rwx
```

cannot be written by the owner or group members but is fully accessible to other users. Modes of this kind are not very useful.

6.3.2 Changing file modes

The mode of a file can be changed by its owner using the chmod command. Early versions of this command only allowed explicit absolute numeric modes to be specified as octal numbers (like those used in umask below). For example,

```
chmod 751 run
```

would result in run having mode

```
rwxr-x--x
```

allowing the owner full access but restricting group members to read and execute and other users to execute only.

chmod allows both relative and absolute specifications. For example,

u-r	Remove user (owner) read permission.
g+w	Add write permission for groups.
o=x	Set execute permission for others.

To make run executable by everyone

```
chmod +x run
```

is sufficient. In this example, run could be replaced by a list of files, in which case, all would be made executable.

The mode of a file is determined when it is created and may be modified by its owner thereafter. A maximum set of permissions given, by default, to any files created by a user can be specified using the umask command.

```
umask 0
```

is equivalent to no restriction and created files would have mode rwxrwxrwx.

```
umask 22
```

is the default on some systems and specifies maximum access permission of
rwxr—xr—x. The chmod command ignores the current umask setting.

The following script will list the mode of a file created with the current
umask setting.

```
> /tmp/$$
ls —l /tmp/$$
rm /tmp/$$
```

Many systems are run with a friendly and cooperative user community
and in these circumstances it may be normal to allow everyone to read all
files. In an environment where privacy is important, umask 77 would restrict
files created to the mode rwx—————— thus providing only the owner with
accessibility.

On many systems ordinary users cannot change the ownership of files or
directories. However, for files this can sometimes be circumvented by copying the file, removing the original and renaming the copy. One side effect of
this operation is to change the created time of the file.

6.3.3 Directory access

The interpretation of read, write and execute for directories is somewhat different than for files.

r   Allow the directory to be read as if it were a file. This is used,
         for example, by file name expansion in the shell.
x   Allow access to the names (files and directories) in this directory.
w   Allow directory entries to be created and removed. (These two
         operations are not distinguished in the UNIX system.)

To print the permissions associated with a directory the —d option of ls
must be used, otherwise ls lists the entries in the directory rather than the
directory itself. For example, the current directory is listed by

```
ls —ld .
```

The output has the form

```
drwxrwxr—x    5    srb    496    May 5 18:06    .
```

where the initial d indicates that the entry is to be interpreted as a directory.
On some systems the group name of the file or directory is also listed by the
ls command.

The access restrictions for files and directories apply to all normal users.
One user, called the *super-user,* is exempt from security checks. Certain
operations, such as directory creation are limited to the super-user to allow
them to be implemented as commands rather than as part of the operating
system. Also, changing the owner or group of a file, is restricted to the
super-user. The login-name root is normally reserved for the super-user.

6.3.4 Groups

As with ownership, the group identity of a file is determined at creation time. When you log in you will have been assigned to a group. On some systems all users are, by default, assigned to a single group. The group identity of a file can be printed using the —g option of ls, so that,

    ls —lg /etc/motd

might print

    rw—rw—r——   1   adm   0   Mar 30 20:03   /etc/motd

where adm is the group name. During a terminal session you can change your group using the command

    newgrp group-name

if you are a member of the group group-name. On some systems, if you are not a member of the group, newgrp will print sorry and log you out. (This is an unfortunate consequence of the way it is implemented and is a bug.)

New groups are created by system administrators and can be used for users involved in a particular project where access to files needs to be restricted to the group. The mechanism is cumbersome and does not lend itself to flexible usage.

Files have both a user (owner) and group identity called the *user-id* and *group-id* respectively. These are represented as integers within the file system and are mapped into names such as srb and root by programs such as ls. These mappings together with some additional information are kept in the two files, /etc/passwd and /etc/group.

The password file /etc/passwd contains entries such as

    srb:yKohajlbawhyg:142:3:mh5967,m044:/usr/srb:

each field being separated by a :. The first field is the login-name, the second field the encrypted password. The third and fourth fields are the (numeric) user-id and group-id. The next field contains information that, historically, was used to contain remote job submission information including the login-name and account number for the local computer center system. The sixth field contains the initial working directory following logging in. This is the home directory referred to earlier. The last field is often empty but is used when a user requests a different command interpreter than /bin/sh.

The group file called /etc/group has a similar format and consists of entries such as

    a68::3:srb,a68

each field being separated by a : as with the password file.

The first field is the group-name, the next field is the password used by newgrp, and the third field is the group-id. The last field is a comma separated list of login-names of users who are group members. The newgrp command is similar to login and changes the group id of the process.

6.4 Advanced input-output

6.4.1 Creating and removing files

Programs are able to create files when necessary. The creat system call is declared as

```
int creat(name, pmode)
        char *name;
        int pmode;
```

A call of creat causes either a new file to be brought into existence or a previously existing file is prepared for overwriting (it is truncated to zero length) and the file is opened for writing.

Recall that in the file system there are nine protection bits controlling the read, write and execute permission for the owner, the owner's group and for all other users; the access mode is normally represented as a three digit octal integer. The access mode described by the pmode argument of creat is modified by the mode mask, umask of the process that attempts the creation. In effect,

```
( ~umask ) & pmode
```

is used. creat will return a file descriptor if successful and −1 otherwise.

A file may be removed by the unlink system call, declared as,

```
int unlink(name)
        char *name;
```

This usually returns 0, but −1 indicates that the associated file does not exist or could not be removed.

The creat system call will not create directories. Instead a call of the mkdir command is used. Similarly, directories can be removed only by executing the rmdir command.

A physical file may have more than one associated file name. The first name is associated when the file is created. Subsequent names are attached using the link system call,

```
int link(name₁, name₂)
        char *name₁, *name₂;
```

where $name_2$ is an alternate for $name_1$. link will fail if $name_2$ already exists.

The ln command is a direct reflection of the system call.

```
ln file newname
```

will make a link called newname to the existing file.

Creating a lock file

To end this section we look at two more examples. A lock file is the exclusive possession of its owner and may be used to ensure exclusive access to a resource. For example, the program that controls the line printer creates a lock file when it is started. If, by accident, another instance of the same program is started it will discover the existence of the lock file and exit.

Such a file can be created as shown in figure 6.4. The method used is to create and open a file, as in

    creat("lock", 0);

The second argument 0 is the mode of the created file, ――――――――. Creating the file so that it cannot be read ensures that another attempt to open it for reading will fail. If creat is successful then the lock has been claimed. Otherwise, another process has the file open.

This version can fail if used by the super-user, since read permission will not be denied. Another technique that can be used is to link to a file that already exists with the name of the lock.

```
/*
 *   mklock file ...
 */
int main(argc, argv)
        Int  argc;
        char *argv[];
{
        int     rc = 0;
        char    *n;
        int     f;

        while (argc-- > 1) {
                if ((f = creat(*++argv, 0)) < 0) {
                        rc++;
                }else{
                        close(f);
                }
        }
        return(rc);
}
```

Figure 6.4 The mklock command

The cp command

The implementation of a simplified version of the cp command is shown in figure 6.5. The program first checks that the correct number of arguments is supplied. If not, it returns from main, and consequently exits from the pro-

gram. Otherwise, the input and output files are opened. If successful, the
copying is implemented within the while loop. A check has also been inserted
to check failure of the write call. This is the subject of further discussion in
section 6.6.3. The function strlen is part of the standard C system library
and returns the length of its argument string.

```c
#define BUFSIZ 512
#define MODE 0644  /* rw- for user, r-- for group and others */
int errflg;

void error(s)
        char s[ ];
{
        write(2, s, strlen(s));
        errflg++;
}

int main(argc, argv)
        int argc;
        char *argv[ ];
{
        int rd, wt, n;
        char b[BUFSIZ];
        if (argc!=3) {    /* wrong number of arguments */
                error("usage: cp fromfile tofile\n");
                return(1);
        }

        if ((rd=open(argv[1], 0)) == -1)
                error("cp: cannot open input\n");

        if ((wt=creat(argv[2], MODE)) == -1)
                error("cp: cannot create output\n");

        if (errflg==0) {
                while ((n=read(rd, b, BUFSIZ)) > 0) {
                        if (write(wt, b, n)!=n) {
                                error("cp: write error\n");
                                break;
                        }
                }
        }

        return(errflg);
}
```

Figure 6.5 A simplified version of the cp command

Creating a temporary file

Temporary files are often created within shell scripts for use within the script. Two directories, /tmp and /usr/tmp, are available in which temporary files may be created by anyone. Files created in these directories should be removed by the program that creates them. When the system is rebooted these directories are usually emptied.

```
#include <stdio.h>
/*
 *        mktemp -- create temp file
 */

char *mktemp();

int main(argc, argv)
        int argc;
        char *argv[];
{
        int rc = 0;
        char *n;
        int f;

        while(argc-- > 1) {
                n = mktomp(*++argv);
                if((f = creat(n, 0644)) < 0) {
                        fprintf(stderr,
                            "mktemp: cannot create '%s'\n", n);
                        rc++;
                } else {
                        fprintf(stdout, "%s\n", n);
                        close(f);
                }
        }
        return(rc);
}
```

Figure 6.6 Creating a temporary file

One convention often used in shell scripts is to create files called

/tmp/$$

This is safe provided everyone follows the convention.

The command mktemp described in figure 6.6 uses the standard C library function mktemp to generate files that do not (already) exist. A typical call of mktemp is

```
mktemp  /tmp/XXXXXX
```

The name of the file created is printed, as for example,

```
/tmp/022780
```

This output is then available for use by shell procedures. For example,

```
tmp=`mktemp  /tmp/XXXXXX`
    . . .
```

will set the shell variable tmp to the name of the temporary file created by
mktemp.

6.4.2 Random access input-output

A file consists of a sequence of characters and access to a file is often sequential. However, a file can be read or written non-sequentially by positioning
within a file using the system call lseek.
   lseek is defined as

```
long lseek(filedescriptor, offset, whence)
        int filedes;
        long offset;
        int whence;
```

and the current position in the file associated with filedescriptor is moved to
the position offset, taken relative to the location specified by whence. Subsequent reading or writing will begin at this position. The argument offset is
a long integer, the filedescriptor and whence are both integers and whence
may be 0, 1 or 2. These three possibilities are as follows:

0   The offset from the start of the file.
1   The current position + offset.
2   The end-of-file + offset.

For example,

```
lseek(filedescriptor, OL, 2)
```
        The current position is moved to the end of the file.
```
lseek(filedescriptor, OL, 0)
```
        The file is rewound to the beginning without loss of information.
        (In early UNIX systems seek was used instead of lseek; the differ-
        ence being that seek did not use the long integer argument.)
   In error situations, such as,

●   an undefined file descriptor,
●   an attempt to seek on a pipe, or
●   an attempt to seek to a position before the start of the file,

the call of lseek returns −1.
   Using lseek it is possible to create files with 'holes'. By writing to a certain point and then seeking beyond the end-of-file a section of file space is

created containing no data. In certain applications, such as a large hash sort, this may be useful. No file space is actually used by these holes.

6.4.3 Status of files

```
struct    stat
{
          dev_t    st_dev;
          ino_t    st_ino;
          unsigned short st_mode;
          short    st_nlink;
          short    st_uid;
          short    st_gid;
          dev_t    st_rdev;
          off_t    st_size;
          time_t   st_atime;
          time_t   st_mtime;
          time_t   st_ctime;
};
#define S_IFMT     0170000 /* mask for the file type */
#define S_IFDIR      0040000 /* directory */
#define S_IFCHR      0020000 /* character special */
#define S_IFBLK      0060000 /* block special */
#define S_IFREG      0100000 /* regular */
#define S_IFMPC      0030000 /* multiplexed char special */
#define S_IFMPB      0070000 /* multiplexed block special */
#define S_ISUID    0004000 /* set user id on execution */
#define S_ISGID    0002000 /* set group id on execution */
#define S_ISVTX    0001000 /* save swapped text */
#define S_IREAD    0000400 /* read permission, owner */
#define S_IWRITE   0000200 /* write permission, owner */
#define S_IEXEC    0000100 /* execute/search permission, owner */
```

Figure 6.7 The system include file <sys/stat.h>

The status of files can be determined using the stat and fstat system calls. A call of stat provides information about any named file. A call of fstat accepts a file descriptor and returns information about open files or pipes. Only stat is described since fstat is otherwise identical. The declarations of the two calls are

```
int stat(name, buf)
        char *name;
        struct stat *buf;
```

and

```
int fstat(filedescriptor, buf);
        int filedescriptor;
        struct stat *buf;
```

The structure stat is declared in the system include file <sys/stat.h>. Also defined in this file are the constants to be used when interpreting the fields. Figure 6.7 is the contents of this system include file. The fields have the following interpretations:

st_mode The type of the file, i.e., whether it is an ordinary file like any user file, a directory, a block special file (unbuffered) or a character special file (buffered).

st_uid   The user's identification.

st_gid   The user's group identification.

st_size   The last (relative) address written to.

st_atime The time when the file was last read (or accessed). This is not set when a directory is searched.

st_mtime The time when the file was last written or created; this is unaffected by changes of owner, group or mode.

st_ctime Set by writing the file or by changing the mode, owner or group.

The ls command provides this information given suitable options. The use of this status information is illustrated by the program chksum in figure 6.8. For each argument chksum produces a line of the form

    chksum.c   170242 Thu Dec 16 03:32:55 1982

The constant S_IFREG is defined in the system header file and denotes the value of (st_mode&S_IFMT) for a regular file. The field st_mode first has to be masked with S_IFMT since the field also contains the permission bits.

6.4.4 Terminal input-output

The file /dev/tty is, in each process, the control terminal associated with the process. It can be used by programs that wish to be sure of sending a message to the terminal, even though the standard and error output have been redirected. It can also be used when input or output is needed from or to the terminal and a command requires a file name.

The first terminal file opened by a process becomes the control terminal for that process. Normally, the open occurs during login and processes that are forked inherit the same control terminal. The control terminal can generate quit and interrupt signals as discussed below. The set of processes that share a control terminal is called a *process group*.

Any terminal associated with one of these files operates in full-duplex. Characters typed at the terminal are transmitted to the host computer where they are passed on to the program and also reflected back to the terminal by the system. Characters may be input at any time, even while output is taking place. There is a limit (usually 256) determined by system buffer sizes on the maximum number of characters that can be typed before they are read by a process. Beyond this limit characters are simply lost.

Input from a terminal is collected a line at a time, so that a **read** will halt the program until an entire line has been entered. Even if more characters are requested by the **read** only a single line will be returned. If fewer characters are requested they will be returned without losing any information. A program can also request input to be read before a full line has been typed using an option of the ioctl system call.

```
/*
 * chksum a list of files
 */
#include <sys/types.h>
#include <sys/stat.h>

char *ctime();

struct stat STATBUF[1];
int fd;
char buff512];

int main(argc, argv)
        int argc;
        char *argv[];
{
        int i;

        for(i = 1; i < argc; i++) {
                close(fd);
                if ((fd = open(argv[i], 0)) < 0)
                        printf("%s: cannot open\n", argv[i]);
                else{
                        fstat(fd, STATBUF);
                        chksum(argv[i]);
                }
        }
        return(0);
} /* main */

chksum(nam)
        char *nam;
{
        register int p, e;
        register unsigned short sum = 0;
        char *c;

        while(e = readb()) {
                for(p = 0; p < e; p++) {
                        if(sum&01) {
                                sum = (sum>>1) | 0x8000;
```

```
                                        }
                                        else{
                                                sum  >>= 1;
                                        }
                                        sum  ^= buf[p];
                                }
                        }
                c  =  ctime(&STATBUF->st_mtime);
                if((STATBUF->st_mode&S_IFMT)  ==  S_IFREG) {
                        printf("%-14s %o\t%s", nam, sum, c);
                }
        } /* chksum */

        int readb()
        {
                register int r;

                r = read(fd, buf, sizeof(buf));
                return((r <= 0) ? 0 : r);
        } /* readb */
```

Figure 6.8 The chksum command

During input, erase and kill processing is normally performed. The character # erases previous characters typed up to the beginning of a line and @ kills the entire line typed so far. These two characters may be changed via an ioctl system call.

Other characters, listed below, also have a special meaning and are not passed on to the reading program except in *raw mode* where they lose their special character.

^D   Generate an end-of-file from a terminal. All characters waiting to be read are passed to the program without waiting for a return and the ^D is discarded. If no characters are waiting, zero characters will be returned by read and this is the standard end-of-file indication.

del   Send an interrupt signal to all processes associated with the control terminal. Unless other arrangements have been made, the processes will terminate.

^\   Generate the quit signal. This signal is identical to an interrupt except that a core image is generated unless the signal is caught. The core file is only written provided that it exists and has write permission or can be created in the current directory.

^S   Delay printing on the terminal until a character is typed.

^Q   This character is ignored except after ^S when printing is resumed.

When a terminal hangs up, the hangup signal is sent to all processes in its group. This signal is generated, for example, if the carrier signal from a dataset drops. If the hangup signal is ignored then any further **read** will return an end-of-file indication.

The treatment of the terminal by the system includes the following:

- Input and output baud rate.
- The parity allowed on input.
- Timing delays for various characters such as **tab, newline.**
- Expand tabs into spaces on input and output.
- The characters used for erase, kill, and interrupt.

These options can be read and rewritten using the **ioctl** system call. This system call is used by **stty** command. In the Sixth Edition UNIX system there were two system calls **stty** and **gtty**; in the Seventh Edition system they were replaced by a single call **ioctl**.

6.4.5 Pipes

Data may be sent between two processes via an inter-process channel called a *pipe*. A pipe is uni-directional and has two ends. These two ends are represented by the file descriptors **p[0]** and **p[1]** returned by the call

```
int p[2];
pipo (p);
```

The file descriptor **p[0]** is the reading end and **p[1]** the writing end of the pipe. The value returned by **pipe** itself is zero if successful and −1 otherwise. A process that reads on a pipe is halted if the pipe is empty and will wait for some characters to be written into the pipe. Similarly, if a process writes to a pipe that is full, it will block until some characters are read by the process at the other end.

Pipes are usually created by a common ancestor of two processes. The shell, for example, when executing the pipeline

```
a | b
```

first creates the pipe and then forks to create the processes for the commands a and b. In the process created to execute the command a, the standard output is closed and the pipe duplicated to take the place of the standard output as shown in the following code

```
close(1);
dup(p[1]);
close(p[1]);
```

The **dup** system call uses the lowest number file descriptor available; it being assumed that file descriptor 0 is already assigned as the standard input. A similar sequence is executed for the command b. Once the standard input and output are suitably redirected the **exec** system call is used to invoke the commands a and b.

The notation provided by the shell is adequate for most needs; however, the shell only allows a simple chain of commands to be connected with pipes and more complex connections are not provided.

6.5 Processes

Using the terminology of Ritchie and Thompson (Ritchie, 1978) an *image* is a computer execution environment. This includes the program, associated data, the states of open files, and the current directory. Some attributes of images such as the user-id and group-id are directly accessible to the user via the system calls getuid and getgid. Other properties, such as the list of child processes are only available (indirectly) via a system call such as wait.

A *process* is the execution of an image. Within the system there is a list of processes maintained by the system. Most of these processes are waiting, either for input from a terminal or file, or for some system function to complete. This list may be printed using the ps command. There is a per user and a system wide limit to the number of processes that may be in existence at one time. The size of the system process table is called NPROC and is kept with the system source files in the directory /usr/sys/h. The per user limit is called MAXUPRC. For a typical VAX 11/780 these two limits are 250 and 50 respectively.

6.5.1 Process execution

During execution a process has three parts to its address space.

- The program text itself is often shared and therefore write protected. This avoids accidental self destruction. (C programs are not self modifying.)
- A data segment that is writable by the user and not shared with, or accessible by, other users. This area begins where the program ends and may be grown or shrunk by the user using the brk system call.
- A non-shared stack segment that grows down from the top of memory. This region is automatically extended when it is exhausted.

The address space of each process is distinct from that of other processes within the system. Communication between processes is possible using pipes and signals.

Four system calls are provided to manage processes: fork, exec, wait and exit.

6.5.2 The fork system call

The system call fork creates two nearly identical copies of a process. One copy is called the parent and the other the child. In the *parent* process, fork returns the process number of the child. The value returned in the child is zero. If fork cannot create a new process then a −1 is returned. This can happen, for example, when the system process table is full, or if the fork call is interrupted.

All parts of the image of the parent process are inherited by the child, including open files. The forked process has its own data and stack segments. The only resources shared by a parent and child are the files that were open when the parent forked. If the parent waits for the child to finish then this presents no problem. However, if the child executes in parallel with its parent then some agreement must be reached to decide to whom these open files belong to.

For example, when the shell executes the command

```
a &
```

a process is created using fork and the standard input is then redirected from /dev/null. The shell thus keeps the terminal for its own use.

6.5.3 The wait system call

Once a process has been created by fork, the parent may elect for the child process to execute independently or it may wait for the child to terminate.

The wait system call will halt the caller until one of its children finishes execution. When more than one child is executing, the order of finish is not defined and to wait for a particular child the following loop is required.

```
int       status;
int       childpid;

while (wait(&status)!=childpid)
          ;
```

A command may not assume that the only children that will be reported by wait have been created by itself. A command may inherit children from a previous user of the process. A command could create children using fork and then invoke another command using exec.

Only a parent may wait for its children and, if the parent dies, the processes are inherited by process 1.

6.5.4 The exec system call

The exec system call overlays the process that is running with a new program and begins execution of the program at its *entry point*. The process-id is unchanged by exec. If successful, this call does not return and the calling program image is lost. There are various forms of exec, the simplest of which is

```
int execv(name, argv)
        char *name;
        char *argv[ ];
```

The name argument is the file name of the program (a.out file) to be executed and argv is a zero-terminated list of pointers to the argument strings that will be available to the called program. By convention, argv[0] is the name of the command being executed.

The second form of exec that is available is declared as

```
int execl(name, arg_0, arg_1, ..., arg_n, 0);
```

and provides the arguments explicitly.

Unless the appropriate option of ioctl is used, files remain open across an exec call. This allows the parent (e.g. the shell) to open files for the child.

Also the states of signals are left unchanged unless they are being caught, then they are reset to zero. The real user-id and group-id are also left unchanged by **exec**. However, if the file to be executed has either the *set-user-id* or *set-group-id* mode then the *effective* user-id or group-id is set to that specified by the file.

As an example, the shell provides input-output redirection by closing and opening files before **exec** is called. If the command is run in background the standard input is also opened from /dev/null to avoid confusion over input and terminal generated signals are turned off.

The most frequent reason for **exec** to fail is likely to be that **name** does not exist or is non-executable. Another common reason, especially when using * for file name generation in the shell, is that the space occupied by the argument list exceeds 5120 bytes. Other reasons include insufficient address space to start execution (more likely on a PDP 11/45 or 11/70 than on the VAX 11/780).

Most programs need not concern themselves with process management; this can be left to the shell using shell scripts. For programs that need to execute a sub-command the **system** subroutine provided in the standard C library may well suffice.

6.5.5 The exit **system call**

```
int status, signal;

while (wait(&status) != childpid)
        ;

if (status&0200) {
        /* Core file was produced */
}
if (status == 0177) {
        /* Child process has been stopped and can be restarted.
         * This is mostly for debuggers that use the ptrace
         * system call to control and monitor another process.
         */
}
signal = status&0177;
if (signal == 0) {
        rc = (status>>8)&0377;
        /* Process terminated normally with exit status in rc. */
}else{
        /* Process terminated abnormally as a result of signal. */
}
```

Figure 6.9 Status returns by a process

A process can finish execution (terminate) either voluntarily using the system call exit or, involuntarily, by receiving a signal. The argument to exit is interpreted as the status of the terminating process. By convention a zero means that the command succeeded and a non-zero value indicates failure.

From a C program the exit call may be used directly, or the program can return a value from the main function.

When a process terminates the status returned to the parent by wait distinguishes various cases. Figure 6.9 shows a program that distinguishes the status values returned by processes. childpid is assumed to contain the process-id of the child process. This program fragment is executed by the parent.

6.5.6 The environment of a process

argv and argc represent explicit (positional) arguments supplied by the exec call. An additional array of strings called the *environment* of a process is also made available by exec when a process begins. The most frequently used names from the environment are discussed in chapter 4.

Conventionally these strings have the form

```
name=value
```

In the previous example, execv passes this environment unchanged. If changes are made they can be passed on using the call

```
int execve(name, argv, envp)
        char *name;
        char *argv[ ];
        char *envp[ ];
```

The argument envp is a zero terminated array of pointers to strings containing the *environment* and is made available to the called program in the external variable environ, declared as

```
char **environ;
```

From C programs values may be retrieved from the environment using the getenv subroutine declared as

```
char *getenv(name)
        char *name;
```

getenv searches for a string of the form name=value in the environment list and returns a pointer to value if the name is found and zero otherwise.

6.6 Signals and interrupts

Various events, such as terminal break, are reported to a program via an asynchronous *signal*. Other events include a program error (e.g. memory fault), and the request of another program (kill). The normal action caused by a signal is to terminate the process. Except for SIGKILL all signals can be either ignored or will cause a jump to a specified C function within the process. Some signals (see list below) will leave a **core** file so that an investigation of the fault can be pursued using **adb** or **sdb**. This can be prevented, for example, by creating a core file that cannot be written.

6.6.1 Signals

A complete list of signals follows. The names used are defined in the system header file <signal.h>. Signal numbers marked by an asterisk will generate a **core** file unless the signal is caught or ignored.

1   **SIGHUP**
A hangup from the terminal. Usually results from loss of carrier on a phone line and can also be generated using

        stty 0 > /dev/tty

2   **SIGINT**
Terminal interrupt. Either **del** or **break** from a terminal keyboard.

3*   **SIGQUIT**
Quit. This is the usual way to abort a program when a core dump is required. Generated using **fs** (**^**) from a terminal.

4*   **SIGILL**
Illegal instruction.

5*   **SIGTRAP***
Trace trap. (Used by **adb**.)

6*   **SIGIOT**
IOT instruction. (Used by **adb**.) This signal is sometimes referred to as *abort*.

7*   **SIGEMT**
EMT instruction. Used on some machines without floating point.

8*   **SIGFPE**
Floating point exception. Overflow has occurred or a zero divisor is used in floating point arithmetic.

9   **SIGKILL**
Kill. This signal can be safely used to get rid of any of your processes. It cannot be caught or ignored by any process.

10* **SIGBUS**
Bus error. This usually results from an illegal pointer indirection in C.

11* **SIGSEGV**
Segmentation violation. This signal can also result from an illegal pointer reference or an array bound error.

12* **SIGSYS**
Bad argument to a system call. This should not occur for C programs.

13   **SIGPIPE**
Write on a pipe with no process to read it. This occurs when a process on the receiving end of a pipe terminates, leaving the writer with a *broken pipe*.

14 SIGALRM

Alarm clock. This is generated following the **pause** system call (see appendix 2).

15 SIGTERM

Software termination signal. This signal is the default for the **kill** command and allows processes receiving it to clean up temporary files and exit gracefully. If this fails, try **kill** −**9** to send a **SIGKILL**.

6.6.2 Sending signals

The **kill** command uses the **kill** system call to send a signal to a process with the same effective user-id.

```
int kill(pid, sig)
        int  pid;
        int  sig;
```

will send the process whose number is **pid** the signal **sig**. If **pid** is zero then all processes with the same effective user-id will be sent the signal. If **sig** is out of range or the process does not exist then **kill** returns on a −1. Only processes with the same effective user-id can send signals using **kill**.

6.6.3 Catching signals

```
#include  <signal.h>

int  sigcnt;

handler(a)
        /* The value of `a` is SIGINT. */
{
        /* Reset the signal so that it can be caught again. */
        signal (a, handler);

        /* Record the interrupt and resume. */
        sigcnt ++;
}
main()
{
        signal(SIGINT, handler);
        . . .
}
```

Figure 6.10 Signal handler

A process can elect to catch a signal, ignore it completely, or allow the system default action. Normally all signals cause termination of the receiving process. The **signal** system call allows a signal to be caught, ignored or the

system default action to be restored. If the signal is caught then control will
be transferred to a user specified location (function in C). For example, the
program shown in figure 6.10 catches SIGINT using the function handler.
When the program receives the signal, the function handler is called with its
argument set to the signal number. This example counts how many times the
signal occurs.

Most signals are reset to the default action when they occur. If it is required to catch every signal, the handler must issue another signal call. To
reset a signal to the system default action the call is, for example,

    signal(SIGINT, SIG_DFL);

A signal may be ignored completely using

    signal(SIGINT, SIG_IGN);

The value returned by a call of signal is the previous state of the signal.

Otherwise, the program is only disturbed by possibly failed system calls.
These system calls can be retried if they fail with errno set to EINTR. For
example, if the program cp in figure 6.4 were interrupted it would still print
a message.

    if(errno != EINTR)
            error("...");

restricts the message to other errors.

6.6.4 Background processes

The states of the signals of a process are inherited by a child process via fork.
By convention if a signal is being ignored when a process starts (following
exec) then it is never changed. This allows processes to be started up at a
terminal and then executed in the background without interference from terminal generated signals, such as interrupt and quit. To ensure that this convention is not violated even for a short time the safe way to set signals is illustrated in the following code:

    if (signal(SIGINT, SIG_IGN)!=SIG_IGN)
            signal(SIGINT, handler);

thus leaving it set to SIG_IGN if it is already set that way.

The subroutine in figure 6.11 may be used from within any C program
to execute a sub-command. While it is waiting for the child process to finish,
interrupts (and quits) are ignored; for the child they are inherited from the
parent. When the child terminates, the parent signal are reset to their original values and the subroutine returns.

```
#include  <signal.h>

int  system(name, argv)
        char *name;
        char *argv[];
{
        int      pid;
        int      status;
        int      del;
        int      quit;

        /* ignore signals in parent */
        del = signal(SIGINT, SIG_IGN);
        quit = signal(SIGQUIT, SIG_IGN);
        switch (pid = fork()) {

        case 0: /* This is the child branch */
                /* signals are reset for child */
                signal(SIGINT, del);
                signal(SIGQUIT, quit);
                exec(name, argv);

                /* exec failed after the fork */
                /* the reason is in errno */
                exit(1);

        case -1: /* fork has failed */
                status = 0;
                break;

        default: /* Wait for the child to terminate. */
                /* This is the parent branch. */
                while (wait(&status)!=pid);
        }
        signal(SIGINT, del);
        signal(SIGQUIT, quit);
        return(status);
}
```

Figure 6.11 The system subroutine

Chapter 7
Document preparation

The preparation of text for letters, reports or books is a time consuming activity requiring considerable attention to detail. The UNIX system provides a set of tools to aid document preparation. These tools include text formatting programs that enable page size, line length, margins, spacing between lines and type fonts to be specified. Other tools combine with these formatters allowing tables and mathematical equations to be produced.

These tools together with a text editor allow documents to be drafted and corrected with considerable ease. Programs are also available to check for correct spelling, make indices or look for wordy or misused phrases. Generally, a high quality result can be achieved with a reasonable expenditure of effort. If a particular tool is not available, it can often be constructed with relatively little effort using the techniques shown in this chapter.

7.1 nroff **and** troff

The basic tools are the text formatters called troff (pronounced *tee-roff)* and nroff. For typewriter quality output nroff is used and for print quality output troff is used. Both programs are descendants of an early text formatter called roff, that was available with the CTSS system (Crisman, 1965). The input contains both text and instructions describing the expected format of the output. The output is suitable for devices ranging from simple ASCII terminals to high-resolution photo-typesetters. Much of this chapter is concerned with nroff that is used mainly for typewriter-like terminals, such as the DASI-450 or the Diablo Hiterm, or for a line printer. With a little care, nroff and troff are compatible and the same input can be used for both. Documents can be printed using a variety of devices including a matrix printer such as the Versatec V80, an Imagen laser printer, or a photo-typesetter such as the APS-5.

Throughout this chapter references to nroff should be understood to include troff as well. troff is only referred to when the facility, such as a font change, is not available in nroff. When a facility is available only in troff, nroff will usually continue processing. A summary of troff requests is given in appendix 7.

nroff provides control over the formatting process including the page size, line length, vertical line spacing, and provides facilities for arbitrary horizontal or vertical movement, indentation, and tabulation. Line filling modes (ragged or smooth) and the level of hyphenation can also be specified. In troff control over different fonts and character size is also provided and finer resolution is available.

nroff provides direct access to these formatting capabilities. In addition there are features that enable nroff to be programmed. String variables and conditional requests are provided as well as numerical registers and the normal arithmetic operations. Macros can be defined and invoked allowing libraries of requests to be encapsulated. Traps can be set to execute a predefined sequence of requests when a given place in a page is reached. Text can be diverted into a named buffer, enabling footnotes to be accumulated and output when the end of the page is reached.

7.1.1 Guidelines for preparing documents

Material submitted to troff contains both text and instructions (or requests) indicating how the text is to be printed. troff requests begin with a special character, either a . or a '. Even when there are no requests, troff will format the output using some primitive defaults. Requests could then be added to produce the required output. This approach is rarely used. Documents are produced with packaged requests that provide for a consistent treatment of paragraphs, titles, displays and headings.

Before entering a document into the machine, you should consider how it is to be formatted and the macro package you intend to use. Macro packages for general use have been written and are suitable for a wide variety of applications. For example, the −ms and −mm libraries are available at Bell Laboratories for producing internal memoranda. The −ms package is distributed with the UNIX system and is summarized in appendix 10. Your own installation may support its own package conforming to local conventions.

Macros should be used to introduce headings, paragraphs, and displays. For example, in this book

    .SH 2.1 "..."

is used for major section headings;

    .LP

appears on the line preceding text for a left blocked paragraph and, similarly,

    .PP

is used before a paragraph with an indented first line. An indented paragraph with a hanging label (a) such as,

    (a)   ...
             ...

would be written as

    .IP (a)
    ...

These macros are similar to those defined in the −ms macro package, although the detailed layout has been modified to suit the publisher's house style.

The use of macros allows final formatting decisions to be delayed, and subsequently varied, to suit individual requirements. When using a macro package care should be taken when using nroff requests directly. Where possible, their use should be avoided since it may interfere with the working of the macro package itself. In any case check with the definitions first to see if the function you need is available.

This chapter introduces some of the capabilities of nroff and troff including a description of the macro library used to format this book. It also provides enough information to allow nroff and troff to be used for simple formatting applications, such as letter writing or viewgraph production. However, writing nroff macros for complex formatting tasks, such as double column output, requires considerable expertise and should be undertaken only by a competent (nroff or troff) programmer.

When preparing documents for nroff, individual lines should be kept reasonably short. Each sentence should begin on a new line and ending a line on each punctuation mark allows modifications to be made more easily. A large document should be split into more than one file. Each chapter of this book, for example, is kept in a separate file enabling text to be easily identified with its chapter when using tools like grep.

The incorporation of the formatting macros into the text is straightforward. Documents can be composed directly at a terminal or entered from the author's handwritten copy, introducing macro requests as needed.

Invoking nroff

nroff is invoked as

    nroff [options ...] document

and the whole document will be printed beginning, by default, at page 1. Some of the options available include the following:

−m*s*	Use the macro package specified by *s*.
−n*p*	Set the first page number to *p*.
−o*list*	Print only the pages listed by number.
−s*n*	Stop after every *n* pages.

For example,

    troff −o3−5,8,12− chapter1

or

    nroff −s1 chapter4

The −o option prints only the pages listed. In the first example, pages 3 through 5, page 8, and pages 12 through to the end of the document will be printed. In the second example, the −s1 option causes nroff to stop printing after every page and wait for a return to be typed. This may be used, for example, when special paper is to be loaded into the typewriter.

7.1.2 Simple requests

In its simplest form nroff absorbs input lines until enough words have been assembled to fill one output line. If an input line begins with white space, any output waiting will be flushed and a new output line is begun preceded by the same number of spaces. A new output line is also started if a blank line appears in the input.

Formatting requests to nroff appear alone on a line and start with a . at the beginning of a line. For example,

```
.sp
```

is equivalent to a blank input line.

Functions are similar to requests and appear within the text introduced by the character \. For example, a comment to nroff is written using a \" as in,

```
.sp        \" output a blank line
```

All requests and functions are embedded within the text of the document and consist of one or two character names. Macro names follow the same rule. Requests may take one or more arguments separated by spaces.

```
.sp 5
```

will move 5 lines down the page and resume output at the start of a new line.

Normally output lines are single spaced. When producing a draft of a document a double spaced format allows room for marking corrections. The request

```
.ls 2
```

sets double spaced output and single spacing can be restored using

```
.ls 1
```

Input lines may be centered using the .ce request. For example,

```
.ce
4. The Shell
```

produces the heading

4. The Shell

Several lines can be centered using the .ce request followed by an integer. In nroff the heading can be underlined using the .ul request, as in,

```
.ce
.ul
4. The Shell
```

In troff this request produces the heading in italic, as in

4. The Shell

Margin control

Both the left and right margins can be controlled. The position of the left margin is altered by the indent request.

   .in 4

indents to the fourth character position on the line.

   .in +4

increases the indentation level by four character positions and

   .in −4

will decrease the indentation level by four positions. At the start of a paragraph the first line is often indented relative to the body. The temporary indent request applies the specified indentation to the next output line only. For example,

   .ti +3

moves the left margin three character positions to the right.
   The right hand margin is controlled by specifying the line length.

   .ll 4i

sets the output line to 4 inches wide. The initial line width is 6.5 inches. The line length can be increased or decreased using a + or −, as in

   .ll −8

that decreases the line length by 8 characters.

Filling and adjusting lines

Once enough words have been read by nroff to fill a line, spaces are inserted between words so that the right hand margin is straight and the line is output. In troff the space between words can be as little as one third the width of the letter m. A ragged (non-adjusted) right margin is requested using the

   .na

request. In this mode no extra spaces are added between words. To restore the right margin alignment, the request

   .ad

is used. For a block of text the

   .nf

request prevents filling of lines during output. Output lines are neither filled nor adjusted following this request; input lines are copied directly to the output without regard for the current line length or word spacing. To resume fill mode, the request

.fi

is used. To break up output text between two lines the .br request is used and causes a *break* to occur; the current line is output and a new output line started.

To adjust the position of the output relative to the physical page the whole page can be offset using the request

.po

Initially, the page offset is set to zero in nroff and to 26/27 inches in troff.

The relationship between line length, indentation, centering and the page offset is illustrated in figure 7.1. The line length is measured from the left margin to the right margin. The current indentation is also measured from the left margin.

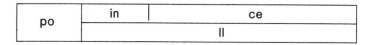

Figure 7.1 nroff **margins**

Without an argument the requests ll, in, and po restore the previous setting. There is only one value remembered so that nesting is most effectively dealt with using an increment and decrement.

nroff normally hyphenates its output. This can be prevented using

.nh

or, if an individual word is not to be hyphenated

.hw word

prevents hyphenation for word. Preferred hyphenations may also be provided, as in

.hw in−di−vid−ual

Vertical positioning

Vertical movement may be specified relative to the current position or from the start of the current page. For example,

.sp 1.5i

moves 1.5 inches down the page starting at the present position, whereas

.sp |1.5i

moves to 1.5 inches from the top of the current page. To move back one line a negative distance is used, as in,

.sp −1

The page length is normally set to 11 inches, by default and may be changed by the

.pl

request. Only movement within the current page is allowed.

Since some devices do not have reverse or half-line feed a special filter, col, is provided to buffer a page and print the lines in order.

Distances

Movements are performed using whatever resolution is available on the output device. A line printer may only be able to resolve to a single line, whereas a Diablo Hiterm has a vertical resolution of 1/48 inches. The CAT typesetter originally used to develop troff is accurate to 1/144 inches vertically and 1/432 inches horizontally. The internal unit size for troff depends on the output device; for the APS-5, used in this document, 1/723 inches is used. For nroff the unit is 1/240 inches.

Requests that specify distances may use the units defined below.

Unit	Meaning	Size
i	inches	
c	centimeters	2.54 inches
p	points	1/72 inch
P	pica	1/6 inch
u	basic units	device dependent
m	ems	the width of an 'm'
n	ens	the width of an 'n' (1/2 an em)
v	vertical line space	variable

When no units are specified the default depends on the request. For horizontally oriented requests the width of the letter m (an *em*) is used. In troff the size of an em is relative to the current character size. For vertically oriented requests a line space is used as the default unit. The line spacing may also be changed using the .vs request (q.v.). Decimal fractions may be used and arithmetic performed. The results are always rounded to the resolution of the output device. Parentheses and the arithmetic operators +, −, /, *, and % (mod) are available within expressions. There is no operator precedence in nroff expressions; parentheses should be used.

Since nroff rounds distances to the horizontal or vertical resolution of the output device inaccuracies can occur, particularly when using absolute specifications, such as

.sp |6.751i

Tabs and columns

Tables and columns of figures are sometimes simple enough to be formatted using nroff directly. However, it is usually better to use a preprocessor such as tbl that was designed specifically for tables.

A tab character in an input line is converted on output into enough unpaddable spaces to move to the next column. The default tab settings in nroff occur every 8 characters, in troff every 0.5 inches. Tabs may be reset. For example,

```
.ta 8 40 60
```

sets the tab positions at 8, 40 and 60 ems. On a typewriter with mechanical tabs, if text is already past a tab position the carriage automatically moves to the next tab. The behavior of nroff is similar. Also, by default, tabs are left justified. For numbers right justified columns are provided and centered columns are also available. For example,

```
.nf
.ta .5i  1.5i  3.5iR
.ul
Ⓣ Name Ⓣ Supplier Ⓣ Cost
Ⓣ Kubik Ⓣ Computer  Technology Ⓣ $183
Ⓣ Anderson Ⓣ System  Memories Ⓣ $79
.fi
```

(where Ⓣ represents a tab character) causes the third field to be right justified at character position 3.5 inches, as in

Name	*Supplier*	*Cost*
Kubik	Computer Technology	$183
Anderson	System Memories	$79

To center a field the C postfix is used.

The fill character used by tabs is usually a space, but may be changed using the tc request. For example,

```
.nf
.ta 20
.ul
Name Ⓣ Phone
.tc .
Hal Alles Ⓣ xxxx
 ...
.fi
```

produces

Name	*Phone*
Hal Alles	xxxx

 ...

To reset the tab character to space use .tc with no argument. .nf appears at the start of the table to prevent output lines from being filled.

Page control

The length of a page is normally 11 inches and may be changed using the page length request, as in,

    .pl 6i

When an explicit page break is required, the request .bp may be used. Page breaks are normally used from within a page end trap (see section 7.1.3). For tabular output it may be required that no page break occurs in the middle of the table. To prevent such a split the .ne request is used. For example, ple,

    .ne 6

continues output if 6 lines are left on the current page, otherwise a break to the next page occurs.

Page titles

The .tl request prints a three part title. The first part of the title is left justified, the second is centered and the last is right justified. For example, the request

    .tl ′February 3, 1982′DRAFT′Chapter 7′

will print

    February 3, 1982   DRAFT   Chapter 7

The delimiter used, in this case a ′, is arbitrary and is the first non-blank character after the request.

The line length and title length are independent. The current indentation does not affect the title but a page offset does. To set the length of the title the .lt request is used.

7.1.3 Advanced requests

Macros

A macro allows a group of requests or plain text to be given a name and invoked using that name. A macro should be defined before it is used, since undefined macro names are ignored. When defining a macro, use can be made of existing definitions. For example, the first version of the control requests for a paragraph in this book was

    .sp
    .ti 4
    .ne 2

requesting a blank line and a temporary indent of 4 ems. These requests are defined in the macro PP as

```
.de PP
.sp
.ti 4
.ne 2
..
```

The first line, .de PP, is the start of the definition and gives the name of the macro, PP. The end of the definition is marked by .. on a line by itself; the line may not contain a comment. Each paragraph of the subsequent text then starts with a call of PP, as in

```
.PP
Upper case names ...
```

Upper case names are used in many macro libraries to avoid conflict with nroff reserved names. Care should be taken to avoid names that are used by troff or by your macro library. To obtain a list of the names defined in a library the .pm request may be used.

Macros may be supplied with parameters on the same line as the call. For example, the section heading macro used in this book is called as

```
.SH 7.2 "Production tools"
```

White space separates arguments and an argument may be enclosed in double quotes if it contains a **space** or **tab**. In the example, the first argument is 7.2 and the second argument is Production tools. In the definition up to 9 arguments are available as \$1 \$2, ... Arguments that are not provided are assumed to be the null string.

In this example, SH is defined as

```
.de SH \" section heading: .SH section-number heading
.sp
\&\\$1 \\$2
..
```

The definition also contains a comment introduced by \" describing the the macro and its arguments.

A macro definition is read twice, once when it is defined and once when it is called. In both cases nroff requests are executed as they appear in the macro text. In the above definition of SH the \ is needed before \$1 to prevent the interpretation of \$1 during the definition scan. Further, if the first argument was an nroff request, such as .bp, a page break would occur. The escape character \& is provided to hide the . at the start of a line.

A pair of double quotes in a quoted argument will be passed to the definition as single double quote. For example,

```
.SH ... "The treatment of the "" character in troff"
```

Page traps

Using the requests introduced so far, ordinary text can be formatted readily although the lack of page control is soon apparent. No direct provision is made within nroff for titles at the top and bottom of the page. Instead, a *trap* may be set at specified vertical positions within the page and when the vertical position is reached the specified request is executed. Often two traps are set, one at the top of the page as

```
.wh 0 ...
```

and the other near the bottom of the page. For example,

```
.wh −5 PE
```

sets a trap 5 lines from the bottom of each page. After the line is output 5 lines before the end of the page, the macro PE is invoked. The definition of the page end macro PE is separate from the trap specification. For example,

```
.de PE
'sp 2
.tl :Unix Programmer's Manual:First Edition 1971:Page %:
'bp
..
```

defines PE to skip two lines and print a title. A : is used as the delimiter since a ' appears in the title string.

Requests introduced by a ' rather than a . prevent any partially processed line from being output. The request 'sp 2 is otherwise identical to .sp 2 and skips two lines. When a . is used, nroff generates a break just as if a .br had been issued and using a ' causes any partially constructed line to be held over to the next page.

A break occurs when a line begins with white space, a blank line occurs, or when one of the following requests is encountered:

```
.bp .br .ce .fi .nf .sp .in .ti
```

.tl may be used, as opposed to 'tl, since the .tl request does not cause a break, although using a ' is equivalent.

The special character %, when used in a title, prints the current page number in decimal. Other print formats may be assigned to the page number character using the .af request. For example,

```
.af % i
```

causes the page number to be printed in lower case Roman numerals i, ii, iii, ...

Writing trap macros requires care, particularly when the title has font or character size changes. This is discussed further in the section on environments.

Horizontal and local vertical motion

Vertical motion within a line is available using \d, \u, or \v. Half a line downwards is provided by \d and upwards by \u. An arbitrary distance downwards is provided by the \v function, as in

   \v′1i′

or upwards as

   \v′−1i′

The half-line motion is useful when dealing with superscripts and subscripts. For example,

   X\d1\u

produces

   X_1

Up and down movements within a line should be balanced otherwise unexpected behavior may result.

Horizontal movement may be specified similarly using the function

   \h′...′

For example, the shell here document symbol

   <<

is written as

   <\h′−.2m′<

bringing the two characters closer together to improve their appearance.

Computing the distance to be moved can be dependent on a string and the width function is provided for this purpose. For example,

   \w′do′

yields the width of the string do in basic units. As an example,

   do\h′−\w′do′u′do

overstrikes the word do to embolden it on a printer. The word is printed once and the \h function returns to the same place horizontally and prints it again. Point size and font changes may occur within a \w function and have no effect on the surrounding text. The u after the width function is strictly unnecessary since the result of \w is in units already.

The same overstriking effect can be achieved using the \k function that marks the current horizontal position on the line and stores the result in a register. For example,

   \kxdo\h′|\nxu′do

will also overprint the word do. The function \kx marks the horizontal position in the register x and the function \h'l...' moves to the absolute horizontal position specified.

The vertical place on the page may be marked using the .mk request. Output can proceed and the .rt request used to return to the same vertical position within a page. This is useful for producing multi-column output.

For example,

```
.mk
o
e
t
n
.rt
.in +4
The page number is odd.
The page number is even.
Using troff.
Using nroff.
.in −4
```

will print two columns, the first at the current indentation and the second indented by 4 more ems as shown below.

```
o          The page number is odd.
e          The page number is even.
t          Using troff.
n          Using nroff.
```

If the vertical height of the two columns differs, arrangements must be made to return to the correct place after the second column is output.

Horizontal and vertical lines may be drawn. The function

```
\l'1i'
```

draws a horizontal line one inch long (like this: _____). The character used to draw the line can also be specified, so that,

```
\l'1i.'
```

will produce

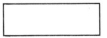

The function \L is similar but draws lines vertically.

For example,

```
\kx\l'1i'\L'2'\l'−1i'\h'l\nx'\L'−2'
```

will produce a box 1 inch wide and 2 lines deep, as in

Conditionals

Requests and text can be processed conditionally, depending on the outcome of a test. Both string and arithmetic comparisons may be specified. The simplest form of a conditional is

.if c anything

where, if the condition c is true, anything is used as input; anything could be text or further nroff requests. The conditions built in to nroff are listed in figure 7.2.

Name	Condition
o	The current page number is odd.
e	The current page number is even.
t	The formatter is troff.
n	The formatter is nroff.

Figure 7.2 nroff test conditions

For example

.if e .tl '%'''
.if o .tl '''%'

places the page number on the left for even pages and on the right for odd pages. Other tests, such as the first page of a document, require the use of register variables provided by nroff.

Several other forms of conditional are available.

.if N anything

accepts anything if the numerical expression N is non-zero and positive.

.if 'string₁'string₂' anything

accepts anything if the two strings are the same. The ! operator may be used in a conditional to negate the sense of the test, so that

.if !N anything

accepts anything if $N \leqslant 0$.

An if-then-else form of conditional is also available of the form

.ie c anything₁
.el anything₂

If c is true then anything₁ is accepted; otherwise, anything₂ is accepted.

When several actions are required, the requests may be enclosed between the delimiters \{ and \} as shown in figure 7.3.

String registers

Whenever a sequence of characters is used frequently it can be defined as a string. Like macros, strings have one or two character names. Strings and macros share the same set of names, so that if a string called xx is defined it will replace any macro of the same name. The define string request is written

.ds *xx string*

where string begins with the first non-blank character and ends at the end of the line. To permit initial blanks, an initial double quote is stripped off from *string*.

```
.ie \\n(sw \{
.nr sw 0
.in 0
.bp
.ns \}
.el \{
.nr sw 1
.rt
.in |3i \}
```

Figure 7.3 An example of a nroff conditional

For example, a subscript 1 could be defined as

.ds s1 \d1\u

where \d and \u are half-line motions down and up, respectively. The string s1 is used in later text as

x*(s1

would appear as x_1.

One character names can also be defined. For example, a bullet can be simulated in nroff as an o overstruck with + using the \o function, as in

.ds b \o'+o'

The string b is referred to within text as

*b

Horizontal movement may be embedded within a string. For example, the here document symbol, used in chapter 4, is defined as

.ds HE <\h'−.2m'<

and is used within text as *(HE.

Number registers

nroff provides a set of number registers for storing numerical values. These registers may be set, incremented and decremented, and used within text. Register names consist of one or two characters and are accessed either as

    \nx

or

    \n(xx

These names do not conflict with those used for macros and strings. Registers can be used within arithmetic expressions, or directly within text. For example, the day, month and year (since 1900) are maintained by nroff in the registers

    dy, mo, yr

so that

    19\n(yr \n(mo \n(dy

would print

    1983 1 24

when the date is January 24, 1983.

The default conversion style for number registers is Roman numerals, as in the example. The af request is used to set the format and has the form

    .af R f

where R is a register name and f is one of the formats listed below. If the format contains n digits then the field width is at least n digits.

Format	Numbering sequence
1	0, 1, 2, 3, 4, 5, ...
001	000, 001, 002, 003, 004, 005, ...
i	0, i, ii, iii, iv, v, ...
I	0, I, II, III, IV, V, ...
a	0, a, b, c, ..., z, aa, ab, ..., zz, aaa, ...
A	0, A, B, C, ..., Z, AA, AB, ..., ZZ, AAA, ...

nroff does not define a string for the name of the month but it can be provided as follows.

    .if \n(mo−0 .ds MO January
    .if \n(mo−1 .ds MO February
    ...

These requests define the string called MO as the current month name.

Number registers are set using the .nr request. For example,

    .nr IN 2m

sets IN to 2m units and

    .nr IN +2m

increases the value of IN by 2 ems.

Registers may be automatically incremented or decremented using the notation

    \n+x   Add m to x.
    \n+(xx   Add m to xx.
    \n−x   Subtract m from x.
    \n−(xx   Subtract m from xx.

The amount, m, added or subtracted is set using the .nr request. For example,

    .nr sn O 1

sets the register sn to O and sets m to 1. This form is useful when providing automatic incrementing of section numbers.

Some requests like .mk also set registers. For example,

    .mk p1

sets the current vertical position, in units, into the register p1. The value of p1 set by this .mk request is 3540. The .sp request

    .sp l\n(p1u

may be used to return to this place where l requests absolute positioning within the page. The value stored in the register by .mk is in basic units and the letter u ensures that nroff treats the value accordingly. The default units for the .sp request are vertical line spaces and if the u were missing this would be the same as

    .sp l3540

requesting 3540 lines. (The numerical values printed in this section depend on the device to which output is being sent.)

To be safe, the u should always be used in arithmetic expressions. For example,

    .sp 1i/2

is the same as

    .sp 3u

since the 2 has been given vertical line spacing as the default units. The above request should be written

    .sp 1i/2u

to divide 1 inch by 2 and this is equivalent to

.sp 361u

The following registers are set by nroff and are read only. The second
column lists the values as they are set for this page using the APS.

Name	Value	Description
.H	1	The available horizontal resolution in basic units.
.V	1	The available vertical resolution in basic units.
.c	2691	The number of input lines read.
.i	270	The current indentation.
.l	3361	The current line length.
.n	3020	The length of text on previous output line.
.o	697	The current page offset.
.p	7953	The current page length.
.s	10	The current point size.
.t	3527	The distance to the next trap.
.v	120	The current vertical spacing.

Further registers are set by troff and may be changed by the user. As in the
previous table the second column lists the values as they are set for this page.

Name	Value	Description
%	159	The current page number.
dw	2	The day of the week (1-7).
dy	24	The day of the month (1-31).
hp	457	The current horizontal input position.
ln	0	The output line number.
nl	4600	The current vertical position.
mo	1	The month (1-12).
yr	83	The last two digits of the year (00-99).

Fonts

So far, except for device resolution, all requests have applied equally well to
both nroff and troff. Printed output of the quality in this book uses a number
of different fonts, such as Times Roman, bold, and italic. The examples use
Helvetica, a sans serif font, to distinguish them from the main text. Modern
phototypesetters have anything from 4 to 32 fonts immediately accessible and
others available by request and a professional printer may well have 1000 different styles of characters available.

troff assumes that Times Roman, italic and bold are the standard fonts.
The current font may be changed using the .ft request. For example,

```
.ft  I
```

causes text to appear in *Times italic,* whereas

```
.ft  B
```

changes to the **Times bold** font. This font change may also be effected within a line as

```
\fB...
```

To return to the previous font

```
.ft
```

or

```
.ft  P
```

may be used. Similarly, within a line

```
\f(HIxx\fP
```

would cause *xx* to appear in Helvetica italic and then revert to the previous font. To return to the Roman font

```
.ft  R
```

or ...\fR is used.

Character size

The size of characters (like these) is usually 10 points, where a point is 1/72 inches. This may be increased or decreased, depending on the output device capabilities. The .ps request or, within text, the \s function is used. For example, to make the heading in the title smaller

```
.tl  '\s−2UNIX  Manual\s0'...
```

decreases the point size by 2 and then reverts to the original size. To make the size of headings 12 points in the SH macro, it would be defined as

```
.de  SH
.ps  12
\&\\$1
.ps
..
```

The .ps request without an argument or \s0 restores the previous font size.

As written this macro can produce unexpected results if there is a point size change as part of the argument \$1. Making the changes relative, as in

```
.de  SH
.ps  +2
\&\\$1
.ps  −2
..
```

avoids this problem. Also, if the point size throughout the document were changed to 9, for example, the headings would still be 2 points larger.

This text has a vertical spacing of 120u (about 12 points) and was set using the request

.vs 12p

The default point size is 10 and the default vertical spacing is 12p. The vertical spacing is the distance between successive lines of text and is the default distance moved vertically by the .sp request.

When the point size is changed the vertical spacing between lines is not automatically changed. As a general rule, the vertical spacing should be about 20% larger than the current point size.

The current point size is available in the register .s and the current vertical spacing is in the register .v.

Special characters

Special characters, such as the Greek letters and certain mathematical symbols are input to troff in the form

\(xx

where xx is a two character name. The Greek letters all have the form

\(*x

where x is the Roman letter equivalent. For example,

$\int \nabla u \, d\tau$

is written

\(is \(gru d\(*t

and

$\alpha^2 = k/\rho$

is written

\(*a\u\s−22\s+2\d \(eq k\(sl\(*r

For applications such as this the eqn preprocessor should be used. The example here illustrates the troff requests to obtain special characters. A complete list of the troff special characters is given in appendix 7.

Escape sequences

With three exceptions, listed below, the ASCII characters are input as themselves.

ASCII input	troff output
´	'
`	'
—	-

Some special characters and functions have already been presented and are reviewed here; a complete list is given in appendix 7.

Character sequence	Effect
\e	Print the escape character.
\´	Print an acute accent.
\`	Print a grave accent.
\-	Print a minus sign.
\kx	Mark horizontal position in register x.
\o´...´	Overstrike the characters enclosed.
..	End of macro definition.
\&	Hide a dot at the start of a line.
\"	Introduce comment.
""	A double quote in macro arguments.

Environments

When crossing a page boundary the point size and font may need to be changed in the page title. Normally this processing is performed in a page-end trap where some text is being held over from the filling process for the next page. To avoid affecting the held over text nroff provides the *environment* mechanism. There are three environments; each containing independent versions of the page layout parameters, font, point size, title length, filling modes, and partially processed text. The request .ev *n* switches to environment *n* where *n* must be 0, 1, or 2. With no argument, .ev reverts to the previous environment; initially processing starts in environment 0.

For example, to change the title length and font for the page end macro PE, defined earlier, it could be rewritten,

```
.de PE
.ev 1
.lt 4i
.ps 12
.ft B
´sp 2
.tl :Unix Programmer´s Manual:First Edition 1971:Page %:
´bp
.ev
..
```

Diversions and traps

Once input text has been filled and adjusted, it is normally output. However, the text for footnotes needs to be stored until the end of a page. Also, the placement of footnotes, and the length of the running page text depends on the size of the accumulated footnote text. Diversions provide a mechanism suitable for footnotes and similar problems.

Output text may be diverted into a named macro enabling the text to be
assembled for footnote processing and its size determined. The diverted text
may be re-read as input at a later time by invoking the macro.

The request

.di *xx*

starts diverting output text into the macro named *xx* replacing the original
contents of the macro. The diversion ends when the request .di with no arguments is read and the text collected may be input again by writing

.*xx*

The vertical and horizontal size of the most recently ended diversion is
available in the registers dn and dl respectively.

nroff provides three types of trap: page traps, the diversion trap, and an
input-line-count trap. The page trap has already been described. The diversion trap is set with the .dt request and allows processing to be interrupted
when a given vertical position is reached in the current diversion. Its use is
similar to the .wh request. For example,

.dt 1 DT

sets the diversion trap to execute the request .DT when one line of output has
been collected in the current diversion. Only one diversion trap exists at any
one time and a second .dt request replaces the trap.

The input-line-count trap is set by the .it request and specifies a macro
to be invoked after some number of input lines has been read. A given trap
is only executed once. For example,

.it 1 IT

invokes the macro IT after one (more) line of input is read. Using this
mechanism, the underline request .ul can be defined as,

```
.de  ul
.it  1  UL
.ft  I
. .
.de  UL
.ft  P
. .
```

7.1.4 A macro library

The use of a macro library is essential when preparing documents and standard packages are available that deal with many formatting needs. A general
purpose package will allow output to be generated in a variety of formats. If
one of these packages does not provide the required capabilities it is sometimes easier to modify the package than to rewrite it from scratch. This section demonstrates the programming techniques used when writing a macro
package. The macros described here were used to format this book and are

similar to those found in a macro library such as —ms. Throughout the discussion that follows reference will be made to appendix 9 that contains a complete listing of the macro library used to produce this book.

The requests provided by the macro library described here are described briefly in the following table. A more complete description is given in the text.

Request	Description
.AH 1 "Commands"	Appendix heading.
.CH 1 "Introduction"	Chapter heading.
.SH 1.1 "History"	Section heading.
.SS 6.3.1 "File permissions"	Subsection heading.
.MS "Use of backslash"	Minor section.
.BU	Bulleted paragraph.
.IP (a)	Indented paragraph with hanging text.
.LP	Blocked paragraph start.
.MP x++	Indented para with hanging program text.
.PP	Normal paragraph start.
.DS 13	Display start.
.DE	End display.
.EX 24	Start of example.
.XE	End example.
.FX 34	Start figure in the text.
.XF	End of figure in text.
.FC 6.3 "Create a lock file"	Caption of a figure.
.FG lock.c 13	Inclusion of figure file.
.RS	Relative section start.
.RE	Relative section end.
.CN "ls"	Command name in text.
.DN "mode"	Definition in text.
.SN "newline"	Symbol (character) name in text.
.HI "heading"	Subsection heading font.
.HL	Half line spacing.
.RU	Horizontal rule.
.CX arg1 arg2	Index arg1,arg2 and arg2,arg1.
.IX arg1 arg2 arg3	Index generation.

nroff is permissive when errors are made and usually allows processing to continue without an error message. This makes debugging difficult. To avoid these difficulties the library described here was constructed incrementally. A small part would be written and tested to provide a working base. Changes to the 'program', in this case nroff macros, were then made one at a time. This technique is applicable to all program writing since many bugs will be introduced as a result of the last modification made to the program. If a large program were to be written without trying out any part of it, it would be difficult to know where to start looking for malfunctions. Starting with something small that works and iterating allows the machine to be used effectively as part of the program construction process.

The first macros written were the section heading and paragraph macros. New macros were added as required and macros already written were revised as deficiencies were found. In the examples that follow the 'final' version of a definition is not necessarily presented. Successive samples, starting with the first approximation, are shown. Appendix 9 lists the version used to format this book.

In common with other macro libraries, the macro definitions have upper case names to avoid potential conflict with nroff requests.

Section headings

The first version of the section heading definition is shown in figure 7.4. A call of this macro would take the form

.SH number heading

If the heading contains any spaces it should be enclosed between double quotes. The section number and heading were provided as separate arguments so that the horizontal distance between them could be adjusted. This allows changes to be made to the spacing between the section number and title without changing each macro call. In later versions this number was incorporated into the title at the top of each page.

No check is made within the definition to ensure that the correct number of arguments is provided.

```
.de SH          \" Section heading:   .SH number title
.sp 2           \" leave blank lines
.ft B           \" bold font (ignored in nroff)
.in 0           \" reset indent
\&\\$1 \\$2     \" first macro argument
.ft R           \" resume normal font
.sp
..
```

Figure 7.4 The first version of section heading macro SH

Lines that begin with a . or a ´ or that contain a \ are processed by nroff each time they are read. For a macro definition this occurs once at the time the definition is assembled and once when it is called. Hence the use of

\&\\$1

to access the argument. The \& at the start of the line prevents an initial . or ´ in the argument from being processed again when the definition is invoked. The \ preceding the \$1 delays the interpretation of the argument until the macro is called.

The return to the Roman font using

```
.ft R
```

instead of .ft P guards against the possibility of a font change within the heading, as in,

```
.SH 7.1 "\fHnroff\fP and \fHtroff\fP"
```

It also assures that the Roman font is selected even if some other font was selected prior to the new section.

Subsequent additions to SH included a change in the point size and a request to ensure that at least 4 lines remain on the page when a new section is started. This prevents a section heading appearing on one page with its associated text on the next page. These are written

```
.ne 4
.ps +2
...
.ps −2
```

A final refinement to SH introduces the number register rs for the left margin.

The left margin is changed for an indented section by changing the value of the rs register. An indented section of text is introduced by the RS macro (Relative Start) and to enable uses of .RS to be nested the associated register is incremented and decremented. The macro definition consists of the request

```
.nr rs +2m
```

that increases the value of the register rs by 2 ems. The initial value is assigned to rs at the start of the macro library by the request

```
.nr rs 0
```

The end of an indented section is marked by the .RE request. No check is made to ensure that uses of .RS and .RE are matched. This is left to a separate program although it could be incorporated in the definitions as follows.

```
.de RS
.nr rs +2m
.nr rc +1
\\n(
..
.de RE
.ie \\n(rc \{
.nr rc −1
.nr rs −2m \}
.el \{
.tm "Unmatched RE"
.nr rc 0 \}
..
```

The register rc is incremented by 1 each time RS is invoked and decremented when RE is invoked. If the value of this count becomes negative, the .tm request prints a message on the error output stream and the register is reset.

```
.de CH \" chapter heading: .CH number text
\\.ds cf \\$1
\\.ds ct \\$2
.ce 2
\\$1
\\$2
.sp 8
..
```

Figure 7.5 The first version of the chapter heading macro CH

Chapter headings

Each chapter of this book is kept in a separate file and begins

```
.so maclib
.CH 7 "Document Preparation"
```

The .so request reads the file maclib and then resumes reading the file containing the .so request. The chapter heading and number are recorded by the CH macro for use later. The initial definition of CH is shown in figure 7.5. The chapter title is stored in the variable ct and the chapter number is stored in cf. The chapter name is required in the page top macro and the chapter number was used in the page bottom text on drafts; both are output at the center of the first page.

```
.de CH            \" chapter heading       .CH 1 "Introduction"
.}H "Chapter \\$1" "\\$2"
..
.de AH            \" appendix heading      .AH 1 "Commands"
.}H "Appendix \\$1" "\\$2"

.de }H            \" macro for chapter and appendix headings
.sp 8
\\.ds cf \\$1
\\.ds ct \\$2
.ce 2
\\$1
.sp
\\$2
.sp 3
..
```

Figure 7.6 Chapter and appendix heading macros

Later versions of this definition have been changed to allow headings for

appendices to be provided. A third macro called }H is introduced as shown in
figure 7.6.

Paragraphs

The first paragraph macros written were LP for left blocked paragraphs like
this one, and PP for paragraphs with an indented first line.

The indented paragraph macro IP is for a completely indented paragraph
with some text projecting into the left margin on the first line. The two additional macros MP and BU follow the same pattern.

```
.de IP  \" Indented paragraph:   .IP (a)
.if n .sp
.if t .sp .5
.ne 3
.in 6
.ta 4
.ti −4
\&\\$1\t\c
\.if \\w\`\\$1´u−4m  .br
..
```

Figure 7.7 The definition of the paragraph macro IP

The MP macro is for hanging text in the program text font, whereas the BU
macro provides for a bullet, •, as the hanging text. All three definitions were
more difficult to write than the section or chapter heading macros. The definition of IP is typical and an initial approximation is shown in figure 7.7.
The indentation for all but the first line of the paragraphs is provided by
.in 6. The argument to IP is processed by the line

    \&\\$1\t\c

The tab (\t) is used to reach the text margin and the label is indented toward
the left margin using a negative temporary indent, .ti −4. The text of the label is provided as an argument and is preceded in the macro definition by \&
to prevent interpretation of arguments that start with a .. The \c prevents a
break from occurring so that text can continue on the same line even though
there is a newline in the input. The break is provided, if required, by the request

    .if \w`\$1´u−4m .br

where one layer of \ has been removed to allow for the defining scan of the
macro by nroff. The form shown here is the request that will be executed
when the macro is called. The condition succeeds if the width of the argument $1 is larger than 4 ems. The u following \w`...´ ensures that the ap-
propriate units are used although is not strictly needed since \w returns a size
in basic units.

Page layout

The top and bottom of each page contain text that is output by two macros. The request

   .wh 0 aa

instructs troff to execute the macro **aa** when the position on the page is 0 units from the top of the page. The definition of **aa** is shown in figure 7.8.

```
.de aa
.ev 1
.lt 7i
.tl '--"--'
.ll 4.65i
.lt 4.65i
'sp 6
.ps 8
.ft R
.tl '%\h'2m'The UNIX System'\\*(ct\h'2m'%'
'sp
.ev
..
```

Figure 7.8 A top of page macro definition

The first line switches to a new environment to avoid disturbing the existing text. The next two lines generate marks on the page that are useful for cutting up continuous paper output. Since the title length is different from the physical paper width the title length is reset to 7 inches and then restored to the normal value for headings.

Initially, page numbers were output both on the left and right of the page using the special character %. A refinement added later was to print the left-hand and right-hand titles depending on whether the page number was even or odd. The even and odd conditions provided by nroff are used as illustrated.

   .if e .tl '%\h'2m'The UNIX System'''
   .if o .tl '''*(ct\h'2m'%'

The end of page activity follows a similar pattern. Another trap, **zz**, is set by the requests

   .if n .wh −5 zz
   .if t .wh 9i zz

In nroff the trap is 5 lines from the bottom of the page, and in troff it is 9 inches from the top.

Within macros executed by traps care is taken to use a ' rather than a . for those requests that cause a break. This prevents any partially accumulated line from being flushed.

Displays

A display is a block of text that is to be kept on the same page and where line filling is not required. The figures in this text are a special kind of display that start and end with a ruled line. The display macros described here require the user to provide the length of the text and a gap is left if there is insufficient room left on the current page.

Two basic macros are provided for displays called DS and DE for display start and display end respectively. The definition of DS is approximately

```
.de DS \" display start  .DS
'in +2m
.ta 4m 8m 12m 16m 20m 24m 28m 32m
'nf
'ne \\$1
..
```

The block of text is indented, and some default tabs are established. No fill mode is set and a .ne request ensures that vertical space is reserved.

The DE request ends a display and is defined as

```
.de DE
.HL
.fi
.in −2m
..
```

Fill mode is resumed and the indent is reduced by 2 ems. The request .HL generates a half-line space.

For displayed examples of programs, the requests .EX and .XE are defined as

```
.de EX
.ft H
.fl
.ss 20
.DS \\$1
..
.de XE
.DE
.ss 12
.ft R
..
```

Two new requests have been introduced in this example. The request .ss 20 sets the minimum spacing between words to be 20/36 ems. The default minimum spacing of 12/36 ems is too small for programs in the Helvetica font. The interpretation of character sizes is the last action taken by troff as output is being copied from its internal buffers into the output stream. The .fl request flushes any output in the buffer and is needed to prevent the change in the space character size from affecting any pending output.

The definitions of .FX and .XF are for figures, where a ruled line is required above and below the figure. Each of these macros is defined in terms of the basic display macros DS and DE.

The last item to note in appendix 9 is a set of string registers designed to provide characters that are more visually appealing than the defaults. For example, the character tilde normally appears as ˜ whereas for programs it is required to be at the same height as an equals =. Character sizes have also been adjusted for cosmetic reasons.

Index generation

An index can be generated by including with the text a macro containing the index item. The macro prints the index item on the error output stream using the .tm request. When nroff is run by the command

        troff chapter 2>ix/chapter

the index items are saved in the file ix/chapter. A subdirectory is used to avoid cluttering the working directory with files that can be regenerated.

The index macro IX is defined as

```
.de IX    \" index maoro
.if t .tm \\$1 \\$2 \\$3 \\$4 \\n%
..
```

and for convenience another macro, CX is defined as

```
.de CX
.IX "\\$1," "\\$2"
.IX "\\$2," "\\$1"
..
```

so that two items can be generated for the index with only a single request. For example,

        .CX "index macro" \fHnroff\fP

will generate the two index items:

        index macro, nroff\n%
        nroff, index macro\n%

The index macro output automatically refers to the page number containing the index request. The output is postprocessed using the shell procedure index shown in section 7.2.

7.2 Production tools

As a project progresses commands are developed and conventions established for naming files. For example, the file containing the index for a given chapter is kept in a subdirectory called ix. The page numbers, similarly are kept in another directory called **page**. The commands described in this sec-

tion were generated and refined during the writing of this book. These include the following:

- Print a chapter using nroff, or troff for various output devices.
- Generate page numbers.
- Generate the index.

Print a chapter

The command to print a chapter has different names depending on the output
device required. It is convenient to keep these variants in one command file
since they all have a similar form and adding a new variant is then easy with
the editor. The command is called by the names listed in the case branches
in figure 7.9.

```
args=`chapters`
for i in ${*-$args}
do      echo "$0        $$      $i      `date`" >>log
        n=`cat page/$i`
        # use tbl and eqn for chapter 7
        case $i in
         t7)    tbl $i | eqn ;;
         *)     cat $i
        esac |
        case $0 in
        t)      # Send to computer center aps
                troff -n$n 2>ix/$i |
                 aps
                ;;
        n)      # use nroff
                nroff -n$n 2>ix/$i
                ;;
        p)      # use proof
                troff -n$n 2>/dev/null |
                 proof
                continue
                ;;
        ix)     # generate index
                troff -n$n 2>ix/$i >/dev/null
                ;;
        esac
        makepage $i
done
```

Figure 7.9 Printing chapters

t   Produce troff output in final, camera ready, form on the APS photo-typesetter.

n   Use nroff and print on the standard output. This was used for viewing the text on simple output devices.

p   Generate output using a troff simulator on a high resolution bit-map terminal. No index is generated with this version since it is used interactively and is often interrupted before all output has been generated.

ix   Only generate the index into the file ix/....

A log of activities is kept in the file log. The command name, $0, the process number, $$, and the chapter name and date are all recorded.

The number of the starting page for each chapter is kept in the file page/*chapter* and is set in the shell variable n by the command

```
n=`cat page/$i`
```

Initially this file is created by hand and when troff is called the page number is passed via the −n option. Page numbers are automatically updated by the makepage command described in figure 7.11.

```
echo tp TC t1 t2 t3 t4 t5 t6 t7 t8
echo A1 A2 A3 a4 a5 a6 a7 a8 a9 a10 a11 tb TX
```

Figure 7.10 The names of the chapter files

The command chapters in figure 7.10 is a simple echo script and is useful since it contains the chapters in the order they appear in the final production. Some chapters are generated automatically by processing other files. These names are capitalized to distinguish them from chapters that cannot be regenerated.

Page numbering

```
args=`chapters`
for i in ${*−$args}
do      set − "`grep LAST <ix/$i`
        start=`expr ${2−0} + 1`
        if test −f page/next$i
        then    next=`cat page/next$i`
                echo $next did start at page `cat page/$next`
                echo now starts at page $start
                echo $start >page/$next
        fi
done
```

Figure 7.11 The makepage script

Each chapter is printed separately and the page numbers are sequential from one chapter to the next. The starting page number for each chapter is kept in the file page/*chapter* and is kept up-to-date by the command makepage listed in figure 7.11.

The index item LAST is generated using the end macro request, .em, provided by nroff as shown in figure 7.12. The makepage script uses this index item to find the number of the last page for a given chapter. One is added to the page number using the expr command and the result stored in a file associated with the appropriate chapter.

```
..                      \" set end of file macro
.em ee
..                      \" end of file macro
.de ee
.af % 1 \" ensure Roman font
.tm LAST \\n%
..
```

Figure 7.12 The end macro request

The set command in the script stores the page number associated with LAST in the shell variable $2 and the variable start is set to the page number for the beginning of the next chapter.

The page directory contains two files for each chapter. One contains the starting page number and the other, called page/next*chapter* is the file name of the next chapter.

Index postprocessing

The index is generated into files and needs to be sorted alphabetically by the index items, and formatted. The index command postprocesses the output from troff and generates troff input containing the final index. If there were no font or point size changes within the index the script would be simple. The sed script described below makes a complete copy of each line, and in the first removes the font and point size changes. This is sorted and then removed by a later sed script.

The cat command on the first line of figure 7.13, generates some fixed troff requests to include the macro library, set the tabs, no fill mode, and the point size. The for loop iterates over the argument file names provided, or uses the standard list.

An initial approximation would sort the index output directly, as in

```
sort ix/*
```

Unfortunately the font changes and point size changes embedded within the index items cause errors in the sorting.

```
cat  <<!
.so  maclib
.}H  "-"  Index
.ta  12m  14m  16m  18m  20m  22m  24m  26m
.ps  8
.nf
!

args="`chapters` see"
for i  in ${*—$args}
do      sed —e "s/    *//
                s/.*/&~~~~&/
                s/\\\\s—*.\(.*\)~~~~/\1~~~~/g
                s/\\\\s—*.\(.*\)~~~~/\1~~~~/g
                s/\\\\s.\(.*\)~~~~/\1~~~~/g
                s/\\\\s.\(.*\)~~~~/\1~~~~/g
                s/\\\\f.\(.*\)~~~~/\1~~~~/g
                s/\\\\f.\(.*\)~~~~/\1~~~~/g
                s/\\\\f.\(.*\)~~~~/\1~~~~/g
                s/    /                    /g"  <ix/$i
done |
  sort —uft'       '  +0 —1 +1n |
    sed —e 's/.*~~~~//' |
      xrefb
```

Figure 7.13 The index postprocessor

The next approximation to the index uses the **sed** command and generates a file with two fields separated by some distinctive string, in this example, ~~~~. The first field is the index item with the point size and font
change requests removed, the second field is the original item unchanged.
The **for** loop in figure 7.13 generates such a list and the output is piped into
sort; the first item being the key. The —uf option to **sort** removes duplicate
entries and ignores (folds) the distinction between upper and lower case
letters.

The final stage is to use the cross reference program described in chapter
8 to take lines of the form

        index-item   page-number
        . . .

and generate a list of the form

        index-item   page-number$_1$ page-number$_2$ . . .

when an index-item has more than one reference.

7.3 Document processing tools

The tools described so far enable text to be created and formatted. Tools are also provided to check spelling, analyze writing style, and to preprocess text enabling tables and mathematical equations to be produced.

col   Post-process nroff output to filter reverse line feeds.
diction Provide feedback on possibly wordy phrases.
eqn   Lay out equations and mathematical notation.
refer   Generate references to a bibliography.
spell   Print dubious or incorrect spelling of words.
style   Compare the readability and sentence structure of each chapter.
tbl   Prepare tabular information.

The programs eqn, refer, and tbl, accept data from the standard input and output modified text on the standard output. The input processed occurs between certain pairs of requests; the remaining text is copied, unaltered.

7.3.1 The col command

The col command accepts output generated by nroff containing reverse line feeds, such as those generated by the .rt request. This request is generated by the tbl preprocessor and by the multi-column options of some macro libraries. Other non-printing characters are also filtered out by the col command making its output suitable for simple printing devices.

The default output produced by nroff is suitable for a model 37 teletype (a mechanical wonder in its time but is no longer in general use). An alternative to using col is to instruct nroff to produce output for a simple terminal such as the DASI-450. This option is invoked as

    nroff −T450 ...

7.3.2 The diction command

The command

    diction <document

finds those sentences in a document containing bad or wordy phrases. Commonly misused phrases are noted on the standard output and although their use may be intentional, overuse detracts from readability.

As with the spell command a file containing those 'errors' that are acceptable can be kept and comm or diff used to print errors not already reported.

7.3.3 The eqn command

The eqn preprocessor is used for typesetting mathematics on a photo-typesetter. A related command, neqn, provides the same function for typewriter-like devices. Using eqn it is possible to produce symbols such as integral signs, summation signs, square roots, as well as complicated expressions. The ideas are simple enough for a non-mathematician to understand.

Text for **eqn** is enclosed by a pair of lines beginning with .EQ and .EN To take a simple example

```
.EQ
x=a+b
.EN
```

produces the italicized version of the equation

$$x = a + b$$

eqn text may also be included between delimiter characters, defined, for example, as

```
.EQ
delim $$
.EN
```

Thus,

Let $ 2 pi omega $ be the ...

produces

Let $2\pi\omega$ be the ...

eqn preprocesses the source text outputting instructions for **nroff** or **troff**. Other document preparing activities such as centering and left justification are performed using the **nroff**/**troff** requests, possibly using a package such as —ms.

Within **eqn** requests, spaces separate items; extra space in the output being produced using a ~. The input is free format and may straddle several lines if necessary. Items may be grouped together using { and }.

eqn also provides for subscripts, limits, partial derivative signs, big brackets for vectors and matrices, sigma signs for summation, and symbols for continued fractions. Some examples of **eqn** are given in figure 7.15 and a brief description follows.

Subscripts and superscripts are generated with the keywords **sub** and **sup**. Fractions are made with **over**. **sqrt** makes square roots. The keywords **from** and **to** introduce lower and upper limits on arbitrary things. Left and right brackets and braces of the right height are made with **left** and **right**. The **right** clause is optional. Legal characters after **left** and **right** are braces, brackets, bars, c and f for ceiling and floor, and "" for nothing at all (useful for a right-side-only bracket).

Vertical piles of things are made with **pile**, **lpile**, **cpile**, and **rpile**. There can be an arbitrary number of elements in a pile. **lpile** left-justifies, **pile** and **cpile** center, with different vertical spacing, and **rpile** right justifies. Matrices are made with **matrix**. In addition, there is **rcol** for a right-justified column.

Diacritical marks are made with **dot**, **dotdot**, **hat**, **tilde**, **bar**, **vec**, **dyad**, and **under**.

eqn *text*	*Output from* troff
x sub i	x_i
a sub i sup 2	a_i^2
e sup {x sup 2 + y sup 2}	$e^{x^2+y^2}$
a over b	$\frac{a}{b}$
x sup 2 over a sup 2	$\frac{x^2}{a^2}$
sqrt {ax sup 2 +bx+c}	$\sqrt{ax^2+bx+c}$
lim from {n−> inf } sum from 0 to n x sub i	$\lim_{n \to \infty} \sum x_i$
left [x sup 2 + y sup 2 over alpha right] ~=~1	$\left[x^2 + \frac{y^2}{\alpha} \right] = 1$
pile {a above b above c}	$\begin{matrix} a \\ b \\ c \end{matrix}$
matrix { lcol { x above y } ccol { 1 above 2 } }	$\begin{matrix} x & 1 \\ y & 2 \end{matrix}$
x dot = f(t) bar	$\dot{x} = \overline{f(t)}$
y dotdot bar ~=~ n under	$\overline{\ddot{y}} = \underline{n}$
x vec ~=~ y dyad	$\vec{x} = \overleftrightarrow{y}$

Sizes and fonts can be changed with size n or size ±n, roman, italic, bold, and font n. Size and fonts can be changed globally in a document by gsize n and gfont n, or by the command-line arguments −sn and −fn.

Normally subscripts and superscripts are reduced by 3 point sizes from the previous size; this may be changed by the command-line argument −pn.

Successive display arguments can be lined up. Place mark before the desired lineup point in the first equation; place lineup at the place that is to line up vertically in subsequent equations.

Keywords like sum ($\sum$), int ($\int$), inf (∞), and shorthands like >= ($\geqslant$), −> ($\rightarrow$), and != ($\neq$) are recognized.

```
.EQ
t ~=~ 2 pi int sub 0 sup 1
sin ( sqrt { x sup 2 + a sup 2 } ) dx
.EN
```

produces

$$t = 2\pi \int_0^1 \sin(\sqrt{x^2+a^2})\,dx$$

Greek letters are spelled out in the desired case, as in alpha or GAMMA. Mathematical words like sin, cos, log are made Roman automatically. troff four-character escapes like \(bs (@) can be used anywhere. Strings enclosed in double quotes "..." are passed through untouched; this permits keywords to be entered as text, and can be used to communicate with troff when all else fails.

If both tables and equations are required tbl should be used first, as in

tbl chapter|eqn|troff −ms

To include references refer should be used first, since both eqn and tbl signi-
ficantly expand the size of the text to be processed. For example,

refer paper|tbl||eqn|troff −ms

7.3.4 ptx - permuted index generation

The permuted index at the front of the *UNIX Programmer's Manual*
was produced using the ptx command.

ptx <input >output

creates a permuted index of the records in input and produces the result on
the file output. The option

−o keywords

is used to specify a file of keywords.

Each line of the input is shifted circularly so that a keyword appears at
the start of the line. The file resulting from a complete set of operations of
this kind is sorted. Finally the sorted lines are rotated so that the keyword
comes to the middle of the page.

7.3.5 The refer command

The refer command finds and formats references; it scans its standard input
looking for citations of the form

.[
references to bibliography
.]

The references to the bibliography are by keywords. For example,

.[
ritchie thompson unix system bstj 1978
.]

The bibliographic data base is scanned and the text between .[and .] is replaced by a set of string definitions in nroff. When using the −ms macros
the complete reference is printed from these strings.

If the −e option is included, as in

refer −e paper

the references are collected and printed wherever

.[
$LIST$
.]

appears, typically at the end of the document. Other options are available for
sorting and numbering references.

The standard bibliography is kept in /usr/dict/papers but may be replaced using the −p option. If references are ambiguous or inadequate then
refer prints a message.

The pubindex command takes files containing the required references
and makes an efficient index into them for use by refer. They contain bibliographic references separated by blank lines. A bibliographic reference is a
set of lines containing bibliographic information fields. Each field starts on a
line beginning with a %, followed by a key-letter, followed by a blank, and
followed by the contents of the field, that continues until the next line starting with %. The most common key-letters and the corresponding fields are

A	Author name.
B	Title of book containing article referenced.
C	City.
D	Date.
d	Alternate date.
E	Editor of book containing article referenced.
G	Government (CFSTI) order number.
I	Issuer (publisher).
J	Journal.
K	Other keywords to use in locating reference.
M	Technical memorandum number.
N	Issue number within volume.
O	Other commentary to be printed at end of reference.
P	Page numbers.
R	Report number.
r	Alternate report number.
T	Title of article, book, etc.
V	Volume number.
X	Commentary, unused by *pubindex*.

Except for A, each field should only be given once. Only relevant fields
should be supplied. For example,

```
%T 5-by-5 Palindromic Word Squares
%A M. D. McIlroy
%J Word Ways
%V 9
%P 199-202
%D 1976
```

The related command lookbib provides an interactive search of the bibliography. For example,

```
lookbib unix bstj
```

prints all references containing the UNIX keyword in the bibliography from the *Bell System Technical Journal.*

7.3.6 The spell command

The spell command checks the words in its input against an on-line dictionary of words. It is run as

    spell document

or

    spell -b document

The latter checks for British, as opposed to American, spelling.

   The output is a list of those words not contained in the dictionary. This list may contain words that are correctly spelled but are not in the standard dictionary. By keeping your own file of strange words the comm command may be used to print only new spelling errors, as in the example below.

```
for i do
        mv spell/$i spell/$i.prev
        <$i spell >spell/$i
        comm -23 spell/$i spell/$i.prev
done
```

Such words could also be added to the standard dictionary by your system administrator or someone who has access to the dictionary file.

   spell strips nroff/troff requests using the deroff filter before checking words against the dictionary.

7.3.7 The style command

The readability of a document may be analyzed using the command

    style document

The percentage use of different grammatical forms is printed. It reports on readability, sentence length, sentence structure, word length, usage, verb type and methods of opening sentences. Although this information is structural and superficial to meaning it is particularly useful for comparing two documents and may also indicate overuse of a given grammatical form.

7.3.8 The tbl command

tbl accepts a simple description of a table and generates nroff requests to print the table. The input to tbl is text with information on the design of tables. Requests to tbl occur between the .TS (table start) and .TE (table end) requests, as in,

```
.TS
table description
.TE
```

tbl leaves all other text unaltered. The .TS and .TE lines are also left unaltered by **tbl** and may be used by other macro requests.

Tables are described as follows:

```
.TS
options governing table design;
format of columns and rows.
data for table
.TE
```

The ; and . are literal and should appear as shown to terminate the appropriate section. The format of the columns and rows generally follows a pattern similar to that of the table itself. In the following example, ⊕ denotes the **tab** character that separates the columns of the table.

```
.TS
center;
c s s s
c c c c
l l n n.
Bell Labs Locations
Name⊕ Address⊕ Area Code⊕ Exchange
Holmdel⊕ Holmdel, NJ 07733⊕ 201 ⊕ 949
Murray Hill⊕ Murray Hill, NJ 07974⊕ 201 ⊕ 582
Whippany⊕ Whippany, NJ 07981 ⊕ 201 ⊕ 386
Indian Hill⊕ Naperville, IL 60540⊕ 312⊕ 690
.TE
```

This example produces a table of the form

Bell Labs Locations			
Name	Address	Area Code	Exchange
Holmdel	Holmdel, NJ 07733	201	949
Murray Hill	Murray Hill, NJ 07974	201	582
Whippany	Whippany, NJ 07981	201	386
Indian Hill	Naperville, IL 60540	312	690

In the format section of the instructions to **tbl** the following options are available.

c   A centered column entry.
l   A left justified column entry.
n   A numerical quantity.
r   A right justified column entry.
s   A spanned heading, i.e., the entry from the previous column continues across into this column.

The **center** option causes the entire table to be centered on the page. The default is left justification. Other options include the following:

allbox	Draw a box around every table entry.
box	Draw a box around the entire table.
center	Center the table, default left justifies.
doublebox	Draw a double box around the table.
expand	Expand the table to use the current line length.
tab(x)	Use x instead of a tab to separate columns.

For example, the allbox request for the above table produces

Bell Labs Locations			
Name	Address	Area Code	Exchange
Holmdel	Holmdel, NJ 07733	201	949
Murray Hill	Murray Hill, NJ 07974	201	582
Whippany	Whippany, NJ 07981	201	386
Indian Hill	Naperville, IL 60540	312	690

The line

        c s s s

defines the fields of the first line of the table. The c indicates that the field
is to be centered and an s says that the previous field is to continue in this
column. The request

        c c c c

formats the second line with four centered headings.
    The format of the remaining entries is described by

        l l n n

and a . ends the format section. The letter l indicates a left justified column
and an n a numerical entry that is to be aligned on the units digits.

Chapter 8

Data Manipulation Tools

The UNIX system is well known for its data manipulation tools. These include:

awk	A pattern matching language and report generator.
cmp	Compare two files.
comm	Select lines common to two sorted files.
diff	Find the differences between two files.
grep	Match patterns in a set of files.
join	Combine two files by joining records with identical keys.
sed	A stream editor like ed but not interactive.
sort	Sort or merge files line by line.
tail	Print the last n lines of input.
tr	One-to-one character translation.
uniq	Remove successive duplicate lines from a file.

In this chapter the tools listed above will be described briefly and examples of their use given. The emphasis is on building new tools from those that already exist.

Combining these tools is achieved via the shell that acts as the glue. Shell scripts are easy to maintain and understand. Shell programming using commands as building blocks can be inefficient unless care is taken. However, it is often possible to produce a working system in a shorter time than if all the programs were written in C. If the design is successful and efficiency is required, parts of the system can be rewritten once it is working.

The following examples are described later in this chapter and illustrate applications well suited to these tools.

Telephone directory

The first example manages a list of phone numbers, names and addresses. A program to update the file with new information is shown. A number may be retrieved by giving a name, or part of a name. Similarly, given a number the associated name can be found. This example treats the file like a notebook.

C language cross-reference

This section illustrates how a C program and a lex program can combine to produce a line and file number cross-reference for C identifiers. Also, a typical makefile is used to keep the compiled versions up-to-date. The cross-reference program itself is a shell script that uses the two tools constructed.

One of these tools is also used in chapter 7 to produce the index for this book.

Tennis ladder maintenance

This example describes a set of shell programs written to maintain a small data base.

Tennis ladder management typically involves keeping up-to-date player rankings. Each week results are reported and the ladder is updated according to some set of rules. Using the UNIX system most of this can be done automatically; updates will happen at a particular time each week without anyone having to issue a command directly.

8.1 Brief description of tools

In this section a brief discussion of the major tools is presented. The details, including the wide variety of available options, can be found in appendix 1, or from the man command.

In the discussion of some of the commands, such as join and sort, the term *fields* within records is used. A record is a line of text. Within a record, fields are separated by a field separator character. Frequently a tab is used as the field separator; this is convenient since it allows easy report generation using nroff. Some commands allow this character to be specified, others do not.

The tools described in some cases perform similar functions. For example, awk, ed, grep, lex, or sed will select lines according to a regular expression. The examples that follow illustrate uses for which these tools are well suited. As a general rule the more specialized the tool the more efficient it is for its stated purpose. For example, wc should be used for counting lines and grep, or egrep, used for selecting lines according to a pattern. sed is used when transformations of the input are required, such as the index generation example in section 7.2. awk is the most general but is slow to get started; lex requires that the C language environment be understood.

Regular expressions

The term *pattern* is used in this book to denote a set of strings. The set is specified using different forms depending on the application. For example, the shell uses a * to match zero or more characters, and ? to match a single character. The shell provides the weakest pattern matching capability. The commands awk, ed, grep, lex, and sed, provide patterns that match input strings. Sometimes the phrase *regular expression* is used to describe these patterns. A short description of regular expressions is given here; a more detailed discussion can be found in Aho, 1977.

A regular expression e is defined as follows, but see also section 3.1.5 for a description of ed patterns. In this description *character* excludes newline.

\c   A \ followed by a single character other than newline matches that character.

^ $ The character ^ ($) matches the beginning (end) of a line.

.   A . matches any character.

c   A single character not otherwise endowed with special meaning
               matches that character.

[...]   A string enclosed in brackets [] matches any single character
               from the string. Ranges of ASCII character codes may be ab-
               breviated as in a−z0−9. A] may occur only as the first char-
               acter of the string. A literal − must be placed where it cannot
               be mistaken as a range indicator.

e*   A regular expression followed by * (+, ?) matches a sequence
               of 0 or more (1 or more, 0 or 1) occurrences of the regular ex-
               pression.

e1 e2   Two regular expressions concatenated match the first followed
               by the second.

The expressions described so far are available in all the programs providing
patterns, namely awk, ed, grep, lex, and sed. Further facilities are provided
in awk, lex, and egrep as described below.

e1 | e2   Two regular expressions separated by | or newline matches ei-
               ther the first or the second expression.

(...)   A regular expression enclosed in parentheses matches the regu-
               lar expression enclosed.

The order of precedence of operators at the same parenthesis level is [],
*+?, concatenation, and |.

8.1.1 awk - report generator

awk is a filter that provides facilities for processing text. It is fully pro-
grammable, providing conditionals, loops, and variables with a notation similar to the C language. The command

    awk program file₁ file₂ ...

executes the awk instructions in the string program with input from the files
listed. If no files are given the standard input is used. Output from awk is
normally sent to the standard output.

awk scans each input line for *selector* and when a match occurs an associated *action* is executed. The general form of a program is

    BEGIN{ initial statements
    }
    {   selector { action }
               . . .
    }
    END{   final statements
    }

Several selector-action pairs may appear. An input line is read and each
selector evaluated, in order. If the selector is true, the associated action is
performed. The selector or action may be absent. If there is no selector the
action is performed for every line of input and if the action is omitted the in-

put line is copied onto the output.

An action may consist of several statements separated by ;. **BEGIN** and **END** introduce actions that are performed once at the beginning of the file and the end of file respectively.

awk reads each line or record of input and breaks it up into fields normally separated by white space. In an expression $0 represents the entire current record and $1, $2, ... represent the first field, second field, and so on. The number of fields in the current record is available in the variable **NF** and the number of input records read is available in **NR**.

The current input field separator and record separator are stored in the variables **FS** and **RS**. The default value for **FS** is white space (space or tab) and for **RS** is a **newline**. To process a file with fields separated by a :, like /etc/passwd, the statement

    FS=":"

should appear in the **BEGIN** section. To revert to the default, the null string should be assigned to **FS**. The output field separator is, by default, a **space** and is kept in the variable **OFS**. The name of the file being processed is kept in the variable **FILENAME**. (Assigning to this variable will not change the input source.)

Examples

    awk '/srb/'
            Print all records of the standard input containing srb.
    awk 'END{print NR}'
            Print the number of input lines.
    awk 'print $3'
            Print the third field from each record.

Expressions

Expressions take on string or numeric values as appropriate and, where necessary, **awk** will convert strings to numbers. The operators +, −, *, /, %, and concatenation (indicated by a **space**) and the C operators ++, −−, +=, −=, *=, /=, and %= are available in expressions. Variables may be scalars, array elements (denoted x[i]), or field names $1, $2, ... Variables are initialized to the null string. The relational operators consist of <, <=, ==, !=, >=, and > with the same meaning as in C. Both strings and numbers are accepted as arguments to these operators. For example,

    NF > 5

is true for records with more than 5 fields.

    $1>"s"

is true when the first field in the line exceeds "s" lexicographically, e.g. for "st" and "tom".

$2>=0

is true whenever the second field is numerically positive.

The explicit pattern matching operators ~ and !~ are also provided. For example,

$1~/srb|SRB/

is true for records whose first field is srb or SRB, and

$1~/[Ss]treet/

is true whenever $1 matches the pattern [Ss]treet. The patterns provided by awk are described in section 8.1.

The range of an action can be restricted using the , operator. For example,

/begin/,/end/{...}

applies the statements enclosed between { and } over sections starting with the line containing begin and ending with the line after that containing end.

Actions

An action in awk consists of one or more statements separated by a ; or newline. A statement can be an assignment, conditional, loop or a built-in function such as print. Generally, the syntax of awk and the set of operators is the same as in C.

A statement is one of the following:

```
if ( conditional ) statement [ else statement ]
while ( conditional ) statement
for ( expression ; conditional ; expression ) statement
for ( identifier in array ) statement
break
continue
{ [ statement ] ... }
variable = expression
print [ expression-list ] [ >expression ]
printf format [ , expression-list ] [ >expression ]
next      # skip remaining selectors on this input line
exit      # skip the rest of the input
```

Statements are terminated by semicolons, newlines or right-braces. An empty expression-list stands for the whole line.

For example,

```
if ($2 > $1) {
        x = $1
        $1 = $2
        $2 = x
}
```

copies the standard input to the standard output and swaps $1 and $2 if $2 exceeds $1. The comparison is numerical if possible and lexicographic otherwise.

Formatted printing

Formatted printing is available in **awk** using the two statements print, and printf. Without arguments, print will output the entire current record. printf is more general than print and allows a C style format to be specified (see chapter 5).

For example,

```
i = 1
while (i <= NF) {
        printf "%s, ", $i
        i++
}
```

prints each field followed by a , . The print statement without arguments prints the entire current record and, with arguments, selected fields may be printed, as in,

```
print $2, $1
```

that prints the second field and then the first field followed by a newline.

No output separators are produced automatically by printf; they must be provided as part of the format. For example,

```
printf "%s, %s\n", $1, $2
```

prints the first two fields separated by a , .

Arrays in **awk** can be indexed by strings thus providing an associative memory. For example, the first field of the password file contains a login-name. The following program checks that each login-name occurs only once.

```
awk '
BEGIN{ FS=":"
}
{       if (user[$1]) {
                print $1, "duplicated"
        }
        user[$1] = NR
}' </etc/passwd
```

All elements of an associative array are accessible via a for statement. For example,

```
for (i in user)
        statement
```

loops over all subscripts of the array **user**.

Standard functions

The only functions available to an **awk** programmer are those that are already built-in to the language and are described below.

sqrt, log, exp, int
: The square root, logarithm to base *e*, exponential, and integer-part of the argument in parentheses.

length
: The length of its string argument. Without an argument the length of the entire current record is given.

substr(s, m, n)
: Produce a substring of s that starts at the m-th character (counting from 1), and that contains at most n characters.

index(s, t)
: The position of the first occurrence of t within s starting at 1. If t is not a substring of s, zero is returned.

8.1.2 cmp - **compare two files**

The command

    cmp file$_1$ file$_2$

compares file$_1$ and file$_2$. If the files are identical then no output is produced; if they are not identical **cmp** responds by giving the byte and line number where the first difference occurs. The exit status returned is as follows:

0   The files are identical.
1   The files are different.
2   The files are inaccessible or arguments are missing.

8.1.3 comm - **select common lines**

This command selects or rejects lines common to two sorted files.

    comm file$_1$ file$_2$

takes file$_1$ and file$_2$ that must both be sorted lexicographically. The output is in three columns consisting of lines only in file$_1$, lines only in file$_2$, and lines common to file$_1$ and file$_2$. Columns may be suppressed using the −[123] option. For example,

    comm −23 f$_1$ f$_2$

suppresses columns 2 and 3, printing lines that are in the first file but not in the second, whereas

    comm −12 f$_1$ f$_2$

prints only lines common to both files.
    For example,

```
for i do
        mv spell/$i spell/$i.prev
        <$i spell >spell/$i
        comm −23 spell/$i spell/$i.prev
done
```

is a script that keeps a file of the words rejected by spell. Each time the script is run the previous file is preserved and the file updated. comm prints the new spelling errors.

8.1.4 diff - file differences

diff is a differential file comparator. It lists the lines from two files that differ and attempts to minimize the length of the differences. It is called as

```
diff file₁ file₂
```

The output resembles that expected by the a, c and d requests to ed. Lines in the first file are preceded by a < and lines from the second by a >. The −e option generates ed requests that will change file₁ into file₂.
    For example,

```
diff −e file1 file2 >diffo
```

will keep in the file diffs an ed script to convert file1 into file2.
    The exit status from diff is:

0   The files are the same.
1   The files differ.
2   An argument is inaccessible or missing.

On some systems the −r option of diff recursively scans two directory hierarchies and executes diff for each file found.

8.1.5 grep - pattern selection

grep is a pattern matching filter and was introduced in chapter 2.

```
grep pattern file ...
```

selects lines matching the given regular expression in one or more files. The expression specifies patterns as described in section 8.1.
    A typical use of grep is to find a variable or function name in a set of C program source files. For example,

```
grep main *.c
```

will search all files with names ending in .c in the current directory, and print lines containing the string main. If more than one file is searched each output line is prefixed by the appropriate file name.
    If the pattern contains characters that have a special meaning to the shell, such as * or ^, the pattern should be quoted. For example,

```
grep '^[0—9][0—9]*'
```

The exit status of **grep** is:

0   No match was found.
1   A match was found.
2   Files are inaccessible or there are syntax errors in **expression**.

The exit status of **grep** may be used to test for the presence of a string within a file. For example,

```
if grep pattern file
then ...
fi
```

will look for *pattern* in *file*. If the pattern is found the **then** clause is executed.

    grep does not provide alternatives within **expression**. **egrep** accepts full regular expressions that include | for alternation, + for one or more occurrences, ? for zero or one occurrence, and parentheses for grouping.

8.1.6 join - combine files

This command combines two files by joining records with identical keys, the key being a field of the file. A typical call is

```
join file₁ file₂
```

where both **file**$_1$ and **file**$_2$ must be sorted lexicographically on the fields to be joined. The default key is the first field in each line.

    There will be one line in the output corresponding to each pair of lines in **file**$_1$ and **file**$_2$ with identical key. By default, each output line will take the form

```
common-field rest-of-line-from-file₁ rest-of-line-from-file₂
```

For example, suppose that the file **dept** contains lines of the form

```
name ⊤ department
```

and the file **cost** contains lines of the form

```
name ⊤ amount ⊤ date-of-purchase
```

⊤ is used to represent the **tab** character and it is assumed that both files are sorted on the first field. The command

```
join dept cost
```

will print a line of the form

```
name department amount date-of-purchase
```

for each pair of lines in the two files that have the same **name**. To illustrate, suppose that the file **dept** contains

```
Leo      13
Shaw     12
```

and the file cost contains

```
Leo      $35      3/82
Shaw     $20      2/82
Shaw     $45      4/82
```

then the output from join dept cost will be

```
Leo 13 $35 3/82
Shaw 12 $20 2/82
Shaw 12 $45 4/82
```

Various options are available. The output just produced is separated by spaces. If the field separator is changed with the −t′⊕′ option, both input and output fields are separated by a **tab**. The −o option accepts a list of fields to be printed. For example,

```
join −o 1.2 2.1 2.2 file₁ file₂
```

will print, in order, field 2 from the first file, and fields 1 and 2 from the second. Using the above example, the output would be

```
13 Leo $35
12 Shaw $20
12 Shaw $45
```

The fields to be joined can be specified by the −j option. The argument

```
−jn m
```

causes joining on the m-th field of the n-th file. For example,

```
join −j1 2 −j2 2 filo₁ filo₂
```

joins on the second field of both files.

When using join the most frequent problem is insufficient output. This can be caused by an incorrect use of the options where white space is significant, or by files not being sorted on the appropriate fields.

Using the two files **dept** and **cost** from the previous example, the script below may be used to print those keys in the cost file not contained in the department file. Again, the first field of each file contains the key.

```
# list names in cost file that are not in dept file

field 1 <cost | sort −u >/tmp/cost$$
field 1 <dept | sort −u >/tmp/dept$$
comm −23 /tmp/cost$$ /tmp/dept$$
rm /tmp/cost$$ /tmp/dept$$
```

The first two lines produce a sorted list of the keys from each file with no duplicates.

The first version of this program was written as shown here but without the −u option for sort. Unexpected results were produced and it took a little time to discover the problem. If this script had been constructed in two stages this might have been avoided. The first stage would construct the temporary files. These files could then be printed to check for unforeseen problems such as duplicated lines.

8.1.7 sed - stream editor

sed is an editor that is used as a filter, not interactively. The operation of sed resembles in many ways that of the awk pattern matcher discussed earlier. Each line of its input is read and the requests that apply are executed. Requests to sed are like those for ed. Repeated global substitutions are more efficient with sed than ed.

sed is invoked as

> sed −e script

or

> sed −f scriptfile

The requests from the script or scriptfile are applied to the standard input. The script may be quoted to prevent characters from being interpreted by the shell.

A general request takes the form

> address$_1$,address$_2$ request argument

If addresses are omitted the request is applied to every line. If two addresses are identical only one need be specified. Otherwise, the address delimits the part of the file that the edit request is applied to. Addresses can be specified numerically as decimal numbers or by context using regular expressions similar to those employed by ed and enclosed between / and /. The + and − operators are not available when addressing lines. Unlike ed, a request is applied to each line that matches address.

The requests available include:

s/.../.../	Substitute a string.
d	Delete a line.
a\	Append text after the current line.
i\	Insert text before the current line.
c\	Change the current line.

Each line of text following a, i or c is terminated by \ except for the last line. Requests for reading files, r, writing files, w, and printing, p, are also available.

```
# print full path name of command found in $PATH
for j do
        for i in `echo $PATH | sed -e 's/:/ /g`
        do      if test -f $i/$j
                then    echo $i/$j
                fi
        done
done
```

Figure 8.1 The path command

The path command in figure 8.1 illustrates a typical use of the sed command. The outer loop sets j to each argument supplied to path. The inner loop sets i to each non-blank word in the output of the command

    echo $PATH | sed -e 's/:/ /g'

The output consists of a blank separated list of directory names from the shell variable PATH.

8.1.8 sort - sort or merge files

When applied in the form

    sort file₁ file₂ ...

all lines of file$_1$, file$_2$, ... are sorted onto the standard output. If no files are specified the standard input is read so that sort can be used as a filter. By default, sorting is done on entire lines using lexical ordering by bytes in the host machine's collating sequence (usually ASCII). This ordering is termed *lexicographic* and is close to the dictionary order for words. An option provides numerical sorting.

The notation

    +pos₁ -pos₂

restricts the sort key to a field beginning at position pos$_1$, and ending just before position pos$_2$. For example,

    sort +0 -1 +3 -4

sorts on the first field followed by the fourth field. (Incorrectly specifying field numbers is a frequent error when using sort.) A starting position may be followed by n to specify numeric comparison for this field. For example,

    sort +0n ...

specifies that sorting on the first field is numerical.

The default field separator is white space and may be changed using the

−t option. Thus

    sort −t: ...

sorts on fields separated by a :.
    Other useful sort options include:

    −n   Sort using the numerical value of the field.
    −r   Reverse the sense of comparisons.
    −u   Suppress all but one instance in each set of identical lines.

    sort and join use a different notation for numbering the fields within a
record and this can be confusing. In sort, +0 −1 means the first field. For
join the first field is specified as 1.

8.1.9 tail - last lines of a file

The tail command is a filter that prints the last few lines of a file. The −n
option, where n is a number, specifies that the last n lines are required. The
−r option is available on some systems and prints the file a line at a time in
reverse. For example, the command uulog is

    tail −r /usr/spool/uucp/SYSLOG

and prints the uucp activity log file in reverse order.

8.1.10 tr - translate characters

The command

    tr string$_1$ string$_2$

copies and translates characters from the standard input to the standard output. All the characters in string$_1$ are mapped onto the corresponding characters in string$_2$. If string$_2$ is shorter than string$_1$, it is padded to the length of
string$_1$ by repeating the last character as often as necessary.
    The command lower in figure 8.2 converts all upper case letters into
lower case. Note that the arguments to the shell are quoted to avoid being
interpreted as file name patterns.

---

    tr '[A−Z]' '[a−z]'

Figure 8.2 The lower command

8.1.11 uniq - remove duplicate lines

This command accepts sorted input and compares adjacent lines. When invoked as

    uniq file

the second and later copies of repeated adjacent lines are removed from file
and printed on the standard output. The standard input is read if no file is

specified. Identical lines must be adjacent to be found; therefore the **sort** command may be needed before uniq is invoked. The —u option of **sort** has a similar specification although **sort** does not provide some of the options of uniq.

The following options are available:

—c Print the number of occurrences of each line followed by the line.
—d Only a single copy of duplicated lines is printed.

The following program generates a list of words from a set of files and produces a frequency count for each word. If no arguments are supplied, the for loop executes once with i set to the null string, causing the standard input to be read by tr.

```
for i in "$@"
do        <$i tr —cs A—Za—z '\012'
done |
  sort —f |
    uniq —c
```

8.1.12 field - **select columns**

The field command is a basic tool, although it is not provided with standard versions of the UNIX system. The implementation of this command is given in section 8.4 and is used as an example to show how new tools are engineered. The arguments to field are the column numbers to be copied from each record. For example, when invoked as

```
field 2 4 3
```

the standard input is read and produces on the standard output fields 2, 4 and 3 separated by a TAB. The **awk** script

```
awk '{print $2, $4, $3}'
```

has a similar effect but separates the output by a **space**.

8.1.13 lex **and** yacc

This section mentions two compiler writing tools lex and yacc. lex accepts a set of regular expressions and associated C program fragments corresponding to actions. A program is produced that partitions its input according to these expressions and executes the associated actions. It is used for the lexical analysis of programming languages such as C, and is particularly well suited as an interface to yacc.

yacc accepts an LALR(1) grammar as input together with fragments of C program and generates a program to partition its input according to the grammar. When a rule is recognized the user program fragment supplied with the rule is executed. yacc expects its input to have been broken up into tokens by a lexical analyzer such as lex.

An example of the use of lex is given in section 8.2.2.

8.2 Simple examples

8.2.1 Maintaining a simple data base

In this example a program is designed to update a file containing names, addresses, and phone numbers. The command is called enter and is shown in
figure 8.3.

The first outline of the program is

```
while read name
do      read address
        read phone
        # append to file
        ...
done
```

The read command provided by the shell is used.

```
read v₁ v₂ ...
```

takes one line of input from the standard input and assigns successive *words*
to the variables v_1, v_2, ... If any words are left over they are assigned to the
last variable. The exit status of read is 0 unless an end-of-file is encountered.
Replacing the read statement by break,

```
read phone || break
```

causes a break out of the while loop to occur if the read fails. For example,
if the end-of-file is reached when reading the data or if an interrupt occurs,
read will fail and break will be executed.

Each entry within the file is kept as a single record so that standard tools
may be used to process the file and the outline given above assumes a single
line address. A multi-line address may be converted into a single line as illustrated below where a ~ is used to separate the various sections of the address in the shell variable address. On input an address is terminated by a
blank line.

```
address=
while read a
do      case $a in
        '')     break ;;
        *)      address="$address~$a" ;;
        esac
done
```

If this program outline were executed, the user would soon get confused,
since there is no prompting. Further, there are no facilities for making
corrections. The prompting is easily added to give a complete version of the
enter command as shown in figure 8.3.

The prompt command used here consists of

```
echo −n $* 1>&2
```

```
date=`date`
while    prompt "name: "
         read name
do       case $name in
         ")        continue ;;
         q)        break ;;
         esac

         prompt "address: "
         address=
         while read a
         do      case $a in
                 ")        # blank line ends address
                           break ;;
                 *)        address="$address~$a" ;;
                 esac
         done

         prompt "phone: "
         read phone || break

         echo  "$name ⊕ $address ⊕ $phone ⊕ $date">> $HOME/tel
done
```

Figure 8.3 The enter command

Looking up numbers

grep is ideally suited to looking up names or numbers in the address-list as illustrated by the following tel script:

```
for i do
         , grep "$i"  <$HOME/tel
done
```

where $HOME/tel is the file containing the checked data. The argument to
grep is quoted to prevent any enclosed meta-characters from being interpreted by the shell.

A file of the kind created here will accumulate entries that are similar,
or even identical, and also will become out of date. One technique that is
useful for detecting potential curiosities in the file is to sort on different
fields. Exact duplicates of lines can be removed using the sort command, as
in

```
sort −u  <$HOME/tel  >$HOME/newtel
```

Duplicate phone numbers are extracted from the file tel by the command

```
field 3 <tel | sort | uniq −d
```

where the −d option results in only one copy of each duplicated record being produced. The entire line from the original file corresponding to duplicate phone numbers may be printed by joining the output with the original **tel** file. The script is shown in figure 8.4.

The join input must be sorted on the fields to be joined and the file /tmp/$$1 is already appropriately sorted. However, since the **tel** file cannot be guaranteed to be sorted, sort is called and the output saved in /tmp/$$2.

```
field 3 <tel | sort | uniq −d >/tmp/$$1
sort −t'Ⓣ' <tel >/tmp/$$2
join −t'Ⓣ' −j1 1 −j2 3 /tmp/$$1 /tmp/$$2
rm /tmp/$$1 /tmp/$$2
```

Figure 8.4 Print duplicate phone numbers

Both **sort** and **join** require the −t'Ⓣ' option specifying that a **tab** is the field separator. In the script a single quote has been used to prevent this **tab** from being absorbed by the shell.

Another improvement that could be made to the original **enter** command is to check to see if numbers that are about to be added are already present. This check takes the form

```
if grep "$phone" <$HOME/tel >/dev/null
then    # the number is already present
else    # the number is missing
fi
```

The output from **grep**, if any, is directed to the null file, /dev/null, that is writable by everyone. Characters sent to this file are 'lost'. The exit status of **grep** is used to determine whether the phone number exists in the file.

A remark should be made about the efficiency of the modification just outlined. **read** is built into the shell and so its use is reasonably efficient. In some versions of the shell an **echo** or **prompt** command is also built-in. **grep** is not built into the shell and each time it is executed a new process is created. This operation is relatively expensive and may cause a noticeable reduction in the response of **enter**. Whether this is serious depends on the local computing environment and the size of the **tel** file.

8.2.2 A C language cross-reference program

The programs described in this section generate cross-references for C programs. The output is a list of the line numbers in each file where the identifiers are used. The result type is printed for function definitions. The output in figure 8.5 is the cross-reference output for the file xrefb.c from figure 8.9.

EOF	xrefb.c	25	64						
MAXW	xrefb.c	5	6	13	65				
argc	xrefb.c	10	17						
argv	xrefb.c	11							
c	xrefb.c	61	64	66	69				
cpstr()	xrefb.c	3	36	40	43				
f1	xrefb.c	13	22	32	40	41			
f2	xrefb.c	13	23	34	36	43	44		
first	xrefb.c	14	27	28					
getchar()	xrefb.c	64							
h	xrefb.c	1							
lastc	xrefb.c	7	46	50	63	69	72		
lastw	xrefb.c	3	6	27	28	32	34	35	48 60 65
main(argc,argv)	xrefb.c	+9							
n	xrefb.c	46	63	64					
p	xrefb.c	60	65	66	71				
printf()	xrefb.c	18	29	35	41	44	48	52	
stdio	xrefb.c	1							
strcmp()	xrefb.c	32	34						
strcpy()	xrefb.c	3							
t	xrefb.c	64							
word()	xrefb.c	25	33	42	47				
word()/int	xrefb.c	+58							
x	xrefb.c	3							

Figure 8.5 xref **output for the file** xrefb.c

The work is divided between two programs xrefa and xrefb. The first program, xrefa, generates a list of the form

identifier ⊕ file-name ⊕ line-number

and is implemented by the lex program whose source is kept in the file xrefa.l. As shown in the shell command xref in figure 8.6, the output from xrefa is sorted and then piped into the layout program xrefb producing output of the form identifier ⓣ file-name ⓣ line₁, line₂ ...

         ...

xrefb is a C program and the source is kept in the file xrefb.c. The index for this book was also partly processed by xrefb (see section 7.2). The vertically oriented output of xrefa is read by xrefb and the line numbers printed across the page.

```
xrefa $*  |
   sort −ut: +0 −1 +1 −2 +2n −3  |
      xrefb
```

Figure 8.6 The xref command

The makefile

The makefile is shown in figure 8.7. Apart from the entries to make the programs, entries are also introduced to *clean* and *install* the system. It is assumed that the files clean and install do not exist in the source directory.

```
xref:          xrefa  xrefb

xrefa:         xrefa.o
               cc −o xrefa xrefa.o −ll
xrefb:         xrefb.o
               cc −o xrefb xrefb.o

clean:;        rm xref[ab].o

install:;      cp xref xrefa xrefb  /usr/local/bin

.c.o:;         cc −O −c $<
```

Figure 8.7 The makefile for the xref system

The first pass, xrefa

This section describes, briefly, the lex program for the first pass of the cross-reference. A complete description of lex is available in Lesk, 1975.

    The program described here has the form

```
% options
%{
C program definitions
%}
%%
lex actions
```

The C program definitions include a definition of the function **main** and the
lex actions consists of a pattern, as described in section 8.1, followed by an
action. The action is a C program statement that is executed when the pattern matches the input. This is similar to the way an **awk** program works except that in lex the input is not automatically divided into records. Further,
lex programs are compiled.

lex *options*

lex uses many internal table and the %option section sets the various table
sizes. The output generated by running the command

    lex xrefa.l

is

    372/500 nodes(%e),
    3188/4000 positions(%p),
    339/400 (%n), 21255 transitions,
    54/100 packed char classes(%k),
    967/1000 packed transitions(%a),
    833/1000 output slots(%o)

and these options have been set so that sufficient space is available and are
not otherwise interesting. In some cases the default lex sizes are sufficient.
The output from lex is left in the file lex.yy.c and is compiled as

    cc lex.yy.c −ll

The lex *environment*

The standard input-output library is automatically provided by lex and is
used in this example to open input files. Other definitions provided by lex include:

yylex()	Invoke the lex analyzer to read the standard input file.
yyinput()	Read a single character from the input.
yytext[]	The string matched by the current rule.
yyleng	The length of the string in yytext.
yylineno	Incremented for each line of input read.

The main routine provided in the definitions section of xrefa.l contains
the argument handling for xrefa just like a C program. lex actions are invoked when the function yylex is called. In this example, if there are no arguments, yylex is called and the standard input is read. If arguments are
provided each file is opened as the standard input by freopen, the file name
remembered and yylex is called.

```
%k  100
%a  1000
%o  1000
%n  400
%e  500
%p  4000
%{
char      *filename="-";

main(argc,argv)
          int       argc;
          char      *argv[];
{
          register int rc=0;
          if(argc<=1) {
                    yylex();
          }else{
                    while(argc>1) {
                              if(freopen(argv[1],"r",stdin)==NULL) {
                                        fprintf(stderr,
                                                  "xref: %s: cannot open\n",
                                                  argv[1]
                                        );
                                        rc++;
                              }else{
                                        filename=argv[1];
                                        yylineno=1;
                                        yylex();
                              }
                              argc--; argv++;
                    }
          }
          return(rc);
}
%}
%%
"/*"        comment();
"\""        strings();
^[a-zA-Z_][a-zA-Z0-9 \t_]*"("[a-zA-Z0-9, ]*")""\n          fndef();
if[ \t]*"("          ;
return[ \t]*"("       ;
while[ \t]*"("        ;
for[ \t]*"("          ;
switch[ \t]*"("       ;
auto              ;
break             ;
```

```
...
[a−zA−Z_][a−zA−Z0−9_]*[ \t]*"(" {
             /* function call */
             printf("%s)\t%s\t%d\n", yytext, filename, yylineno);
             }
[a−zA−Z_][a−zA−Z0−9_]* {
             /* identifier reference */
             printf("%s\t%s\t%d\n", yytext, filename, yylineno);
             }
  .         ;
\n          ;
```

Figure 8.8 The lex source for xrefa.l

Figure 8.8 contains lex rules for the cross-reference program. One caveat should be noted in the BUGS section of the manual page. The rule for recognizing function definitions is not exactly correct since the result type can appear on the line preceding the function name.

The lex rules are described below:

"/*" The start of a comment. The function comment is called and is defined below.

```
comment() {
           /* comments */
           char c;
           while(c = yyinput()) {
                       if(c == '*' && yyinput() == '/')
                                break;

           }
}
```

"\"" The opening quote of a string constant. The function strings, defined below, is called and skips characters up to the closing quote.

```
strings() {
           /* strings */
           char c;
           while(c = yyinput()) {
                       if(c == '"')
                                break;
                       else if(c == '\\')
                                yyinput();
           }
}
```

^[a−zA−Z_][a−zA−Z0−9 \t_]*"("[a−zA−Z0−9,]*")"\n
    The pattern describes an identifier at the start of a line, followed by a (,

a list of identifiers and commas, a) and a **newline**. It is assumed to be a function definition. This rule is not strictly correct but is adequate for C programs using standard layout such as that produced by the cb command. Within a rule lex metacharacters, like (and) may be enclosed within double quotes to remove their special meaning. The C function fndef listed below is called and scans backwards through the text recognized by the rule looking for the end of the identifier and the result type, if any. The result type is printed after the function name and argument list.

```
fndef()
{
        /* fn defs */
        register char *p = &yytext[yyleng];

        *--p = 0;          /* remove ) */
        while(*--p != '(');
        while(*p==' ' || *p=='\t') {
                p--;
                if(p < yytext) break;
        }
        while(*p!=' ' && *p!='\t') {
                p--;
                if(p < yytext) break;
        }
        p++;
        printf("%s", p);
        if(p != yytext) {
                *--p=0;
                printf("/%s", yytext);
        }
        printf("\t%s\t+%d\n", filename, yylineno-1);
```

The remaining rules are similar to those already described. Once function definitions have been recognized, the language constructions involving parentheses are read and ignored. Any identifiers remaining that are followed by a (are treated as function calls. Identifier references are recognized last and the two rules

```
.         ;
\n        ;
```

absorb any characters that remain.

The second pass, xrefb

The second pass of the cross-reference takes the sorted output from the first pass and lays it out horizontally across the page. The program, as presented here, could easily be written as an **awk** script; the original program had more options to control the output format.

```
#include <stdio.h>

#define MAXW 128
char    lastw[MAXW];    /* last word read */
char    lastc;

main(argc,argv)
        int     argc;
        char    *argv[];
{
        char f1[MAXW], f2[MAXW];
        char first=0;

        /* args ? */
        if(argc>1) {
                printf("unexpected argument\n");
                return(1);
        }

        f1[0]=0;
        f2[0]=0;

        while(word() != EOF){
                if(lastw[0]!=first) {
                        first=lastw[0];
                        printf("\n");
                }

                if(strcmp(lastw, f1)==0) {
                        word();
                        if(!strcmp(lastw, f2) == 0) {
                                printf("\n\t%s", lastw);
                                strcpy(f2, lastw);
                        }
                }
                else{
                        strcpy(f1, lastw);
                        printf("\n%s", f1);
                        word();
                        strcpy(f2, lastw);
                        printf("\t%s", f2);
                }
                if(lastc != '\n'){
                        word();
                        printf("\t%s", lastw);
                }
                lastc = 0;
        }
```

```
                printf("\n");
                return(0);
        } /* main */

        /* read a word from the input */
        /* result is stored in lastw */
        int word()
        {
                register char *p = lastw;
                register int c;

                if(lastc != '\n'){
                        while((c = getchar())!='\t' && c!='\n' && c!=EOF) {
                                if(p < &lastw[MAXW]) {
                                        *p++ = c;
                                }
                        }
                        lastc = c;
                }
                *p++ = 0;
                return(lastc);
        } /* word */
```

Figure 8.9 The C source for xrefb.c

8.3 A tennis ladder system

This section describes the use of the UNIX system tool kit through a complete example. The programs in this section are written using standard commands with the addition of the field described in section 8.4.

The system maintains a tennis ladder for staff members at the Murray Hill laboratory. The ladder itself is a file containing a rank ordered list of players. Each line of the file consists of the following fields:

- The player's identity (initials if unique).
- The numerical rank of the player.
- The player's name.
- The player's phone number.
- The player's office number.
- The number of matches won.
- The number of matches lost.
- The movement up or down the ladder since last week.
- The number of weeks the player has been inactive.

The ladder operates as follows. All matches played between Monday and Sunday are recorded in a file. On Tuesday of each week (allowing Monday for delays in reporting matches) the ladder is updated according to the previous week's match results. If a player beats a player higher in the ladder, the winner is moved just above the loser. Otherwise, no movement occurs as a result of the match. However, if a player is inactive for 3 or more consecutive weeks then that player drops two places down the ladder each subsequent week. A player who is inactive for 7 weeks is dropped entirely from the ladder.

8.3.1 Organization

All files relating to this system reside in the directory $HOME/tennis or in a subdirectory of this directory. This directory is considered to be the current directory in the following description.

The commands to support and implement this system are kept in ./bin (i.e. $HOME/tennis/bin). This separation of commands and data files avoids congestion in the main directory and enables commands to be easily identified. A suitable setting of the PATH variable in the shell is:

    PATH=.:/bin:/usr/bin:./bin:$HOME/bin

A directory is created each year for use as an archive for results. It also serves as a backup in case of failure. For most of the commands that follow, the ladder file is assumed to exist and be named .ladder. When testing the system the file name was kept in the variable $ladder that was set and exported from the shell.

The remainder of this section describes the commands that implement the ladder maintenance including:

- Enter match results.
- Update the ladder weekly.
- Print the ladder.
- Determine prize winners.
- Clean up of files at the end of the season.

Commands scripts

The scripts are summarized here for reference. The level of indentation indicates the execution hierarchy. For example, cron calls weekly and weekly calls both run and send.

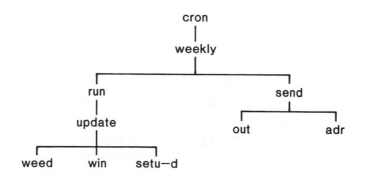

8.3.2 Entering results

Each game result consists of the identity of the winner and loser, the score and the date. Players are identified by their initials although, given a name, the initials can be looked up. Both are stored in the ladder file.

The program to enter results follows closely the style of the example in section 8.2.1.

The program record, is accessible from the tennis directory when the $PATH variable has been set appropriately. As shown in figure 8.9, record prompts for the following fields for each match played:

```
date:
winner:
loser:
score:
```

```
NL='
'

# read ladder into L_id
. readL

while   true
do      prompt 'date: '
        read D || break

        case $D in
        [0-9]*) # assume it is a date ;;
        q)      break ;;
        *)      look $D || prompt "\'$D' not found$NL"
                continue
                ;;
        esac

        prompt 'winner: '
        read WP || break
        # check player is in the ladder
        eval namew\=\$L_$WP
        case $namew in
        '')     prompt "$WP not in the ladder$NL"
                continue
        esac
        set $namew; rank1=$1; name1=$2;

        prompt 'loser: '
        read LP || break
        eval namel\=\$L_$LP
        case $namel in
        '')     prompt "$LP not in the ladder$NL"
```

```
                continue
        esac
        set $namel; rank2=$1; name2=$2;

        prompt 'score: '
        read S || break

        prompt "$NL$D  $name1($rank1)  over $name2($rank2)"
        prompt "${NL}ok? "
        read ok
        case $ok in
        y|ok|") echo "$D ⓣ $WP ⓣ $LP ⓣ $S" >> .matches
                ;;
        *)      prompt "result not recorded$NL"
                ;;
        esac
done
```

Figure 8.10 The record script

After the prompt, if a valid date, such as 12/7, is entered the remaining
fields are requested. An end-of-file or a q will cause a break and exit. Otherwise, if the name of a player is entered, look (figure 8.11) is called to print
an entry from the ladder file. If more than one entry is found by look then
all such entries are printed.

Next the winner and loser are read and checked to ensure that they are
on the ladder and finally the match score is requested and read. The full
name and ladder position of the participants is reflected back to the user for
confirmation before being added to the .matches file.

The discussion of the shell commands that read and check the player
identities is deferred until after the description of the readL script.

The look *script*

look finds lines in the ladder file containing all of its arguments. In the simple case, when called with a single argument, $# is 1 and the first branch of
the case statement is executed.

```
case $# in
        1)      tr [A–Z] [a–z] < .ladder | grep "$1" ;;
        0)      ;;
        *)      a="$1"; shift; look "$*" | grep "$a"
esac
```

Figure 8.11 The look script

When more than one argument is provided, as, for example, in

```
look bob lucky
```

the default branch of the case is executed. The first argument is recorded in
the variable $a and look is called again with the second argument. The out-
put from the second call of look is filtered by

```
... | grep "$a"
```

so that only lines containing both bob and lucky are printed.

The readL *script*

Certain aspects of record will be discussed further since they involve less frequently used parts of the shell. The command

```
. readL
```

in figure 8.10 executes the commands in readL as if they were part of the file
record. The effect of readL (figure 8.12) is to store information in shell
variables about each player in the ladder. These variables are used later to
check that players are on the ladder.

```
# read ladder into L_id
exec 3<&0 <.ladder

while read id rest
do eval L_$id='"$rest"'
done

exec 0<&3 3<&-
```

Figure 8.12 The readL script

The body of readL consists of the while loop

```
while read id rest
do eval L_$id='"$rest"'
done
```

with input being read from the file .ladder. If the first lines of the ladder file
were

```
hga ...
jmg ...
...
```

then, after execution of readL, the shell variables L_hga and L_jmg would be
set as

```
L_hga=...
L_jmg=...
...
```

where the value assigned is the line from the ladder file corresponding to the player. This use of **eval** provides an array-like mechanism from within the shell.

The statement

```
read id rest
```

reads the next line from the ladder and places the first word in the variable id, and the remainder of the line is placed in the variable rest.

If id is set to hga then

```
eval L_$id='"$rest"'
```

is interpreted as

```
L_hga="..."
```

where ... is the value of the variable rest.

The **exec** statement of **readL** redirects input in the shell to allow the .ladder file to be read by the **while** loop. Using shell input redirection with the while loop, as in,

```
while ...
do ...
done <.ladder
```

will not work as required since a new process is created to execute the while loop when redirection (<.ladder) is present. The new process cannot return the values of shell variables to its parent.

```
exec 3<&0
```

duplicates the file descriptor 0 using the **dup** system call and saves it as file descriptor 3.

```
exec <.ladder
```

then redirects the standard input. These two commands can be combined as shown. The reverse operation occurs when the **while** loop is complete with the command

```
exec 0<&3 3<&−
```

Checking player identities

Now that the appropriate variables have been set by **readL** the remainder of the record script from figure 8.10 can be described.

After the winner's name has been entered it is checked to ensure that the player is on the ladder.

Names are recovered from the variables, set by **readL**, also using **eval**.

```
eval namew\=\$L_$WP
```

assigns to namew the value of the variable $L_... where ... is the value of

$WP. Suppose that jmg won his match, then $WP would be set to jmg and this line would be interpreted as

```
namew=$L_jmg
```

On the first evaluation, only $WP is interpreted by the shell. eval passes this string to the shell for interpretation causing the variable namew to be assigned the value contained in the variable

```
$L_jmg
```

If jmg is in the ladder namew will be set, otherwise a message is printed and the loop resumed at the beginning.

8.3.3 Weekly activities

The remainder of the work involving the ladder is left to be run in the early hours of the morning when many machines are lightly loaded and have cycles to spare. Such work is scheduled for a later time using the at command.

```
at 0300 cron
```

will copy the file cron into a system directory (/usr/spool/at) to be run at 3 a.m. The cron file for tennis is shown in figure 8.13. The first line reschedules cron to be run again the next day and

```
exec >>cron.1 2>>cron.2
```

redirects the standard output and error output into a file, otherwise the output would be lost.

```
at 0300 cron
exec >>cron.1   2>>cron.2

set `date`
echo $*
case $1 in
        Tue)    weekly ;;
        Sun)    date >.sunday
esac
```

Figure 8.13 The cron script

Each Tuesday the program weekly in figure 8.14 is run and each Sunday the output from the date command is recorded in the file .sunday. This is used later in the ladder printing program.

weekly updates the ladder by executing run (figure 8.15) and send is called to print out the ladder, one copy to each player. Lastly, the date of printing is recorded in the file .lastweek. This file has been used in the output to indicate when the previous printing occurred. Participants can then check that all ladder print-outs have been received. The next two sections describe the ladder update and printing commands.

```
# run this week's ladder
run

# print this week's results
send
date > .lastweek
```

Figure 8.14 The weekly **script**

8.3.4 The ladder update

Having dealt with the organization of the ladder and how to schedule a weekly, daily or monthly activity, the details of updating the ladder from week-to-
week are described in this section. Although this description is 'top down', in
practice these high level organizational programs would be left to last when
writing a set of programs of this kind.

The run *script*

The shell script run in figure 8.15 is called by the weekly cron file. It contains more organizational commands and requires little explanation.

```
set - `date`
year=$6 month=$2 day=$3
date=$month-$day

# wait for lock
trap "" 1 2 3 15
until mklock .lock
do sleep 60; done

echo $month $day weekly tennis run starting

cp .ladder $year/${date}L
cp .matches $year/${date}G
trap 'rm -f .lock; exit' 0 1 2 3 15

# update ladder from weeks matches
update <.matches >.results

# save for printing
cp .results $year/${date}R

# empty the match file
>.matches

echo $month $day weekly tennis run ending
```

Figure 8.15 The run script

The command mklock (section 6.4.1) guarantees exclusive access to the file .lock. If the command fails the lock file is unavailable, otherwise the lock has been obtained. The lock may be used to prevent weekly results from being entered at the same time that the ladder update is running, although the version of enter presented earlier does not make use of this facility.

The update *script*

The updating activity is broken up into file management, kept in the run command, and the changes required to the ladder file itself that are dealt with in update (figure 8.16). Both the current ladder and the week's matches are copied into the backup directory as a safeguard against system crashes and program bugs. Also, the player identities are again checked since the win script assumes that the players are present.

```
NL='
'

# read ladder into L_id
. readL

# set u-d field to zero
setu-d

# read from match record file
while    read D WP LP S
do       eval namew\=\$L_$WP
         case $namew in
         ")       prompt "winner \'$WP\' not known$NL"
                  continue
         esac
         set $namew; rank1=$1; name1=$2;

         eval namel\=\$L_$LP
         case $namel in
         ")       prompt "loser \'$LP\' not known$NL"
                  continue
         esac
         set $namel; rank2=$1; name2=$2;

         win $WP $LP

         # generate output for results service
         echo "$D⊤ $name1($rank1)⊤ over⊤ $name2($rank2)⊤ $S"
done

# remove inactive players and penalize 3 week non players
weed
```

Figure 8.16 The update script

When the update of the ladder is complete the results are stored in .results and in the backup directory. In addition, the ladder manager is kept informed, by mail, of the state of the ladder update.

win is called once for each match played from within the while loop of update. Each line is read from the standard input (usually .matches) into the variables D, W, L and S. Use is again made of readL to set shell variables L_id. As in the record script, these variables are used to check that players are on the ladder. The output from update is a list of matches including the name of each player (rather than identity) and that player's position last week.

Field 8 of the ladder file shows the number of places up or down each player has moved since the previous week. The program setu−d (figure 8.17) sets this field to zero using an awk script. This field is used by win to record the movement up or down the ladder. Since awk is a filter, a temporary file is required to store intermediate output. When setu−d is complete this temporary file is renamed as .ladder using the mv command.

```
trap 'rm −f $tmp; exit' 0 1 2 3 15
tmp=`mktemp /tmp/tennisXXXXXX`

awk < .ladder >$tmp '
BEGIN {
        FS="    "
        OFS="   "
}
{       $8 = 0
        print
}'

trap " 1 2 3 15
mv $tmp .ladder
```

Figure 8.17 The setu−d script

The win *script*

An individual match result is recorded in the .matches file as

　　　date ⊤ winner ⊤ loser ⊤ score

where the winner and loser correspond to the identity of the players. The win command (figure 8.18) scans the ladder using an awk script, and changes the second field containing the rank of each player. The number of wins or losses is incremented and the number of weeks idle is set to −1. This output is then sorted on the new rankings and the ladder file replaced with the updated version.

```
# called as: win winner loser
trap 'rm −f $tmpa; exit' 1 2 3 15
tmpa=`mktemp .tmpaXXXXX`

awk <$ladder '
BEGIN {
        FS="    "
        OFS="   "
        W=0
        L=0
        N=1
}
{       if($1=="'$1'") {
                W = 1;
                $6 = $6 + 1;
                $9 = −1;
                if(L!=0) {
                        $2 = L;
                        N = NR;
                }
        }
        else if($1=="'$2'") {
                L = NR;
                $7 = $7 + 1;
                $9 = −1;
                if(W==0) {
                        N = NR + 1;
                        $2 = N;
                }
                else {
                        $2 = N;
                }
        }
        else {
                $2 = N;
        }
        $8 = $8 + NR − $2;
        N = N + 1;
        print
}' |
sort +1n −2 >$tmpa

trap " 1 2 3 15
mv $tmpa $ladder
```

Figure 8.18 The win script

The first test

```
if($1=="'$1'") {
```

requires explanation. The first $1 represents the first field in each line as it is read from the standard input by **awk**. The double quotes are interpreted by **awk** and enclose the string passed as the first argument by the shell (the identity of the winner). The single quote belongs to the shell and ends the first part of the argument.

```
awk '
BEGIN{ ...
        ...'$1'
```

The bold text is interpreted by the shell. The single quote after the $1 is the resumption of the quoted argument by the shell. The $1 itself is outside the single quotes and is substituted by the shell before **awk** begins execution.

If **win** is called as

```
win hga img
```

then the argument to **awk** would be

```
BEGIN{
        ...
}
{
        if($1=="hga") {
        ...
```

the single quotes having been stripped by the shell.

The remainder of **win** can be read as if it were a C program. **awk** takes care of string to integer conversions and the body of the **awk** program is executed for each line of the standard input.

The variable W is set when the winner is encountered during the scan of the file. The variable L is set to the (old) rank of the losing player and two cases are distinguished.

- *The winner is higher on the ladder than the loser.* The test

  ```
  if($1=="'$1'") {
  ```

  will succeed and L will be zero since the loser has not yet been encountered. No adjustments to the ladder are necessary.
- *The winner appears below the loser in the ladder file.* W is zero and the test W==0 succeeds. A gap is left in the numbering for the winner (N=NR+1) and the loser is assigned the next rank below. When the winner is reached L is already set to the original rank of the loser and the test L!=0 succeeds. The loser's original rank is assigned to the winner ($2=L). The remaining rankings can be left unchanged and N is reset to account for this (N=NR).

The resulting output is sorted on the new ranking field and stored in a temporary file. The last line restores the ladder from the temporary file.

Although it may seem that there is a profusion of commands, each of which does little, constructing the system in this way allows each part of the system to be tested as it is built. For example, win can be called directly from the shell and input presented interactively. Similarly, update can be run by hand once a week until the at script can be made to work.

The weed *script*

```
: ${ladder=.ladder}
trap 'rm −f $tmp; exit' 0 1 2 3 15
tmp=`mktemp /tmp/tennisXXXXXX`

# remove inactive players and penalise 3 week non players
awk <$ladder '
BEGIN {
        OFS="Ⓣ"
        FS="Ⓣ"
}
{       $9 = $9 + 1;
        $8 = $8 + $2;
        R = 2*NR;
        if($9 >= 3 && NR!=1) R = R + 5;
        if($9 < 7 || NR==1) {
                $2 = R;
                print
        }
}' |
  sort +1n −2 |
  awk >$tmp '
  BEGIN {
        FS="Ⓣ"
        OFS="Ⓣ"
}
{       $8 = $8 − NR;
        $2 = NR
        print
}'
trap "" 1 2 3 15
mv $tmp $ladder
```

Figure 8.19 The weed script

The last program that makes ladder changes is called **weed** (figure 8.19) and deals with players who have been inactive for more than 3 weeks. These players are moved down two places to encourage active participation. The top player is exempt from the 3 week rule since he is unable to challenge other players. Players who are inactive for 7 weeks are removed from the ladder.

The form of the **awk** scripts is, by now, familiar. The up-down movement in field 8 is maintained and the rank field is renumbered as

    2R

where R is the real rank (R=2*NR). If a player is demoted then the rank is adjusted (R=R+5). The output is then sorted on the new rankings and the rank recomputed by the second **awk** script.

8.3.5 Weekly ladder printing

The ladder is printed every week and addressed to each player so that the output can by fed directly into the company mail. The **send** script (figure 8.20) organizes the printing activity.

```
trap 'rm −f $out; exit' 0 1 2 3 15
out=`mktemp /tmp/otXXXXXX`

# generate one copy of the output
out .ladder >$out

# send to everyone
while read line
do      adr $line <$out
done <.ladder | lpr
```

Figure 8.20 The send script

The program out (figure 8.21) is called by **send** and formats the weekly ladder results. nroff is used as a formatting program with a here document providing the standard input, after substitution of shell variables. The page length for the heading is set to 6, from the default 66, since nroff fills the remainder of the page with blank lines.

```
# print the ladder and results

set `date`
year=$6 month=$2 day=$3

set − `cat .lastweek`
L_year=$6 L_month=$2 L_day=$3

# output heading
nroff <<!
.pl 6
.ll 80
.ce 2
```

```
.nf
M U R R A Y    H I L L    T E N N I S    L A D D E R
.ce 2
Standings as of $year $month $day
(Previous Listing $L_year $L_month $L_day)

rank Ⓣ name Ⓣ phone Ⓣ room Ⓣ won Ⓣ lost Ⓣ u−d Ⓣ idle
!

# output ladder itself
field 2 3 4 5 6 7 8 9 <$ladder |
 sed −e 's/^/	/' |
  ta="3R 5 32 42 56R 62R 68R 74C" detab

set − `cat .sunday`
S_year=$6 S_month=$2 S_day=$3

if test −s .results
then      # if results file non empty
          nroff <<! − .results
.ll 80
.pl 5
.sp 2
.ce
Match results for the week ending $S_month $S_day
.sp
.tr _
.nf
.ta 5 34 39 68
!

fi
```

Figure 8.21 The out script

field selects all but the first **tab** separated fields and **detab** formats the
result according to the **tab** setting passed as an argument. The **tab** inserted
by **sed** at the start of each line allows the first field to be right justified in
nroff using the ta request.

```
(cat <<! ; cat $*) | nroff
.pl 1
.nf
.ta $ta
!
```

Figure 8.22 The detab script

The text of the **detab** command is shown in figure 8.22.

If the results file (produced by **update**) is not empty then it is printed with a heading giving the previous Sunday's date and formatted according to the tab setting.

The program **adr** (figure 8.23) paginates the ladder output taking its input from the standard input. A banner is also added using the line drawing function of **nroff**. The shell variable **banner** is set depending on whether any positional parameters have been provided. $# is set to the number of positional parameters.

```
case $#  in
        0)        banner=`date` ;;
        *)        banner="$3    MH $5" ;;
esac
(cat  <<!;  cat)Inroff
.nf
.tr _
.ll  80
.wh  0  SP
.wh  −4  EP
.de  EP
.bp
. .
.de  SP
.sp  4
. .
.SP
.ce
\l'\w'$banner'u+4\&−'
.in  70
$2
.in
.ce
$banner
.sp
.ce
\l'\w'$banner'u+4\&−'
.sp  3
!
```

Figure 8.23 The adr script

The line drawing functions in nroff are used to enclose the mailing address.

    \l'\w'$adr'u+4\&−'

draws a line to enclose the mailing address ($banner).

\w´$adr´u

computes the width of the string $adr and the result is in basic units (u). To allow for an overlap on each side 4 is added (2 each side since this line is centered).

\l´...´

is the line drawing function where ... is the length computed by the previous expression. The & separates this width expression from the trailing − that would otherwise be absorbed as part of the expression.

8.3.6 The start and end of season

The initial ladder is entered into the file .initial. Each player may request a starting rank and, where possible, this is honored by ordering the initial requests. The startup script (figure 8.24) initializes the files required to run the system and makes the backup directory. The cron file also needs to be started.

```
# create files
cat <<! >.lastweek
− − none
!
>.results
>.matches
>.ladder

sort +0n <.initial |
awk ´
BEGIN {
        FS="Ⓣ"
        OFS="Ⓣ"
        N = 1;
}
{       F = $1;
        $1 = $2;
        $2 = N;
        $6 = 0;
        $7 = 0;
        $8 = 0;
        $9 = 0;
        NF = 9;
        if(F != "−") {print; N=N+1;}
}
´ >.ladder
```

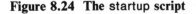

Figure 8.24 The startup script

End of season awards

Two prizes are awarded, one for the player who plays the most matches, the other for the player who wins the most matches. In both cases only two matches against the same opponent count. Two scripts are provided to determine the prize winners and each uses the atmost script, shown in figure 8.25. The command **atmost** produces at most two entries from the output of a command passed as the argument $1.

```
($\{1?\}  |  uniq  −d ;  $1  |  sort  −u)  |  sort
```

Figure 8.25 The atmost script

The command $1 is executed twice and is required to generate a sorted list.

```
${1?}  |  uniq  −d
```

is executed first and generates a single line for each line occurring two or more times.

```
$1  |  sort  −u
```

is executed second and generates a single line for each entry. The construction

```
( ... )  |  sort
```

collects the output from the first command followed by the output form the second and sorts the result.

The player with the most wins

The player with most wins is determined by the command **most−wins** shown in figure 8.26.

```
atmost list−matches  |
   field  1  |
      uniq  −c  |
      sort  +0nr
```

Figure 8.26 The most-wins script

The first line, **atmost list-matches**, generates a list of pairs of players,

```
W  L
```

corresponding to matches between the players **W** and **L**, where **W** won the match. The rest of the pipeline selects the field containing the winner and counts how many times it occurs. Since the output of **atmost** is sorted, the first field can be passed directly to **uniq**. The −c option produces count winner

where count is the number of occurrences of winner in the input list. The final call to sort arranges the output according to the player with the most wins as required. The argument +Onr sorts in decreasing numerical order on the first field of the input. The list—matches script is shown in figure 8.27.

```
cd 1982; cat *G | field 2 3 | sort
```

Figure 8.27 The list—matches **script**

The player with the most matches played

This prize is for the player with the most matches played with no more than two counting against the same opponent. The command list—players (figure 8.28) generates a list of matches with the player in the first column alphabetically preceding the player in the second column. Thus, who won the match is not important, only the pair of players matters.

```
cat *G | field 2 3 |
awk 'BEGIN
{
        FS="Ⓣ"
        OFS="Ⓣ"
}
{       if($1  >  $2) {
                t  =  $1;
                $1  =  $2;
                $2  =  t;
        }
        print
}' | sort
```

Figure 8.28 The list-players **script**

The output from atmost list-players is a list of the matches played by any two players with at most two against a given opponent that count. The first line of most—matches (figure 8.29) produces the list of players that needs sorting so that uniq −c can be run.

```
(atmost list—players | field 1; atmost list—players | field 2) |
   sort |
     uniq −c |
       sort +Onr
```

Figure 8.29 The most-matches script

8.4 Implementing the field command

The manual page for the field command reads

DESCRIPTION
>   field — select fields or columns from a file

SYNOPSIS
>   field [n] ...

DESCRIPTION
>   The field command copies selected, tab-separated fields from the standard input to the standard output. Fields are numbered from 1 and a field may be requested more than once.

BUGS
>   The number of input or output fields may not exceed 256 and the maximum line length is 4096 characters.

The field command selects **tab** separated fields from its standard input and prints the result on the standard output.

The implementation of field illustrates some useful techniques. The first step is to look for a program that does something similar. Since field is a filter that copies its input to its output the **cat** command is a good place to start. The source for system commands is usually kept in the directory /usr/src/cmd making it easy to use one command as the starting point for another.

The program is shown in figure 8.30.

The stages in the writing of this program were simple.

- Write a program to read a line into the array L and print it out again. (This is the **cat** command with buffering added.)
- Add the code to record the field boundaries and print out a fixed field.
- Add the code to read the arguments and print the columns specified.
- Add the checks for exceeding the sizes of the fixed arrays.

Other options that are easy to add but have been omitted here include:

−c   Check that all input records contain the same number of fields.
−tc   Set the field separator to c.

The version presented in figure 8.30 does not check for exceeding array bounds. Also, the bounds of fv, fp, and L are fixed at compile time using the defined constants MAXF, and MAXL. A production program should check these limits or, better still, allocate the arrays dynamically. The number of output fields can be determined from the number of arguments. The number of input fields and the maximum line length are not easily found. Another solution to the fixed limits imposed in this implementation is to have options to change them. This is left as an exercise to the reader.

The limitations of this command have been documented under the BUGS section of the manual page.

```
#include <stdio.h>

#define MAXF    256
#define MAXL    4096
#define IFS     '\t'
#define OFS     '\t'

int fv[MAXF];    /* numerical equivalent of arguments */
int nf;          /* number of columns to print */
int mf;          /* number of fields in the current record */
char *fp[MAXF];  /* pointers into `L' at field boundaries */
char L[MAXL];    /* current line buffer */

main(argc,argv)
        int argc;
        char *argv[];
{
        register char *cp;
        register char **ap;
        register int c;
        int f;

        /* read arguments into fv[...] */
        while (argc>1) {
                if(sscanf(argv[1], "%d", &fv[nf++]) != 1) {
                        printf("usage: field [ n ] ...\n");
                        return(2);
                }
                argc--; argv++;
        }

        /* read and copy input */
        nf--;
        cp = L;
        ap = fp;
        *ap++ = cp;
        while(1){
                c = getc(stdin);
                if(c=='\n' || c==EOF) {
                        int fc;
                        if(cp==L && c==EOF) break;
                        *cp++ = 0;
                        mf = ap-fp;

                        /* print this line */
                        for(fc = 0; fc <= nf; fc++) {
                                putf(fv[fc]-1);
                                if(fc != nf) putchar(OFS);
```

```
                              }
                              if(c  ==  EOF) break;
                              putchar('\n');
                              cp  =  L;
                              ap  =  fp;
                              *ap++  =  cp;
                    }
                    else if(c  ==  IFS) {
                              *cp++  =  0;
                              *ap++  =  cp;
                    }
                    else *cp++  =  c;
          }

          return(0);
}

/* output field n from the current line */
putf(n)
{
          register char *cp  =  fp[n];
          register char c;

          if(n<0 || n>=mf) return;
          while (c = *cp++) putchar(c);
}
```

Figure 8.30 The field command

Appendix 1
Commands

---

adb — debugger   ADB(1)

adb [—w] [objfil [corfil]]

    adb is a general purpose debugging program. It may be used to examine files and to provide a controlled environment for the execution of UNIX programs.

    objfil is normally an executable program file, preferably containing a symbol table. Without a symbol table the symbolic features of **adb** cannot be used although the file can still be examined; the default for objfil is *a.out*. corfil is assumed to be a core image file produced after executing objfil; the default for corfil is *core.*

    Requests to **adb** are read from the standard input and responses are written to the standard output. If the —w flag is present then both objfil and corfil are created, if necessary, and opened for reading and writing enabling files to be modified using **adb**. An interrupt causes return to the next **adb** request and the quit signal is ignored.

---

ar — archive and library maintainer   AR(1)

ar key [posname] afile name ...

    ar maintains groups of files combined into a single archive file. Its main use is to create and update the library files as used by the loader. It can be used, though, for any similar purpose.

    key is one character from the set *drtpx,* optionally concatenated with one or more of *vuaibcl.* afile is the archive file. The names are constituent files in the archive file. The meanings of the key characters are:

    d   Delete the named files from the archive file.

    r   Replace the named files in the archive file. If the optional character u is used with r, then only those files with modified dates later than the archive files are replaced. If an optional positioning character from the set **abi** is used, then the **posname** argument must be present and specifies that new files are to be placed after (**a**) or before (**b** or **i**) **posname**. Otherwise, new files are placed at the end.

    t   Print a table of contents of the archive file. If no names are given, all files in the archive are tabled. If names are given, only those files are tabled.

p   Print the named files in the archive.

x   Extract the named files. If no names are given, all files in the archive are extracted. In neither case does x alter the archive file.

v   Verbose. Under the verbose option, ar gives a file-by-file description of the making of a new archive file from the old archive and the constituent files. When used with t, it gives a long listing of all information about the files. When used with p, it precedes each file with a name.

c   Create. Normally ar will create afile when it needs to. The create option suppresses the normal message that is produced when afile is created.

---

at — execute commands at a later time   AT(1)

at time [day] [file]

at copies the named file (standard input default) to be used as input to sh(1) at a specified later time. A cd command to the current directory is inserted at the beginning, followed by assignments to all environment variables (excepting the variable TERM, that is useless in this context.) When the script is run, it uses the user-id and group-id of the creator of the copy file.

The time is 1 to 4 digits, with an optional trailing A, P, N or M for AM, PM, noon, or midnight. One and two digit numbers are taken to be hours, three and four digits to be hours and minutes. If no letters follow the digits, a 24 hour clock is understood.

The optional day is either a month name followed by a day number, or a day of the week; if the word week follows invocation is moved seven days further off. Names of months and days may be recognizably truncated.

---

awk — pattern scanning and processing language   AWK(1)

awk [prog] [file] ...

awk scans each input file for lines that match any of a set of patterns specified in prog. With each pattern in prog there can be an associated action that will be performed when a line of a file matches the pattern. The set of patterns may appear literally as the single argument prog, or in a file specified as —f file.

Files are read in order; if there are no files, the standard input is read. The file name — means the standard input.

awk is described in chapter 8.

---

basename — strip filename affixes   BASENAME(1)

basename string [suffix]

basename deletes any prefix ending in / and the specified suffix from string and prints the result on the standard output.

---

cal — print calendar   CAL(1)

cal [month] year

   cal prints a calendar for the specified year. If a month is also specified,
a calendar for that month is printed. year can be between 1 and 9999. The
month is a number between 1 and 12. The calendar produced is that for
England and her colonies.

---

calendar — reminder service   CALENDAR(1)

calendar [−]

   calendar consults the file calendar in the current directory and prints
out lines that contain today's or tomorrow's date anywhere in the line. Most
reasonable month-day dates such as Dec. 7, december 7, and 12/7, are
recognized, but not 7 December or 7/12. If you give just a date, i.e. 1, that
day in any month will do. On weekends tomorrow extends through Monday.
   When an argument is present, calendar looks in all users' login directories for a file called calendar and sends any positive results by mail(1) to
those users.

---

cat — catenate and print   CAT(1)

cat [−u] file ...

   cat reads each file in sequence and writes it on the standard output. If
no input file is given, or if the argument − is encountered, cat reads from the
standard input file. Output is buffered in blocks unless the standard output is
a terminal, in which case it is line buffered. The −u option causes the output
to be completely unbuffered.

---

cb — C program beautifier   CB(1)

cb

   cb places a copy of the C program from the standard input on the standard output with spacing and indentation that displays the structure of the
program.

---

cc — C compiler   CC(1)

cc [option] ... file ...

   cc is the UNIX C compiler. Arguments to cc whose names end with .c
are taken to be C source programs; they are compiled, and each object program is left in the file whose name is that of the source with .o substituted
for .c. The .o file is normally deleted if a single C program is compiled and
loaded at one time.
   In the same way, arguments whose names end with .s are taken to be as-

sembly source programs and are assembled, producing a .o file.

Options

−c   Suppress the loading phase of the compilation, and force an object file to be produced even if only one program is compiled.

−g   Generate symbol table information for sdb(1).

−w   Suppress warning diagnostics.

−p   Generate code that counts the number of times each routine is called; also, if loading takes place, replace the standard startup routine by one that automatically calls monitor(3) at the start and arranges to write out a mon.out file at normal termination of execution of the object program. An execution profile can then be generated by use of prof(1).

−O   Invoke an object-code improver.

−R   Passed on to **as**, making initialized variables shared and read-only.

−S   Compile the named C programs, and leave the assembler-language output on corresponding files suffixed .s.

−E   Run only the macro preprocessor on the named C programs, and send the result to the standard output.

−C   Prevent the macro preprocessor from eliding comments.

−o output

     Name the final output file output. If this option is used the file a.out will be left undisturbed.

−D name=def

−D name

     Define the name to the preprocessor, as if by #define. If no definition is given, the name is defined as 1.

−U name

     Remove any initial definition of name.

−I dir   #include files whose names do not begin with / are always sought first in the directory of the file argument, then in directories named in −I options, then in directories on a standard list.

Other arguments are taken to be either loader option arguments, or C-compatible object programs, typically produced by an earlier cc run, or perhaps libraries of C-compatible routines. These programs, together with the results of any compilations specified, are loaded (in the order given) to produce an executable program with name *a.out*.

---

chmod − change mode   CHMOD (1)

chmod mode file ...

The mode of each named file is changed according to mode, which may be absolute or symbolic. An absolute **mode** is an octal number constructed from the OR of the modes described in chmod(2).

A symbolic **mode** has the form:

[who] op permission [op permission] ...

The **who** part is a combination of the letters *u* (for user's permissions), *g* (group) and *o* (other). The letter *a* stands for *ugo*. If **who** is omitted, the default is *a* but the setting of the file creation mask (see umask(2)) is taken into account.

op can be + to add **permission** to the file's mode, − to take away **permission** and = to assign **permission** absolutely (all other bits will be reset).

permission is any combination of the letters *r* (read), *w* (write), *x* (execute), *s* (set user-id or group-id) and *t* (save text − sticky). Letters *u*, *g* or *o* indicate that **permission** is to be taken from the current mode. Omitting **permission** is only useful with = to take away all permissions.

Multiple symbolic modes separated by commas may be given. Operations are performed in the order specified. The letter *s* is only useful with *u* or *g*.

Only the owner of a file (or the super-user) may change its mode.

---

cmp − compare two files   CMP(1)

cmp [−l] [−s] file1 file2

The two files are compared. If file1 is −, the standard input is used. Under default options, **cmp** makes no comment if the files are the same; if they differ, it announces the byte and line number at which the difference occurred. If one file is an initial subsequence of the other, that fact is noted.

Options

    −l   Print the byte number (decimal) and the differing bytes (octal) for each difference.

    −s   Print nothing for differing files; return codes only.

---

col − filter reverse line feeds   COL(1)

col [−bfx]

col reads the standard input and writes the standard output. It performs the line overlays implied by reverse line feeds **(esc-7)** and by forward and reverse half line feeds **(esc-9)** and **(esc-8)**. **col** is particularly useful for filtering multi-column output made with the .rt command of **nroff** and output resulting from use of the **tbl**(1) preprocessor.

Although **col** accepts half-line motions in its input, it normally does not emit them on output. Instead, text that would appear between lines is moved to the next lower full line boundary. This treatment can be suppressed by the −f (fine) option; in this case the output from **col** may contain forward half line feeds **(esc-9)**, but will still never contain either kind of reverse line motion.

If the −b option is given, **col** assumes that the output device in use is not capable of backspacing. In this case, if several characters are to appear in the same place, only the last one read will be taken.

The control characters so (016), and si (017) are assumed to start and end text in an alternate character set. The character set (primary or alternate) associated with each printing character read is remembered; on output, so and si characters are generated where necessary to maintain the correct treatment of each character.

col normally converts white space to tabs to shorten printing time. If the −x option is given, this conversion is suppressed.

All control characters are removed from the input except space, backspace, tab, return, newline, esc (033) followed by one of 7, 8, 9, si, so, and vt (013). This last character is an alternate form of full reverse line feed, for compatibility with some other hardware conventions. All other non-printing characters are ignored.

---

comm − select or reject lines common to two sorted files   COMM(1)

comm [− [123]] file1 file2

comm reads file1 and file2, that should be ordered lexicographically, and produces a three column output: lines only in file1; lines only in file2; and lines in both files. The filename − means the standard input.

The flags 1, 2, or 3 suppress printing of the corresponding column.

---

cp − copy   CP(1)

cp file1 file2
cp file ... directory

file1 is copied onto file2. The mode and owner of file2 are preserved if file2 already existed; otherwise, the mode of the source file is used.

In the second form, one or more files are copied into the directory with their original file-names.

cp refuses to copy a file onto itself.

---

crypt − encode/decode   CRYPT(1)

crypt [password]

crypt reads from the standard input and writes on the standard output. The password is a key that selects a particular transformation. If no password is given, crypt demands a key from the terminal and turns off printing while the key is being typed in. crypt encrypts and decrypts with the same key:

crypt key <clear >cypher
crypt key <cypher | pr

will print the clear text.

Files encrypted by crypt are compatible with those required by the editor ed in encryption mode.

The security of encrypted files depends on three factors: the fundamental method must be hard to solve; direct search of the key space must not be feasible; 'sneak paths' by which keys or cleartext can become visible must be minimized.

crypt implements a one-rotor machine designed along the lines of the German Enigma, but with a 256-element rotor. Methods of attack on such machines are known, but not widely; moreover the amount of work required is likely to be large.

The transformation of a key into the internal settings of the machine is deliberately designed to be expensive, i.e. to take a substantial fraction of a second to compute. However, if keys are restricted to (say) three lower-case letters, then encrypted files can be read by expending only a few minutes of machine time.

Since the key is an argument to the crypt command, it is potentially visible to users executing ps(1) or a derivative. To minimize this possibility, crypt takes care to destroy any record of the key immediately upon entry. No doubt the choice of keys and key security are the most vulnerable aspect of crypt.

---

date — print and set the date   DATE(1)

date

The current date and time are printed. The system operates in GMT and **date** takes care of the conversion to and from local standard and daylight time.

---

dd — convert and copy a file   DD(1)

dd [option=value] ...

dd copies the specified input file to the specified output with possible conversions. The standard input and output are used by default. The input and output block size may be specified to take advantage of the physical block sizes of the devices being used. Options are specified by keywords.

Options

if=	The input file name; standard input is default.
of=	The output file name; standard output is default.
ibs=n	Use an input block size of n bytes (default 512).
obs=n	Use an output block size of n bytes (default 512).
bs=n	Set both input and output block size, superseding ibs and obs; also, if no conversion is specified, it is particularly efficient since no copy need be made.
cbs=n	The conversion buffer size.
skip=n	Skip n input records before starting copy.
files=n	Skip n input files before starting copy.
seek=n	Seek n records from beginning of output file before copying.
count=n	Copy only n input records.
conv=ascii	Convert EBCDIC to ASCII.
ebcdic	Convert ASCII to EBCDIC.
block	Convert variable length records to fixed length.

unblock	Convert fixed length records to variable length.
lcase	Map alphabetics to lower case.
ucase	Map alphabetics to upper case.
swab	Swap every pair of bytes.
noerror	Do not stop processing on an error.
sync	Pad every input record to ibs.
..., ...	Several comma-separated conversions.

Where sizes are specified, a number of bytes is expected. A number may end with k, b or w to specify multiplication by 1024, 512, or 2 respectively; a pair of numbers may be separated by x to indicate a product.

cbs is used only if ascii, unblock, ebcdic, or block conversion is specified. In the first two cases, cbs characters are placed into the conversion buffer, any specified character mapping is done, trailing blanks trimmed and newline added before sending the line to the output. In the latter three cases, characters are read into the conversion buffer, and spaces added to make up an output record of size cbs.

After completion, dd reports the number of whole and partial input and output blocks.

---

deroff — remove nroff, troff, tbl and eqn constructs   DEROFF(1)

deroff [−w] file ...

deroff reads each file and removes all nroff and troff request lines, backslash constructions, macro definitions, eqn constructs (between .EQ and .EN lines or between delimiters), and table descriptions and writes the remainder on the standard output. deroff follows chains of included files (.so and .nx requests); if a file has already been included, a .so is ignored and a .nx terminates execution. If no input file is given, deroff reads from the standard input file.

If the −w flag is given, the output is a word list, one word (string of letters, digits, and apostrophes, beginning with a letter; apostrophes are removed) per line, and all other characters ignored. Otherwise, the output follows the original.

---

df — disk free   DF(1)

df filesystem

df prints the number of free blocks available on the specified filesystem, e.g. /dev/rp0a'. If no file system is specified, the free space on all of the normally mounted file systems is printed.

The reported numbers are in file system block units. On some UNIX systems each filesystem block is 1024 bytes long, twice the size of the blocks reported by du(1) or ls(1) with the −s option.

---

diction, explain — print wordy sentences; thesaurus for diction DICTION(1)

diction [—ml] [—mm] [—n] [—f pfile] file ...
explain

    diction finds all sentences in a document that contain phrases from a data base of bad or wordy diction. Each phrase is bracketed with [ ]. Because diction runs deroff before looking at the text, formatting header files should be included as part of the input. The default macro package is —ms. The —mm option uses the —mm macro library. The flag —ml causes deroff to skip lists and should be used if the document contains many lists of non-sentences. The user may supply a pattern file to be used in addition to the default file with —f pfile. If the flag —n is also supplied the default file will be suppressed.

    explain is an interactive thesaurus for the phrases found by diction.

---

diff — differential file comparator   DIFF(1)

diff [option] file1 file2

    diff lists the lines that must be changed in the files to bring them into agreement. Except in rare circumstances, diff finds a smallest sufficient set of file differences. If file1 or file2 is a —, the standard input is used.

    There are several options for output format; the default output format contains lines of these forms:

    $n1$ a $n3,n4$
    $n1,n2$ d $n3$
    $n1,n2$ c $n3,n4$

These lines resemble ed commands to convert file1 into file2. The numbers after the letters pertain to file2. By exchanging a for d and reading backward one may ascertain equally how to convert file2 into file1. As in ed, identical pairs where $n1=n2$ or $n3=n4$ are abbreviated as a single number.

    Following each of these lines come all the lines that are affected in the first file flagged by <, then all the lines that are affected in the second file flagged by >.

    Except for —b, which may be given with any of the others, the options are mutually exclusive.

Options

    —e   Produce a script of a, c and d commands for the editor ed, that will recreate file2 from file1.
    —h   Do a fast, half-hearted job. It works when changed stretches are short and well separated, and on files of unlimited length.
    —b   Trailing blanks (spaces and tabs) are ignored, and other strings of blanks compare equal.

du — summarize disk usage   DU(1)

du [−s] [−a] [name ...]

du gives the number of blocks contained in all files and (recursively) directories within each specified directory or file name. If name is missing, the current directory is used.

The optional argument −s causes only the grand total to be given. The optional argument −a causes an entry to be generated for each file. Absence of either causes an entry to be generated for each directory only.

A file which has two or more links to it is only counted once.

---

echo — echo arguments   ECHO(1)

echo [−n] [arg] ...

echo writes its arguments separated by blanks and terminated by a newline on the standard output. If the flag −n is used, no newline is added to the output.

---

ed — text editor   ED(1)

ed [−] [−x] [name]

ed is the standard text editor.

If a name argument is given, ed simulates an e command (see below) on the named file; that is to say, the file is read into ed's buffer so that it can be edited. If −x is present, an x request is simulated first to handle an encrypted file. The optional − suppresses the printing of explanatory output and should be used when the standard input is an editor script.

If an interrupt signal is sent, ed prints ?interrupted and returns to its request level.

Some size limitations: 512 characters per line, 256 characters per global request list, 64 characters per file name and, on mini computers, 128K characters in the temporary file. The limit on the number of lines depends on the memory available.

When reading a file, ed discards ASCII nul characters and all characters after the last newline. It refuses to read files containing non-printing characters.

---

eqn, neqn — typeset mathematics   EQN(1)

eqn [file] ...

eqn is a troff(1) preprocessor for typesetting mathematics on a Graphic Systems phototypesetter. neqn provides similar facilities with output suitable for terminals.

Usage is typically

```
eqn file ... | troff
neqn file ... | nroff
```

and if no files are specified, eqn and neqn read from the standard input.

---

expr — evaluate arguments as an expression   EXPR(1)

expr arg ...

The arguments are taken as an expression. After evaluation, the result is written on the standard output. Each token of the expression is a separate argument.

The operators and keywords are listed below. The list is in order of increasing precedence, with equal precedence operators grouped.

expr | expr   Yield the first expr if it is neither null nor 0, otherwise yield the second expr.

expr & expr   Yield the first expr if neither expr is null or 0, otherwise yield 0.

expr op expr Yield 1 if the indicated comparison is true, 0 if false. op is one of < <= = != >= >. The comparison is numeric if both expr are integers, and lexicographic otherwise.

expr + expr

expr − expr   Add or subtract the arguments.

expr * expr

expr / expr

expr % expr   Multiply, divide, or take the remainder after division, of the arguments.

expr : expr   The matching operator compares the string first argument with the regular expression second argument; regular expression syntax is the same as that of ed(1). The symbols \(and \) can be used to select a portion of the first argument. Otherwise, the matching operator yields the number of characters matched (0 on failure).

(expr)   Parentheses are for grouping.

---

f77 — Fortran 77 compiler   F77(1)

f77 [option] ... file ...

Arguments whose names end with .f are taken to be Fortran 77 source programs; they are compiled, and each object program is left in the file in the current directory whose name is that of the source with .o substituted for .f.

Arguments whose names end with .r or .e are taken to be Ratfor or EFL source programs, respectively; these are first transformed by the appropriate preprocessor, then compiled by the f77 command.

In the same way, arguments whose names end with .c or .s are taken to be C or assembly source programs and are compiled or assembled, producing a .o file.

Options

The following options have the same meaning as in cc(1). See ld(1) for load-time options.

—c   Suppress loading and produce .o files for each source file.

—g   Produce symbol table information for sdb(1). Also pass the —lg flag to ld(1).

—w   Suppress all warning messages. If the option is —w66, only Fortran 66 compatibility warnings are suppressed.

—p   Prepare object files for profiling, see prof(1).

—O   Invoke an object-code optimizer.

—S   Compile the named programs, and leave the assembler-language output on corresponding files suffixed .s. (No .o is created.)

—o *output*
     Name the final output file *output* instead of a.out.

The following options are peculiar to f77.

—onetrip Compile DO loops that are performed at least once if reached. (Fortran 77 DO loops are not performed at all if the upper limit is smaller than the lower limit.)

—u   Make the default type of a variable *undefined* rather than using the default Fortran rules.

—C   Compile code to check that subscripts are within declared array bounds.

—F   Apply EFL and Ratfor preprocessor to relevant files, put the result in the file with the suffix changed to .f, but do not compile.

—E *x*   Use the string *x* as an EFL option in processing .e files.

—R *x*   Use the string *x* as a Ratfor option in processing .r files.

Other arguments are taken to be either loader option arguments, or f77-compatible object programs, typically produced by an earlier run, or perhaps libraries of f77-compatible routines. These programs, together with the results of any compilations specified, are loaded (in the order given) to produce an executable program with name a.out.

---

find — find files   FIND (1)

find pathname-list expression

find recursively descends the directory hierarchy for each pathname in the pathname-list (i.e., one or more pathnames) seeking files that match a Boolean expression written in the primaries given below. In the descriptions, the argument n is used as a decimal integer where +n means more than n, —n means less than n and n means exactly n.

—name *file*   True if the *file* argument matches the current file name. Normal shell argument syntax may be used if escaped (watch out for [, ? and *).

—perm *onum*	True if the file permission flags exactly match the octal number *onum* (see chmod(1)). If *onum* is prefixed by a minus sign, more flag bits (017777, see stat(2)) become significant and the flags are compared: (flags&onum) == onum.
—type *c*	True if the type of the file is *c,* where *c* is b, c, d or f for block special file, character special file, directory or plain file.
—links *n*	True if the file has *n* links.
—user *name*	True if the file belongs to the user *name* (login-name or numeric user-id).
—group *name*	True if the file belongs to group *name* (group-name or numeric group-id).
—size *n*	True if the file is *n* blocks long (512 bytes per block).
—inum *n*	True if the file has inode number *n.*
—atime *n*	True if the file has been accessed in *n* days.
—mtime *n*	True if the file has been modified in *n* days.
—exec *cmd* ;	True if the executed command returns a zero value as exit status. The command must be terminated by a ; that is normally quoted to prevent its interpretation by the shell. A command argument {} is replaced by the current pathname.
—ok *cmd* ;	Like —exec except that the generated command is written on the standard output, then the standard input is read and the command executed only upon response y.
—print	Always true; causes the current pathname to be printed.
—newer *file*	True if the current file has been modified more recently than the argument file.

The primaries may be combined using the following operators (in order of decreasing precedence):

(...)	A parenthesized group of primaries and operators (parentheses are special to the Shell and must be escaped).
!p	! is the unary not operator.
p p	Concatenation of primaries. The and operation is implied by the juxtaposition of two primaries.
P —o p	Alternation of primaries. —o is the or operator.

---

grep, egrep, fgrep — search a file for a pattern   GREP(1)

grep [option ...] expression [file] ...
egrep [option ...] [expression] [file] ...
fgrep [option ...] [strings] [file] ...

Commands of the **grep** family search the input files (standard input default) for lines matching a pattern. Normally, each line found is copied to the standard output. **grep** patterns are limited regular expressions in the style of ed(1); it uses a compact non-deterministic algorithm. **egrep** patterns are full regular expressions; it uses a fast deterministic algorithm that sometimes needs exponential space. **fgrep** patterns are fixed strings; it is fast and compact.

Options

−c	Only a count of matching lines is printed.
−e *exp*	Same as a simple **expression** argument, but useful when *exp* begins with a −.
−f *file*	The regular expression (**egrep**) or string list (**fgrep**) is taken from the file.
−h	Do not print file name headers with output lines.
−i	The case of letters is ignored in making comparisons. (**grep** and **fgrep** only.) On some systems this option is called −y.
−l	The names of files with matching lines are listed (once) separated by newlines.
−n	Each line is preceded by its relative line number in the file.
−s	Silent mode. Nothing is printed (except error messages). This is useful for checking the error status.
−v	All lines but those matching are printed.
−x	Only lines that match exactly are printed (**fgrep** only).

In all cases the file name precedes printed lines if there is more than one input file. Care should be taken when using the characters $ * [^ | ( ) and \fR in the *expression* as they are also meaningful to the shell. It is safest to enclose the entire *expression* argument in single quotes ´ ´.

fgrep searches for lines that contain one of the (newline-separated) strings.

egrep accepts extended regular expressions as described in chapter 8.

---

join − relational database operator   JOIN(1)

join [options] ... file1 file2

join forms, on the standard output, a join of the two relations specified by the lines of file1 and file2. If file1 is −, the standard input is used.

file1 and file2 must be sorted lexicographically on the fields on which they are to be joined, normally the first in each line.

There is one line in the output for each pair of lines in file1 and file2 that have identical join fields. The output line normally consists of the common field, then the rest of the line from file1, then the rest of the line from file2.

Fields are normally separated by white space. Multiple separators count as one, and leading separators are discarded.

Options

−a *n*	In addition to the normal output, produce a line for each unpairable line in file *n*, where *n* is 1 or 2.
−e *s*	Replace empty output fields by string *s*.
−j *n m*	Join on the *m-th* field of file *n*. If *n* is missing, use the *m-th* field in each file.
−o *list*	Each output line comprises the fields specified in *list*, each ele-

ment of which has the form n.m, where n is a file number and
m is a field number.

−t c   Use character c as separator (tab character). Every appearance of c in a line is significant.

---

kill — terminate a process

kill [− sig] processid ...

   kill sends the signal sig to the specified processes. If no signal is specified as first argument, the signal SIGTERM (15) is sent by default.
   The terminate signal kills processes that do not catch the signal;

   kill −9 ...

is a sure kill, since this signal cannot be caught. By convention, if process
number 0 is specified, all members in the process group (i.e. processes resulting from the current login) are signaled. The killed processes must belong to
the current user.

---

ld — link editor

ld [option] ... file ...

   ld combines several object programs into one, resolves external references, and searches libraries. In the simplest case several object files are
given, and ld combines them, producing an object module which can be either
executed or become the input for a further ld run. (In the latter case, the −r
option must be given to preserve the relocation bits.) The output of ld is left
on a.out. This file is made executable only if no errors occurred during loading.
   The argument routines are concatenated in the order specified. The entry point of the output is the beginning of the first routine (unless the −e option is specified).
   If any argument is a library, it is searched exactly once at the point it is
encountered in the argument list. Only those routines defining an unresolved
external reference are loaded. If a routine from a library references another
routine in the library, and the library has not been processed by ranlib(1), the
referenced routine must appear after the referencing routine in the library.
Thus the order of programs within libraries may be important. The first
member of a library should be a file named __.SYMDEF, which is understood
to be a dictionary for the library as produced by ranlib(1); the dictionary is
searched iteratively to satisfy as many references as possible.
   The symbols _etext, _edata, and _end, (etext, edata and end in C) are
reserved, and if referred to, are set to the first location above the program,
the first location above initialized data, and the first location above all data
respectively. It is erroneous to define these symbols.

Options

   −d   Force definition of common storage even if the −r flag is
present.

—e   The following argument is taken to be the name of the entry point of the loaded program; location 0 is the default.

—l*x*   This option is an abbreviation for the library name /lib/lib*x*.a, where *x* is a string. If that does not exist, ld tries /usr/lib/lib*x*.a, A library is searched when its name is encountered, so the placement of a —l is significant.

—M   Produce a primitive load map, listing the names of the files which will be loaded.

—n   Arrange that, when the output file is executed, the text portion will be read-only and shared among all users executing the file.

—o   The name argument after —o is used as the name of the ld output file, instead of *a.out*.

—r   Generate relocation bits in the output file so that it can be the subject of another ld run. This flag also prevents final definitions from being given to common symbols, and suppresses the undefined symbol diagnostics.

—S   Remove all symbols except locals and globals from the output.

—s   Remove the symbol table and relocation bits from the output to save space (but impair the usefulness of the debuggers). This information can also be removed by strip(1).

—u   Take the following argument as a symbol and enter it as undefined in the symbol table. This is useful for loading wholly from a library, since initially the symbol table is empty and an unresolved reference is needed to force the loading of the first routine.

—X   Save local symbols except for those whose names begin with L. This option is used by cc(1) to discard internally-generated labels while retaining symbols local to routines.

—x   Do not preserve local (non-global) symbols in the output symbol table; only enter external symbols. This option saves some space in the output file.

---

learn — computer aided instruction about UNIX   LEARN(1)

learn [subject [lesson [speed]]]

learn gives CAI courses and practice in the use of UNIX. To get started simply type learn. The program will ask questions to find out what you want to do. The questions may be bypassed by naming a subject, and the last lesson number that learn told you in the previous session. You may also include a speed number that was given with the lesson number (but without the parentheses that learn places around the speed number). If lesson is —, learn prompts for each lesson; this is useful for debugging. The special command bye terminates a learn session.

The subjects presently handled are: editor, eqn, files, macros, morefiles, and C.

---

lex — generator of lexical analysis programs   LEX(1)

lex [option] [file] ...

lex generates programs to be used in simple lexical analysis of text. The input files (standard input default) contain regular expressions to be searched for, and actions written in C to be executed when expressions are found.

A C source program, lex.yy.c is generated, to be compiled thus:

    cc lex.yy.c —ll

This program, when run, copies unrecognized portions of the input to the output, and executes the associated C action for each regular expression that is recognized.

Options

—t	Place the result on the standard output instead of in file lex.yy.c.
—v	Print a one-line summary of statistics of the generated analyzer.
—n	Opposite of —v; —n is default.
—f	Faster compilation: don't bother to pack the resulting tables; limited to small programs.

---

lint — a C program verifier   LINT(1)

lint [option] file ...

lint attempts to detect features of the C program files that are likely to be bugs, non-portable, or wasteful. It also checks the type usage of the program more strictly than the compilers. Among the things found are unreachable statements, loops not entered at the top, automatic variables declared but not used, and logical expressions whose value is constant. Moreover, the usage of functions is checked to find functions that return values in some places but not in others, functions called with varying numbers of arguments, and functions whose values are not used.

By default, it is assumed that all the files are to be loaded together; they are checked for mutual compatibility. Function definitions for certain libraries are available to lint; these libraries are referred to by a conventional name, such as —lm, in the style of ld(1).

Options

Any number of the options in the following list may be used. The —D, —U, and —I options of cc(1) are also recognized as separate arguments.

—a	Report assignments of long values to int variables.
—b	Report **break** statements that cannot be reached. (This is not the default because, unfortunately, most lex and many yacc outputs produce dozens of such comments.)
—c	Complain about casts that have questionable portability.
—h	Apply a number of heuristic tests to attempt to intuit bugs, improve style, and reduce waste.

−n   Do not check compatibility against the standard library.
−p   Attempt to check portability to the IBM and GCOS dialects of
           C.
−u   Do not complain about functions and variables used but not de-
           fined, or defined but not used (this is suitable for running lint
           on a subset of files out of a larger program).
−v   Suppress complaints about unused arguments in functions.
−x   Report variables referred to by extern declarations, but never
           used.

exit(2) and other functions that do not return are not understood; this
causes various lies.

Certain conventional comments in the C source will change the behavior
of lint.

/ * NOTREACHED * /
           At appropriate points stops comments about unreachable code.
/ * VARARGS n * /
           Suppress the usual checking for variable numbers of arguments
           in the following function declaration. The data types of the
           first n arguments are checked; a missing n is taken to be 0.
/ * NOSTRICT * /
           Shut off strict type checking in the next expression.
/ * ARGSUSED * /
           Turn on the −v option for the next function.
/ * LINTLIBRARY * /
           At the beginning of a file shuts off complaints about unused
           functions in this file.

---

ln − make links   LN(1)

ln name1 [name2]

A link is a directory entry referring to a file; the same file (together with
its size, all its protection information, etc.) may have several links to it.
There is no way to distinguish a link to a file from its original directory entry;
any changes in the file are effective regardless of the name by which the file
is known.

Given one or two arguments, ln creates a link to an existing file name1.
If name2 is given, the link has that name.

It is forbidden to link to a directory or to link across file systems.

---

login − sign on   LOGIN(1)

login [username]

The login command is used when a user initially signs on, or it may be
used at any time to change from one user to another.

If login is invoked without an argument, it asks for a user name, and, if
appropriate, a password. Echoing is turned off (if possible) during the typing
of the password, so it will not appear on the written record of the session.

After a successful login the user is informed of the existence of mail, and the message of the day is printed.

login initializes the user-id and group-id and the working directory, then executes a command interpreter (usually sh(1)) according to specifications found in a password file. Argument 0 of the command interpreter is —sh, or more generally the name of the command interpreter with a leading dash (—) prepended.

login also initializes the environment with information specifying home directory, command interpreter, terminal type (if available) and user name.

login is recognized by sh(1) and executed directly (without forking).

---

look — find lines in a sorted list   LOOK(1)

look [—df] string [file]

look consults a sorted file and prints all lines that begin with string. It uses binary search. If no file is specified, /usr/dict/words is assumed.

Options

—d   Lexicographic (dictionary) order: only letters, digits, tabs and spaces participate in comparisons.

—f   Fold. Upper case letters compare equal to lower case.

---

lorder — find ordering relation for an object library   LORDER(1)

lorder file ...

The input is one or more object or library archive (see ar(1)) files. The standard output is a list of pairs of object file names, meaning that the first file of the pair refers to external identifiers defined in the second. The output may be processed by tsort(1) to find an ordering of a library suitable for one-pass access by ld(1).

The need for lorder may be vitiated by use of ranlib(1), which converts an ordered archive into a randomly accessed library.

---

lpr — line printer spooler   LPR(1)

lpr [option] [name ...]

lpr causes the named files to be queued for printing. If no files are named, the standard input is read. The option —m causes notification via mail(1) to be sent to the user when the job completes.

ls — list contents of directory   LS(1)

ls [option] name ...

For each directory argument, ls lists the contents of the directory; for each file argument, ls repeats its name and any other information requested. The output is sorted alphabetically by default. When no argument is given, the current directory is listed. When several arguments are given, the arguments are first sorted appropriately, but file arguments appear before directories and their contents.

Options

Versions of ls differ in output format and some versions have options not listed below.

—l	List in long format, giving mode, number of links, owner, size in bytes, and time of last modification for each file.
—t	Sort by time modified (latest first) instead of by name, as is normal.
—a	List all entries; usually . and .. are suppressed.
—s	Give size in blocks for each entry.
—d	If name is a directory, list only its name, not its contents (mostly used with —l to get status on directory).
—r	Reverse the order of sort to get reverse alphabetic or oldest first as appropriate.
—u	Use time of last access instead of last modification for sorting (—t) or printing (—l).
—c	Use time of file creation for sorting or printing.
—i	Print the inode-number in first column for each file listed.
—f	Force each argument to be interpreted as a directory and list the name found in each slot. This option turns off —l, —t, —s, and —r, and turns on —a; the list is in the order in which entries appear in the directory.
—g	Give the group-id instead of user-id in long listing.

mail — send or receive mail among users   MAIL(1)

mail [—r] [—f file]

mail with no argument prints a user's mail, message-by-message, in last-in, first-out order; the optional argument —r causes first-in, first-out order. For each message, mail reads a line from the standard input as follows.

return	Go on to next message.
d	Delete message and go on to the next.
p	Print message again.
—	Go back to previous message.
s [file] ...	
	Save the message in the named *files* (mbox default).
w [file] ...	

> Save the message, without a header, in the named *files* (mbox default).

m [*person*] ...
> Mail the message to the named *persons* (yourself is default).

end-of-file
> Put unexamined mail back in the mailbox and stop.

q   Same as end-of-file.

! *cmd*   Escape to the Shell to execute *cmd*.

An interrupt normally causes termination of the command; the mail file is unchanged. The optional argument −i causes mail to continue after interrupts.

When persons are named, mail takes the standard input up to an end-of-file (or a line with just .) and adds it to each person's mail file. The message is preceded by the sender's name and a postmark. Lines that look like postmarks are prepended with >. A person is usually a user name recognized by login(1). To denote a recipient on a remote system, prefix person by the system name and exclamation mark (see uucp(1)).

The −f option causes the named file, e.g. mbox, to be printed as if it were the mail file.

---

make — maintain program groups   MAKE(1)

make [−f makefile] [option] ... name ...

make executes commands in makefile to update one or more target names. name is typically a program. If no −f option is present, makefile and Makefile are tried in order. If makefile is −, the standard input is taken. More than one −f option may appear

Commands returning non-zero status cause make to terminate unless the special target .IGNORE is in makefile.

Interrupt and quit cause the target to be deleted unless the target depends on the special name .PRECIOUS.

Options

−i   Equivalent to the special entry .IGNORE:.

−k   When a command returns non-zero status, abandon work on the current entry, but continue on branches that do not depend on the current entry.

−n   Trace and print, but do not execute the commands needed to update the targets.

−t   Touch, i.e. update the modified date of targets, without executing any commands.

−s   make operates silently.

man — print out the manual   MAN(1)

man [section] title ...

man formats a specified set of manual pages. If a section is requested man looks in that section of the manual for the given titles. section is an arabic section number, e.g. 3, possibly followed by a single letter classifier, e.g. 3M indicating a Mathematical subroutine in section 3. If section is omitted, man searches all sections of the manual, giving preference to commands over subroutines in system libraries, and printing the first section it finds, if any.

mesg — permit or deny messages   MESG(1)

mesg [n] [y]

mesg with argument n forbids messages via write(1) by revoking non-user write permission on the user's terminal. mesg with argument y reinstates permission. Without arguments, mesg reports the current state without changing it.

mkdir — make a directory   MKDIR(1)

mkdir dirname ...

mkdir creates specified directories with the mode determined by the umask setting. Standard entries, . for the directory itself, and .. for its parent, are made automatically.

mkdir requires write permission in the parent directory.

mv — move or rename files   MV(1)

mv file1 file2

mv file ... directory

mv moves (changes the name of) file1 to file2. If file2 already exists, it is removed before file1 is moved. If file2 has a mode which forbids writing, mv prints the mode (see chmod(2)) and reads the standard input to obtain a line; if the line begins with y, the move takes place; if not, mv exits. In the second form, one or more files are moved to the directory with their original file-names. Some versions of this command allow directories to be renamed.

mv refuses to move a file onto itself.

newgrp — log in to a new group   NEWGRP(1)

newgrp group

    newgrp changes the group identification of its caller, analogously to lo-
gin(1). The same person remains logged in, and the current directory is unchanged, but access permissions to files are evaluated with respect to the new
group-id.
    newgrp is built-in to the shell, which executes it directly without a fork.

nice — run a command at low priority   NICE(1)

nice [— number] command [arguments]

    nice executes command with low scheduling priority. If the number ar-
gument is present, the priority is incremented (higher numbers mean lower
priorities) by that amount up to a limit of 20. The default number is 10.
    The super-user may run commands with priority higher than normal by
using a negative priority, e.g. ——10.

nm — print name list   NM(1)

nm [option] [file ...]

    nm prints the name list (symbol table) of each object file in the argu-
ment list. If an argument is an archive, a listing for each object file in the
archive will be produced. If no file is given, the symbols in *a.out* are listed.
    Each symbol name is preceded by its value (blanks if undefined) and one
of the letters U (undefined), A (absolute), T (text segment symbol), D (data
segment symbol), B (bss segment symbol), C (common symbol), f file name,
or — for sdb symbol table entries (see —a below). If the symbol is local
(non-external) the type letter is in lower case. The output is sorted alphabetically.

Options

    —a   Include all symbols for printing; normally symbols destined for
            sdb(1) are excluded.
    —g   Print only global (external) symbols.
    —n   Sort numerically rather than alphabetically.
    —o   Prepend file or archive element name to each output line rather
            than only once.
    —p   Print in symbol-table order without sorting.
    —r   Sort in reverse order.
    —u   Print only undefined symbols.

nohup — run a command immune to interrupts   NOHUP(1)

nohup command [arguments]

   nohup executes command immune to hangup and terminate signals from
the controlling terminal. nohup should be invoked from the shell with & in
order to prevent it from responding to interrupts by or stealing the input from
the next person who logs in on the same terminal.

---

od — octal dump   OD(1)

od [option] [file]

   od dumps file in one or more formats as selected by the first argument.
If the first argument is missing, —o is default.
   The file argument specifies which file is to be dumped. If no file argu-
ment is specified, the standard input is used.

Options

   —b   Interpret bytes in octal.
   —c   Interpret bytes in ASCII. Certain non-graphic characters appear
         as the equivalent C character escape; others appear as 3-digit oc-
         tal numbers.
   —d   Interpret shorts (16 bit words) in decimal.
   —o   Interpret shorts (16 bit words) in octal.
   —x   Interpret shorts (16 bit words) in hexadecimal.
   —D   Interpret longs (32 bit words) in decimal.
   —O   Interpret longs (32 bit words) in octal.
   —X   Interpret longs (32 bit words) in hexadecimal.

---

passwd — change login password   PASSWD(1)

passwd [name]

   This command changes (or installs) a password associated with the user
name (your own name by default).
   The program prompts for the old password and then for the new one.
The caller must supply both. The new password must be typed twice, to fore-
stall mistakes.
   New passwords must be at least four characters long if they use a sufficiently rich alphabet and at least six characters long if monocase. These
rules are relaxed if you are insistent enough.
   Only the owner of the name or the super-user may change a password;
the owner must prove knowledge of the old password.

---

pr — print file   PR(1)

pr [option] ... [file] ...

    pr produces a printed listing of one or more files. The output is separated into pages headed by a date, the name of the file or a specified header, and the page number. If there are no file arguments, the standard input is printed.

    Inter-terminal messages via write(1) are forbidden during a pr.

Options

Options apply to all following files but may be reset between files:

− *n*	Produce *n*-column output.
+ *n*	Begin printing with page *n*.
−h	Take the next argument as a page header.
−w *n*	For purposes of multi-column output, take the width of the page to be *n* characters instead of the default 72.
−f	Use formfeeds instead of newlines to separate pages. A formfeed is assumed to use up two blank lines at the top of a page. (Thus this option does not affect the effective page length.)
−l *n*	Take the length of the page to be *n* lines instead of the default 66.
−t	Do not print the 5-line header or the 5-line trailer normally supplied for each page.
−s *c*	Separate columns by the single character *c* instead of by the appropriate amount of white space. A missing *c* is taken to be a tab.
−m	Print all files simultaneously, each in one column.

---

prof — display profile data   PROF(1)

prof [option] [a.out [mon.out ...]]

    prof interprets the file produced by the monitor(3) subroutine. Under default modes, the symbol table in the named object file (*a.out* default) is read and correlated with the profile file (*mon.out* default). For each external symbol, the percentage of time spent executing between that symbol and the next is printed (in decreasing order), together with the number of times that routine was called and the number of milliseconds per call. If more than one profile file is specified, the output represents the sum of the profiles.

    In order for the number of calls to a routine to be tallied, the −p option of cc, or f77 must have been given when the file containing the routine was compiled. This option also arranges for the profile file to be produced automatically.

Options

−a	All symbols are reported rather than just external symbols.
−l	The output is sorted by symbol value.

−n   The output is sorted by number of calls.

−s   A summary profile file is produced in *mon.sum*. This is only useful when more than one profile file is specified.

−z   Routines which have zero usage (as indicated by call counts and accumulated time) are nevertheless printed in the output.

---

ps − process status   PS(1)

ps [option]

    ps prints information about processes. Normally, only your processes are printed by **ps**; specifying **a** causes other users' processes to be printed; specifying x prints processes without control terminals.

    All output formats include, for each process, the process-id PID, control terminal of the process TT, cpu time used by the process TIME (this includes both user and system time), the state STAT of the process, and an indication of the COMMAND which is running. The state is given by a sequence of four letters, e.g. RWNA. The first letter indicates the runnability of the process: R for runnable processes, T for stopped processes, D for those in disk (or other short term) waits, S for those sleeping for less than about 20 seconds, and I for idle (sleeping longer than about 20 seconds) processes. The second letter indicates whether a process is swapped out, showing W if it is, or a blank if it is loaded (in-memory).

Options

a   Provide information about all processes with terminals (ordinarily only one's own processes are displayed). The environment is printed as well as the arguments to the command.

g   List all processes. Without this option, **ps** only prints interesting processes. Processes are deemed to be uninteresting if they are process group leaders. This normally eliminates top-level command interpreters and processes waiting for users to login on free terminals.

l   Produce a long listing, with fields PPID, CP, PRI, NI, ADDR, SIZE, RSS and WCHAN as described below.

x   Include processes with no terminal.

If a process number is given, indicated here by a #, the output is restricted to that process. This option must be last.

    A process that has terminated and has a parent, but has not yet been waited for by the parent is marked <defunct>; a process which is blocked trying to exit is marked <exiting>; **ps** makes an educated guess as to the file name and arguments given when the process was created by examining memory or the swap area. The method is inherently somewhat unreliable and in any event a process is entitled to destroy this information, so the names cannot be counted on too much.

---

ptx — permuted index   PTX(1)

ptx [option ...] [input [output]]

    ptx generates a permuted index to file input on file output (standard input and output default). It has three phases: the first does the permutation, generating one line for each keyword in an input line. The keyword is rotated to the front. The permuted file is then sorted. Finally, the sorted lines are rotated so the keyword comes at the middle of the page. ptx produces output in the form:

    .xx "tail" "before keyword" "keyword and after" "head"

where .xx may be an nroff or troff(1) macro for user-defined formatting. The before keyword and keyword and after fields incorporate as much of the line as will fit around the keyword when it is printed at the middle of the page. tail and head, at least one of which is an empty string "", are wrapped-around pieces small enough to fit in the unused space at the opposite end of the line. When original text must be discarded, / marks the spot.

Options

    −f   Fold upper and lower case letters for sorting.

    −t   Prepare the output for the phototypesetter; the default line length is 100 characters.

    −w *n*   Use the next argument, *n,* as the width of the output line. The default line length is 72 characters.

    −g *n*   Use the next argument, *n,* as the number of characters to allow for each gap among the four parts of the line as finally printed. The default gap is 3 characters.

    −o *only* Use as keywords only the words given in the *only* file.

    −i *ignore*

            Do not use as keywords any words given in the *ignore* file. If the −i and −o options are missing, use /usr/lib/eign as the *ignore* file.

    −b *break*

            Use the characters in the *break* file to separate words. In any case, white space characters are always used as break characters.

    −r   Take any leading non-blank characters of each input line to be a reference identifier (as to a page or chapter) separate from the text of the line. Attach that identifier as a 5th field on each output line.

pubindex − make inverted bibliographic index   PUBINDEX(1)

pubindex [file] ...

   pubindex makes a hashed inverted index to the named files for use by
refer(1). The files contain bibliographic references separated by blank lines.
A bibliographic reference is a set of lines that contain bibliographic information fields. Each field starts on a line beginning with a %, followed by a
key-letter, followed by a blank, and followed by the contents of the field,
which continues until the next line starting with %.

---

pwd − working directory name   PWD(1)

pwd

   pwd prints the pathname of the working (current) directory.

---

ranlib − convert archives to random libraries   RANLIB(1)

ranlib archive ...

   ranlib converts each archive to a form that can be loaded more rapidly
by the loader, by adding a table of contents named __.SYMDEF to the beginning of the archive. It uses ar(1) to reconstruct the archive, so that sufficient
temporary file space must be available in the file system containing the
current directory.

---

refer, lookbib − find and insert literature references in document REFER(1)

refer [option] ...

lookbib [file] ...

   lookbib accepts keywords from the standard input and searches a bibliographic data base for references that contain those keywords anywhere in title, author, journal name, etc. Matching references are printed on the standard output. Blank lines are taken as delimiters between queries.
   refer is a preprocessor for nroff or troff(1) that finds and formats references. The input files (standard input default) are copied to the standard
output, except for lines between .[and .] request lines, that are assumed to
contain keywords as for lookbib, and are replaced by information from the
bibliographic data base. The user may avoid the search, override fields from
it, or add new fields. The reference data, from whatever source, are assigned
to a set of troff strings. Macro packages such as ms print the finished reference text from these strings. A flag is placed in the text at the point of reference. By default the references are indicated by numbers.

Options

   −a*r*   Reverse the first *r* author names (Jones, J. A. instead of J. A.
            Jones). If *r* is omitted all author names are reversed.

−b   Bare mode. Do not put any flags in text (neither numbers nor labels).

−c *string*
        Capitalize the fields whose key-letters are in *string*.

−e   Instead of leaving the references where encountered, accumulate them until a sequence of the form

        $LIST$

        is encountered, and then write out all references collected so far. Collapse references to the same source.

−k *x*   Instead of numbering references, use labels as specified in a reference data line beginning %*x;* by default *x* is **L**.

−l *m,n* Instead of numbering references, use labels made from the senior author's last name and the year of publication. Only the first *m* letters of the last name and the last *n* digits of the date are used. If either *m* or *n* is omitted the entire name or date respectively is used.

−p   Take the next argument as a file of references to be searched. The default file is searched last.

−n   Do not search the default file.

−s *keys* Sort references by fields whose key-letters are in the *keys* string; permute reference numbers in text accordingly. Implies −e. The key-letters in *keys* may be followed by a number to indicate how many such fields are used, with + taken as a very large number. The default is **AD** that sorts on the senior author and then date; to sort, for example, on all authors and then title use −s**A+T**.

To use your own references, put them in the format described in **pubindex**(1). They can be searched more rapidly by running **pubindex**(1) on them before using **refer**; failure to index results in a linear search.

----

rm, rmdir − remove (unlink) files   RM (1)

rm [option] file ...

rmdir dir ...

rm removes the entries for one or more files from a directory. If an entry was the last link to the file, the file is destroyed. Removal of a file requires write permission in its directory, but neither read nor write permission on the file itself.

If a file has no write permission and the standard input is a terminal, its permissions are printed and a line is read from the standard input. If that line begins with y the file is deleted, otherwise the file remains. No questions are asked and no errors are reported when the −f (force) option is given.

If a designated file is a directory, an error comment is printed unless the optional argument −r has been used. In that case, rm recursively deletes the entire contents of the specified directory, and the directory itself.

If the −i (interactive) option is in effect, rm asks whether to delete each file, and, under −r, whether to examine each directory.

The null option − indicates that all the arguments following it are to be treated as file names. This allows the specification of file names starting with a minus.

rmdir removes entries for the named directories, that must be empty.

---

sdb − symbolic debugger   SDB(1)

sdb [objfil [corfil [directory]]]

sdb is a symbolic debugger that can be used with C, Pascal, and f77 programs. It may be used to examine their files and to provide a controlled environment for their execution.

objfil is an executable program file that has been compiled with the −g (debug) option; the default for **objfil** is *a.out*. corfil is assumed to be a core image file produced after executing objfil; the default for corfil is *core*. The core file need not be present.

At any time there is a **current line** and **current file**. If corfil exists then they are initially set to the line and file containing the source statement at which the process terminated or stopped. Otherwise, they are set to the first line in main. The current line and file may be changed with the source file examination requests.

Names of variables are written just as they are in C, Pascal, or f77. Variables local to a procedure may be accessed using the form **procedure:variable**. If no procedure name is given, the procedure containing the current line is used by default. It is also possible to refer to structure members as **variable.member**, pointers to structure members as **variable−>member** and array elements as **variable[number]**. Combinations of these forms may also be used.

It is also possible to specify a variable by its address. All forms of integer constants that are valid in C may be used, so that addresses may be input in decimal, octal or hexadecimal.

Line numbers in the source program are referred to as **filename:number** or **procedure:number**. In either case the number is relative to the beginning of the file. If no procedure or file name is given, the current file is used by default. If no number is given, the first line of the named procedure or file is used.

Data examination requests

t	Print a stack trace (the names of the most recently called functions) for the terminated or stopped program.
T	Print the top line of the stack trace.
variable / *lm*	
	Print the value of variable according to length *l* and format *m*. If *l* and *m* are omitted, **sdb** chooses a length and format suitable for the variable's type as declared in the program. The length specifiers are:
	b One byte.

h   Two bytes (half word).
l   Four bytes (long word).
number
         String length for formats s and a (see below).

Legal values for m are:
c   character
d   decimal
u   decimal, unsigned
o   octal
x   hexadecimal
f   32 bit single precision floating point
g   64 bit double precision floating point
s   Assume variable is a string pointer and print characters until a null is reached.
a   Print characters starting at the variable's address until a null is reached.
p   A pointer to procedure.

The length specifiers are only effective with the formats d, u, o and x. If one of these formats is specified and l is omitted, the length defaults to the word length of the host machine; 4 for the VAX 11/780. The last variable may be redisplayed with the request ./.

The sh(1) metacharacters * and ? may be used within procedure and variable names, providing a limited form of pattern matching. If no procedure name is given, both variables local to the current procedure and global (common for f77) variables are matched; while if a procedure name is specified then only variables local to that procedure and matched. To match only global variables (or blank common for f77), the form :pattern is used. The name of a common block may be specified instead of a procedure name for f77 programs.

variable=*lm*
linenumber=*lm*
number=*lm*
         Print the address of the variable, line number, or the value of the number, in the specified format. If no format is given, then lx is used. The last variant of this request provides a convenient way to convert between decimal, octal and hexadecimal.

variable!value
         Set the variable to the given value. The value may be a number, character constant, or a variable. If the variable is of type float or double, the value may also be a floating constant.

Source files requests

e procedure
e filename.c
         Set the current file to the file containing the named procedure

or the named filename. Set the current line to the first line in
the named procedure or file. All source files are assumed to be
in directory. The default for directory is the working directory.
If no procedure or file name is given, the current procedure and
file names are reported.

/ regular expression /
Search forward from the current line for a line containing a
string matching the regular expression as in section 8.1. The
trailing / may be elided.

?regular expression?
Search backward from the current line for a line containing a
string matching the regular expression. The trailing ? may be
elided.

p   Print the current line.

z   Print the current line followed by the next 9 lines. Set the
          current line to the last line printed.

^D   Scroll. Print the next 10 lines. Set the current line to the last
          line printed.

w   Window. Print the 10 lines around the current line.

number   Set the current line to the given line number. Print the new
          current line.

count +   Advance the current line by count lines. Print the new current
          line.

count −   Retreat the current line by count lines. Print the new current
          line.

Execution control requests

count r args
count R   Run the program with the given arguments. The r request with
          no arguments reuses the previous arguments to the program
          while the R request runs the program with no arguments. An
          argument beginning with < or > causes redirection for the
          standard input or output respectively. If count is given, it
          specifies the number of breakpoints to be ignored.

linenumber c count
linenumber C count
          Continue after a breakpoint or interrupt. If count is given, it
          specifies the number of breakpoints to be ignored. C continues
          with the signal that caused the program to stop and c ignores
          it. If a linenumber is specified then a temporary breakpoint is
          placed at the line and execution is continued. The breakpoint is
          deleted when the command finishes.

count s   Single step. Run the program through count lines. If no count
          is given then the program is run for one line.

count S   Single step, but step through subroutine calls.

k   Kill the debugged program.

procedure(arg1,arg2,...)
procedure(arg1,arg2,...)/m

Execute the named procedure with the given arguments. Arguments can be integer, character or string constants or names of variables accessible from the current procedure. The second form causes the value returned by the procedure to be printed according to format *m*. If no format is given, the default is d.

linenumber b *requests*
Set a breakpoint at the given line. If a procedure name without a line number is given (e.g. proc:), a breakpoint is placed at the first line in the procedure even if it was not compiled with the debug flag. If no *linenumber* is given, a breakpoint is placed at the current line. If no **requests** are given then execution stops just before the breakpoint and control is returned to **sdb**. Otherwise the **requests** are executed when the breakpoint is encountered and execution continues. Multiple requests are separated by ;.

linenumber d
Delete a breakpoint at the given line. If no *linenumber* is given then the breakpoints are deleted interactively. Each breakpoint location is printed and a line is read from the standard input. If the line begins with a y or d then the breakpoint is deleted.

B   Print a list of the currently active breakpoints.
D   Delete all breakpoints.
l   Print the last executed line.

linenumber a
Announce. If *linenumber* is of the form proc:number, the request effectively executes a linenumber b l. If *linenumber* is of the form proc:, the request executed is proc: b T.

Miscellaneous requests

! *cmd*   The command is interpreted by sh(1).
return   If the previous request printed a source line then advance the current line by 1 line and print the new current line. If the previous request displayed a core location then display the next core location.
"   Print the given string.
q   Exit the debugger.

---

sed — stream editor   SED(1)

sed [−n] [−e script] [−f sfile] [file] ...

sed copies the named files (standard input default) to the standard output, edited according to a script of requests. The −f option causes the script to be taken from file sfile; these options accumulate. If there is just one −e option and no −f, the flag −e may be omitted. The −n option suppresses the default output.

A script consists of editing requests, one per line, of the following form:

[address [, address]] function [arguments]

In normal operation **sed** cyclically copies a line of input into a **pattern space** (unless there is something left after a D request), applies in sequence all requests whose **addresses** select that pattern space, and at the end of the script copies the pattern space to the standard output (except under the −n flag) and deletes the pattern space.

An **address** is either a decimal number that counts input lines cumulatively across files, a **$** that addresses the last line of input, or a context address, /**regular expression**/, as described in section 8.1 modified thus:

The escape sequence \n matches a **newline** embedded in the pattern space.

A request line with no addresses selects every pattern space.

A request line with one address selects each pattern space that matches the address.

A request line with two addresses selects the inclusive range from the first pattern space that matches the first address through the next pattern space that matches the second. (If the second address is a number less than or equal to the line number first selected, only one line is selected.) Thereafter the process is repeated, looking again for the first address.

Editing requests can be applied only to non-selected pattern spaces by use of the negation function **!** (below).

An argument denoted **text** consists of one or more lines, all but the last of which end with \ to hide the **newline**. Backslashes in text are treated like backslashes in the replacement string of an s request, and may be used to protect initial blanks and tabs against the stripping that is done on every script line.

An argument denoted **rfile** or **wfile** must terminate the request line and must be preceded by exactly one blank. Each wfile is created before processing begins. There can be at most 10 distinct wfile arguments.

a\
text
> Append. Place **text** on the output before reading the next input line.

b label Branch to the : request bearing the **label**. If **label** is empty, branch to the end of the script.

c\
text
> Change. Delete the pattern space. With 0 or 1 address or at the end of a 2-address range, place text on the output. Start the next cycle.

d   Delete the pattern space. Start the next cycle.

D   Delete the initial segment of the pattern space through the first **newline**. Start the next cycle.

g   Replace the contents of the pattern space by the contents of the hold space.

G   Append the contents of the hold space to the pattern space.

h   Replace the contents of the hold space by the contents of the pattern space.

H   Append the contents of the pattern space to the hold space.

i\
text
            Insert. Place text on the standard output.

n   Copy the pattern space to the standard output. Replace the
            pattern space with the next line of input.

N   Append the next line of input to the pattern space with an em-
            bedded newline. (The current line number changes.)

p   Print. Copy the pattern space to the standard output.

P   Copy the initial segment of the pattern space through the first
            newline to the standard output.

q   Quit. Branch to the end of the script. Do not start a new cy-
            cle.

r   rfile   Read the contents of rfile. Place them on the output before
            reading the next input line.

s /regular expression/replacement/flags
            Substitute the replacement string for instances of the regular
            expression in the pattern space. As in the editor ed any char-
            acter may be used instead of /. flags is zero or more of

            g   Global. Substitute for all non-overlapping instances of
                        the regular expression rather than just the first one.

            p   Print the pattern space if a replacement was made.

            w file   Write. Append the pattern space to file if a replace-
                        ment was made.

t label   Test. Branch to the : request bearing the label if any substitu-
            tions have been made since the most recent reading of an input
            line or execution of a t. If label is empty, branch to the end of
            the script.

w file   Write. Append the pattern space to file.

x   Exchange the contents of the pattern and hold spaces.

y /string1/string2/
            Transform. Replace all occurrences of characters in string1
            with the corresponding character in string2. The lengths of
            string1 and string2 must be equal.

! function
            Don't. Apply the function (or group, if function is {...}) only
            to lines not selected by the address(es).

: label   This request does nothing; it bears a label for b and t requests
            to branch to.

=   Place the current line number on the standard output as a line.

{   Execute the following requests through a matching } only when
            the pattern space is selected.
            An empty request is ignored.

sh — command language   SH(1)

sh [options] [arg] ...

   sh is a command programming language that executes commands read
from a terminal or a file.
   If the first character of argument zero is —, commands are read from
$HOME/.profile, if the file exists. Commands are then read as described
below.
   The interpretation of other flags is described with the **set** command in
chapter 4.

Options

The following flags are interpreted by the shell when it is invoked.

   —c *s*   If the —c flag is present then commands are read from *s*.
   —s   If the —s flag is present or if no arguments remain then com-
             mands are read from the standard input. Shell output is writ-
             ten to file descriptor 2.
   —i   If the —i flag is present or if the shell input and output are at-
             tached to a terminal (as told by gtty) then this shell is *interac-
             tive*. In this case the terminate signal is ignored (so that *kill 0*
             does not kill an interactive shell) and the interrupt signal is
             caught and ignored (so that *wait* is interruptable). In all cases
             the quit signal is ignored by the shell.

size — size of an object file   SIZE(1)

size [object ...]

   size prints the (decimal) number of bytes required by the text, data, and
bss portions, and their sum in hexadecimal and decimal, of each object-file
argument. If no file is specified, *a.out* is used.

sleep — suspend execution for an interval   SLEEP(1)

sleep time

   sleep suspends execution for *time* seconds.

sort — sort or merge files   SORT(1)

sort [options] [+pos1 [—pos2]] ... [options] [name] ...

   sort reads the named files and sorts the result onto the standard output.
The name — means the standard input. If no input files are named, the standard input is sorted.
   The default sort key is an entire line and the default ordering is lexicographic.

Options

The ordering is affected globally by the following options, one or more of which may appear.

    −b   Ignore leading blanks (spaces and tabs) in field comparisons.

    −d   Dictionary order: only letters, digits and blanks are significant in comparisons.

    −f   Fold upper case letters onto lower case.

    −i   Ignore characters outside the ASCII range 040-0176 in non-numeric comparisons.

    −n   An initial numeric string, consisting of optional blanks, optional minus sign, and zero or more digits with optional decimal point, is sorted by arithmetic value. Option −n implies option −b.

    −r   Reverse the sense of comparisons.

    −tx The field separator (tab character) is x.

The notation + pos1 −pos2 restricts a sort key to a field beginning at pos1 and ending just before pos2. Both pos1 and pos2 have the form $m.n$, optionally followed by one or more of the flags bdfinr, where m gives the number of fields to skip from the beginning of the line and n gives the number of characters to skip further. If any flags are present they override all the global ordering options for this key. If the b option is in effect n is counted from the first non-blank in the field; b is attached independently to pos2. A missing .n means .0; a missing − pos2 means the end of the line. Under the −tx option, fields are strings separated by the character x; otherwise fields are non-empty non-blank strings separated by blanks.

When there are multiple sort keys, later keys are compared only after all earlier keys compare equal. Lines that otherwise compare equal are ordered with all bytes significant. These options are:

    −c   Check that the input file is sorted according to the ordering rules; give no output unless the file is out of sort.

    −m   Merge only, the input files are already sorted.

    −o   The next argument is the name of an output file to use instead of the standard output. This file may be the same as one of the inputs.

    −T   The next argument is the name of a directory in which temporary files should be made.

    −u   Suppress all but one in each set of equal lines. Ignored bytes and bytes outside keys do not participate in this comparison.

---

spell − find spelling errors   SPELL (1)

spell [option] ...   [file] ...

spell collects words from the named documents, and looks them up in a spelling list. Words that neither occur among nor are derivable (by applying certain inflections, prefixes or suffixes) from words in the spelling list are printed on the standard output. If no files are named, words are collected from the standard input.

spell ignores most troff, tbl and eqn(1) constructions.

Under the −v option, all words not literally in the spelling list are printed, and plausible derivations from spelling list words are indicated.

Under the −b option, British spelling is checked. Besides preferring *centre, colour, speciality, travelled,* etc., this option insists upon *-ise* in words like *standardise,* Fowler and the OED to the contrary notwithstanding.

Under the −x option, every plausible stem is printed with = for each word.

The spelling list is based on many sources, and while more haphazard than an ordinary dictionary, is also more effective in respect to proper names and popular technical words. Coverage of the specialized vocabularies of biology, medicine and chemistry is light.

---

strip — remove symbols and relocation bits   STRIP(1)

strip name ...

strip removes the symbol table and relocation bits ordinarily attached to the output of the assembler and loader. This is useful to save space after a program has been debugged.

The effect of strip is the same as use of the −s option of ld.

---

stty — set terminal options   STTY(1)

stty [option ...]

stty sets certain input-output options for the current output terminal, placing its output on the diagnostic output. With no argument, it reports the speed of the terminal and the settings of the options that are different from their defaults. With the argument all, all normally used option settings are reported. With the argument everything, everything stty knows about is printed.

Options

even	Allow even parity input.
−even	Disallow even parity input.
odd	Allow odd parity input.
−odd	Disallow odd parity input.
raw	Raw mode input (no input processing (erase, kill, interrupt, ...); parity bit passed back).
−raw	Negate raw mode.
cooked	Same as −raw.
cbreak	Make each character available to read(2) as received; no erase and kill processing, but all other processing (interrupt, ...) is performed.
−cbreak	Make characters available to read only when a newline is received.
−nl	Allow carriage return for newline, and output CR-LF for carriage return or newline.
nl	Accept only newline to end lines.

echo   Echo back every character typed.

−echo   Do not echo characters.

lcase   Map upper case to lower case.

−lcase   Do not map case.

tandem   Enable flow control, so that the system sends out the stop char-
           acter when its internal queue is in danger of overflowing on in-
           put, and sends the start character when it is ready to accept
           further input.

−tandem Disable flow control.

−tabs   Replace tabs by spaces when printing.

tabs   Preserve tabs.

ek   Set erase and kill characters to # and @.

erase c Set erase character to c (default #).

kill   c   Set kill character to c (default @).

intr   c   Set interrupt character to c (default del or ∧? (delete)).

quit   c   Set quit character to c (default ∧\).

start c   Set start character to c (default ∧Q).

stop   c   Set stop character to c (default ∧S).

eof   c   Set end of file character to c (default ∧D).

brk   c   Set break character to c (default undefined). This character is
           an extra wakeup causing character.

cr0 cr1 cr2 cr3
           Select style of delay for carriage return (see ioctl(2)).

nl0 nl1 nl2 nl3
           Select style of delay for linefeed.

tab0 tab1 tab2 tab3
           Select style of delay for tab.

ff0 ff1   Select style of delay for formfeed.

bs0 bs1 Select style of delay for backspace.

tty33   Set all modes suitable for the Teletype Corporation Model 33
           terminal.

tty37   Set all modes suitable for the Teletype Corporation Model 37
           terminal.

vt05   Set all modes suitable for Digital Equipment Corp. VT05 ter-
           minal.

dec   Set all modes suitable for Digital Equipment Corp. operating
           systems users; (erase, kill, and interrupt characters to ∧?, ∧U,
           and ∧C, decctlq and newcrt).

tn300   Set all modes suitable for a General Electric TermiNet 300.

ti700   Set all modes suitable for Texas Instruments 700 series termi-
           nal.

tek   Set all modes suitable for Tektronix 4014 terminal.

0   Hang up phone line immediately.

50 75 110 134 150 200 300 600 1200 1800 2400 4800 9600 exta
           extb Set terminal baud rate to the number given, if possible.

---

style — analyze surface characteristics of a document   STYLE(1)

style [−ml] [−mm] [option ...] file ...

   style analyzes the surface characteristics of the writing style of a document. It reports on readability, sentence length and structure, word length
and usage, verb type, and sentence openers. Because **style** runs **deroff** before
looking at the text, formatting header files should be included as part of the
input. The default macro package −ms may be overridden with the option
−mm. The option −ml, that causes **deroff** to skip lists, should be used if the
document contains many lists of non-sentences.

Options

The remaining options are used to locate sentences with certain characteristics.

−a	Print all sentences with their length and readability index.
−e	Print all sentences that begin with an expletive.
−p	Print all sentences that contain a passive verb.
−l num	Print all sentences longer than num.
−r num	Print all sentences whose readability index is greater than num.
P	Print parts of speech of the words in the document.

---

tabs — set terminal tabs   TABS(1)

tabs [−n] [terminal]

   tabs sets the tabs on a variety of terminals. Various terminal names are
recognized; the default is, however, suitable for most 300 baud terminals. If
the −n flag is present then the left margin is not indented as is normal.

---

tail — deliver the last part of a file   TAIL(1)

tail [±number [lbc] [fr]] [file]

   tail copies the named file to the standard output beginning at a designated place. If no file is named, the standard input is used.
   Copying begins at distance +number from the beginning, or −number
from the end of the input. number is counted in units of lines, blocks or
characters, according to the appended option l, b or c. When no units are
specified, counting is by lines.
   Specifying r causes tail to print lines from the end of the file in reverse
order. The default for r is to print the entire file this way. Specifying f
causes **tail** to not quit at end of file, but rather wait and try to read repeatedly in hopes that the file will grow.

tar — tape archiver   TAR(1)

tar [key] [name ...]

   tar saves and restores files on magtape. Its actions are controlled by the
key argument. The key is a string of characters containing at most one function letter and possibly one or more function modifiers. Other arguments to
the command are file or directory names specifying which files are to be
dumped or restored. In all cases, appearance of a directory name refers to
the files and (recursively) subdirectories of that directory.
   The function portion of the key is specified by one of the following
letters:

r   The named files are written on the end of the tape. The c func-
        tion implies this.

x   The named files are extracted from the tape. If the named file
        matches a directory whose contents had been written onto the
        tape, this directory is (recursively) extracted. The owner, modifi-
        cation time, and mode are restored (if possible). If no file argu-
        ment is given, the entire content of the tape is extracted. Note
        that if multiple entries specifying the same file are on the tape,
        the last one overwrites all earlier entries.

t   The names of the specified files are listed each time they occur on
        the tape. If no file argument is given, all of the names on the
        tape are listed.

u   The named files are added to the tape if either they are not al-
        ready there or have been modified since last put on the tape.

c   Create a new tape; writing begins on the beginning of the tape in-
        stead of after the last file. This command implies r.

o   On output, tar normally places information specifying owner and
        modes of directories in the archive.

p   This option restores files to their original modes, ignoring the
        present umask(2). Set-user-id and sticky information will also be
        restored to the super-user.

   The following characters may be used in addition to the letter which
selects the function desired.

0,...,7 This modifier selects an alternate drive on which the tape is
        mounted. (The default is drive 0 at 1600 bpi, which is normally
        /dev/rmt8.)

v   Normally tar does its work silently. The v (verbose) option
        causes it to type the name of each file it treats preceded by the
        function letter. With the t function, v gives more information
        about the tape entries than just the name.

w   Print the action to be taken followed by file name, then wait for
        user confirmation. If a word beginning with y is given, the action
        is performed. Otherwise there is no action.

f   Use the next argument as the name of the archive instead of
        /dev/rmt?. If the name of the file is —, tar writes to the standard

output or reads from the standard input, whichever is appropriate. Thus, tar can be used as the head or tail of a filter chain, for example, to move hierarchies with the command

cd fromdir; tar cf — . | (cd todir; tar xf —)

b   Use the next argument as the blocking factor for tape records. The default is 20 (the maximum). This option should only be used with raw magnetic tape archives (see f above). The block size is determined automatically when reading tapes (key letters x and t).

l   Complain if it cannot resolve all of the links to the files dumped. If this is not specified, no error messages are printed.

m   Do not restore the modification times. The modification time of files will be the time of extraction.

---

tbl — format tables for nroff or troff

tbl [files] ...

   tbl is a preprocessor for formatting tables for nroff or troff(1). The input files are copied to the standard output, except for lines between .TS and .TE command lines, that are assumed to describe tables and are reformatted.

   If no arguments are given, tbl reads the standard input, so it may be used as a filter. When it is used with eqn or neqn the tbl command should be first, to minimize the volume of data passed through pipes.

---

test — condition command

test expr

   test evaluates the expression expr, and if its value is true then returns zero exit status; otherwise, a non-zero exit status is returned. test returns a non-zero exit if there are no arguments.

   The following are used to construct expr. All the operators and flags are separate arguments to test.

−r file	The file exists and is readable.
−w file	The file exists and is writable.
−f file	The file exists and is not a directory.
−d file	The file exists and is a directory.
−s file	The file exists and has a size greater than zero.
−t [fildes]	The open file whose file descriptor number is fildes (1 by default) is associated with a terminal device.
−z s1	The length of string s1 is zero.
−n s1	The length of the string s1 is non-zero.
s1 = s2	The strings s1 and s2 are equal.
s1 != s2	The strings s1 and s2 are not equal.
s1	s1 is not the null string.
n1 −eq n2	The integers n1 and n2 are algebraically equal. Any of the comparisons −ne, −gt, −ge, −lt, or −le may be used in

place of −eq.

These primaries may be combined with the following operators where, −a has higher precedence than −o.

!   Unary negate.
−a   Binary AND.
−o   Binary OR.
(expr)   Parentheses for grouping.

---

time − time a command   TIME (1)

time command

The given command is executed. When it terminates, time prints the elapsed time of the command, the time spent in the system, and the time spent in execution of the command. Times are reported in seconds on the error output stream.

On a PDP 11, the execution time can depend on what kind of memory the program happens to land in; the user time in MOS is often half what it is in core.

---

touch − update date last modified of a file   TOUCH(1)

touch [−c] file ...

touch attempts to set the modified date of each file. This is done by reading a character from the file and writing it back.

If a file does not exist, an attempt will be made to create it unless the −c option is specified.

---

tr − translate characters   TR(1)

tr [option] [string1 [string2]]

tr copies the standard input to the standard output with substitution or deletion of selected characters. Input characters found in string1 are mapped into the corresponding characters of string2. When string2 is short it is padded to the length of string1 by duplicating its last character. Any combination of the options −cds may be used.

Options

−c   Complement the set of characters in string1 with respect to the universe of characters whose ASCII codes are 01 through 0377 octal;
−d   Delete all input characters in string1;
−s   Squeeze all strings of repeated output characters that are in string2 to single characters.

In either string the notation a−b means a range of characters from a to b in increasing ASCII order. The character \ followed by 1, 2 or 3 octal digits stands for the character whose ASCII code is given by those digits. A \

followed by any other character stands for that character.

---

troff, nroff — text formatting and typesetting   TROFF(1)

troff [option ...] [file] ...

nroff [option ...] [file] ...

    troff formats text in the named files for printing on a phototypesetter; nroff for typewriter-like devices.

    If no file argument is present, the standard input is read. An argument consisting of a — is taken as a file name corresponding to the standard input.

Options

The options may appear in any order so long as they appear before the files.

    —o list   Print only pages whose page numbers appear in the comma-separated list of numbers and ranges. A range $n-m$ means pages n through m; an initial $-n$ means from the beginning to page n; and a final $n-$ means from n to the end.

    —n p Number first generated page p.

    —s n Stop every n pages. nroff will halt prior to every n pages (default $n=1$) to allow paper loading or changing, and will resume upon receipt of a newline. troff will stop the phototypesetter every n pages, produce a trailer to allow changing cassettes, and resume when the typesetter's start button is pressed. Prepend the macro file /usr/lib/tmac/tmac. name to the input files.

    —r a n   Set register a (one-character) to n.

    —i   Read standard input after the input files are exhausted.

nroff only

    —T name Prepare output for specified terminal. Known names are *37* for the (default) Teletype Corporation Model 37 terminal, *tn300* for the GE TermiNet 300 (or any terminal without half-line capability), *300S* for the DASI-300S, *300* for the DASI-300, and *450* for the DASI-450 (Diablo Hiterm).

    —e   Produce equally-spaced words in adjusted lines, using full terminal resolution.

    —h   Use output tabs during horizontal spacing to speed output and reduce output character count. Tab settings are assumed to be every 8 nominal character widths.

troff only

    —t   Direct output to the standard output instead of the phototypesetter.

    —f   Refrain from feeding out paper and stopping the phototypesetter at the end of the run.

    —w   Wait until the phototypesetter is available, if currently busy.

    —b   Report whether the phototypesetter is busy or available. No text processing is done.

   -a   Send a printable ASCII approximation of the results to the
             standard output.
   -p n   Print all characters in point size *n* while retaining all prescribed
             spacings and motions, to reduce phototypesetter elapsed time.

---

tsort — topological sort   TSORT(1)

tsort [file]

   tsort produces on the standard output a totally ordered list of items consistent with a partial ordering of items mentioned in the input file. If no file
is specified, the standard input is understood.
   The input consists of pairs of items (non-empty strings) separated by
blanks. Pairs of different items indicate ordering. Pairs of identical items indicate presence, but not ordering.

---

uniq — report repeated lines in a file   UNIQ(1)

uniq [−udc [+ n] [− n]] [input [output]]

   uniq reads the input file comparing adjacent lines. In the normal case,
the second and succeeding copies of repeated lines are removed; the
remainder is written on the output file. Repeated lines must be adjacent in
order to be found; see sort(1). If the −u flag is used, the lines that are not
repeated in the original file are output. The −d option specifies that one copy
of the repeated lines is to be written. The normal mode of output is the union of the −u and −d mode outputs.
   The −c option supersedes −u and −d and generates an output report in
default style but with each line preceded by a count of the number of times it
occurred.
   The *n* arguments specify skipping an initial portion of each line in the
comparison:

   −n   The first *n* fields together with any blanks before each are ig-
             nored. A field is defined as a string of non-blank characters
             separated by white space from its neighbors.
   +n   The first *n* characters are ignored. Fields are skipped before
             characters.

---

units — conversion program   UNITS(1)

units

   units converts quantities expressed in various standard scales to their
equivalents in other scales. It works interactively in this fashion:

                   You have: *inch*
                   You want: *cm*
                         * 2.54000e+00
                         / 3.93701e−01

A quantity is specified as a multiplicative combination of units optionally preceded by a numeric multiplier. Powers are indicated by suffixed positive integers, division by the usual sign:

> You have: *15 pounds force/in2*
> You want: *atm*
>   * 1.02069e+00
>   / 9.79730e−01

units only does multiplicative scale changes. Thus it can convert Kelvin to Rankine, but not Centigrade to Fahrenheit. Most familiar units, abbreviations, and metric prefixes are recognized, together with a generous leavening of exotica and a few constants of nature including:

pi	Ratio of circumference to diameter.
c	Speed of light.
e	Charge on an electron.
g	Acceleration of gravity.
force	Same as g.
mole	Avogadro's number.
water	Pressure head per unit height of water.
au	Astronomical unit.

pound is a unit of mass. Compound names are run together, e.g. **lightyear**. British units that differ from their US counterparts are prefixed thus: **brgallon**. Currency is denoted **belgiumfranc, britainpound,** ....

For a complete list of units, **cat /usr/lib/units**.

---

uucp − unix to unix copy   UUCP(1)

uucp [option] ... source-file ... destination-file

uucp copies files named by the source-file arguments to the destination-file argument. A file name may be a path name on your machine, or may have the form

system-name!pathname

where **system-name** is taken from a list of system names which uucp knows about. Shell metacharacters ?*[] appearing in the pathname part will be expanded on the appropriate system.

Pathnames may be one of the following.

- A full pathname.
- A pathname preceded by ~user; where **user** is a login-name on the specified system and is replaced by that user's login directory.
- Anything else is prefixed by the current directory.

If the result is an erroneous pathname for the remote system the copy will fail. If the destination-file is a directory, the last part of the source-file name is used. If a simple ~user destination is inaccessible to uucp, data is copied to a spool directory and the user is notified by mail(1).

uucp preserves execute permissions across the transmission and gives 0666 read and write permissions (see chmod(2)).

Options

-d   Make all necessary directories for the file copy.
-c   Use the source file when copying out rather than copying the
          file to the spool directory.
-m   Send mail to the requester when the copy is complete.

---

vi — screen oriented (visual) display editor   VI(1)

vi [-r] [+request] [-l] [-wn] name ...

   vi (visual) is the display oriented text editor described in chapter 3.

Options

-r x   Recover file x following a system crash or terminal hangup.
-r   Type a list of saved files.
-w n   Set the initial window size to *n.*
-x   Prompt for a key that will be used to encrypt and decrypt the
          file contents. (See also crypt(1).)
+ *request*
          Execute *request* before reading requests from the terminal;
          useful for initial positioning of the file. The default is to start
          at the last line of the document.

---

wc — word count   WC(1)

wc [-lwc]

   wc counts lines, words and characters in the named files, or in the standard input if no name appears. A word is a maximal string of characters delimited by white space.
   If an argument beginning with one of lwc is present, the specified counts
(lines, words or characters) are selected by the letters l, w, or c. The default
is -lwc.

---

who — who is on the system   WHO(1)

who [who-file] [am i]

   Without an argument, who lists the login name, terminal name, and login time for each logged in user. The system file /etc/utmp is examined to
obtain its information. If a file is given, that file is examined instead. Typically the given file will be /usr/adm/wtmp, which contains a record of all
the logins since it was created. Then who lists logins, logouts, and crashes
since the creation of the wtmp file. Each login is listed with user name, terminal name (with /dev/ suppressed), and date and time. When an argument is given, logouts produce a similar line without a user name.
   With two arguments, as in who am I (and also who are you), who tells
who you are logged in as.

---

write — write to another user   WRITE(1)

write user [ttyname]

write copies lines from your terminal to that of another user. When first
called, it sends the message

Message from yourname yourttyname...

The recipient of the message should write back at this point. Communication
continues until an end-of-file is read from the terminal or an interrupt is sent.
At that point write writes EOT on the other terminal and exits.

If you want to write to a user who is logged in more than once, the
ttyname argument may be used to indicate the appropriate terminal name.

Permission to write may be denied or granted by use of the mesg command. At the outset writing is allowed. Certain commands, in particular
nroff and pr(1) disallow messages in order to prevent messy output.

If the character ! occurs at the beginning of a line, write calls the shell to
execute the rest of the line as a command.

---

yacc — yet another compiler-compiler   YACC(1)

yacc [−vd] grammar

yacc converts a context-free grammar into a set of tables for a simple
automaton that executes an LR(1) parsing algorithm. The grammar may be
ambiguous; specified precedence rules are used to break ambiguities.

The output file, y.tab.c, is compiled by the C compiler to produce a program yyparse. This program is loaded with the lexical analyzer program,
yylex, as well as main and yyerror, an error handling routine. These routines
are supplied by the user; lex(1) is useful for creating lexical analyzers usable
by yacc.

If the −v flag is given, the file y.output is prepared, that contains a
description of the parsing tables and a report on conflicts generated by ambiguities in the grammar.

If the −d flag is used, the file y.tab.h is generated with the define statements that associate the yacc-assigned 'token codes' with the user-declared
'token names'. This allows source files other than y.tab.c to access the token
codes.

Appendix 2
System Calls

---

access — determine accessibility of file   ACCESS(2)

access(name, mode)
char *name;

    access checks the given file **name** for accessibility according to **mode**, which is 4 (read), 2 (write) or 1 (execute) or a combination thereof. Specifying mode 0 tests whether the directories leading to the file can be searched and the file exists.

    An appropriate error indication is returned if **name** cannot be found or if any of the desired access modes would not be granted. On disallowed accesses −1 is returned and the error code is in **errno**(2). 0 is returned from successful tests.

    The user-id and group-id with respect to which permission is checked are the real user-id and group-id of the process, so this call is useful to set-uid programs.

    Only the access bits are checked. A directory may be announced as writable by **access**, but an attempt to open it for writing will fail (although files may be created there); a file may look executable, but **exec** will fail unless it is in the proper format.

---

alarm — schedule signal after specified time   ALARM(2)

alarm(seconds)
unsigned seconds;

    alarm causes the signal **SIGALRM** (14) to be sent to the invoking process in a number of seconds given by the argument. Unless caught or ignored, the signal terminates the process.

    Alarm requests are not stacked; successive calls reset the alarm clock. If the argument is 0, any alarm request is canceled. Because the clock has a 1-second resolution, the signal may occur up to one second early; because of scheduling delays, resumption of execution of when the signal is caught may be delayed an arbitrary amount. The longest specifiable delay time is limited by the size of an unsigned integer.

    The return value is the amount of time remaining in the previously called alarm clock.

brk, sbrk — change core allocation   BRK(2)

```
char *brk(addr)
char *sbrk(incr)
```

brk sets the system's idea of the lowest location not used by the program (called the break) to addr (rounded up to the next multiple of 64 bytes on the PDP 11, 256 bytes on the Interdata 8/32, and 1024 bytes on a VAX 11). Locations not less than addr and below the stack pointer are not in the address space and will thus cause a memory violation if accessed.

In the alternate function sbrk, incr more bytes are added to the program's data space and a pointer to the start of the new area is returned.

When a program begins execution via exec the break is set at the highest location defined by the program and data storage areas. Ordinarily, therefore, only programs with growing data areas need to use these system calls.

chdir — change current working directory   CHDIR(2)

```
chdir(dirname)
char *dirname;
```

dirname is the address of the pathname of a directory, terminated by a null byte. chdir causes this directory to become the current working directory, the starting point for path names not beginning with /.

chmod — change mode of file   CHMOD(2)

```
chmod(name, mode)
char *name;
```

The file whose name is given as the null-terminated string pointed to by name has its mode changed to mode. Modes are constructed by a combination of the following:

04000	Set user-id on execution.
02000	Set group-id on execution.
01000	Save text image after execution.
00400	Read by owner.
00200	Write by owner.
00100	Execute (search on directory) by owner.
00070	Read, write, execute (search) by group.
00007	Read, write, execute (search) by others.

If an executable file is shared-text (the default) then mode 1000 prevents the system from abandoning the swap-space image of the program-text portion of the file when its last user terminates.

Only the owner of a file (or the super-user) may change the mode. Only the super-user can set the 1000 mode.

On some systems, writing or changing the owner of a file turns off the set-user-id bit. This makes the system somewhat more secure by protecting set-user-id files from remaining set-user-id if they are modified.

---

close — close a file   CLOSE(2)

close(fildes)

Given a file descriptor, **close** closes the associated file. A close of all files is automatic on **exit**, but since there is a limit on the number of open files per process, **close** is necessary for programs that deal with many files.

Files are closed upon termination of a process, and certain high-numbered file descriptors are closed automatically by **exec**(2).

---

creat — create a new file   CREAT(2)

creat(name, mode)
char *name;

creat creates a new file or prepares to rewrite an existing file called **name**, given as the address of a null-terminated string. If the file did not exist, it is given mode **mode**, as modified by the process's mode mask (see **umask**(2)). See **chmod**(2) for the definition of **mode**.

If the file did exist, its mode and owner remain unchanged but it is truncated to 0 length.

The file is also opened for writing, and its file descriptor is returned.

The **mode** given is arbitrary; it need not allow writing. However, the super-user can read any file regardless of its mode.

---

dup, dup2 — duplicate an open file descriptor   DUP(2)

dup(fildes)
int fildes;

dup2(fildes, fildes2)
int fildes, fildes2;

Given a file descriptor, **dup** allocates another file descriptor synonymous with the original. The new file descriptor is returned.

In the second form of the call, **fildes** is a file descriptor referring to an open file, and **fildes2** is a non-negative integer less than the maximum value allowed for file descriptors (approximately 19). **dup2** causes **fildes2** to refer to the same file as **fildes**. If **fildes2** already referred to an open file, it is closed first.

errno — system call error numbers   ERRNO(2)

#include <errno.h>

An error condition is indicated by an otherwise impossible value returned from a system call. Almost always this is −1; the individual sections specify the details. An error number is also made available in the external variable **errno. errno** is not cleared on successful calls, so it should be tested only after an error has occurred.

There is a table of messages associated with each error, and a routine for printing the message; see perror(3). Here is a list of the error numbers, their names as defined in the include file <errno.h>, and the messages available using **perror.**

1 EPERM Not owner

Typically this error indicates an attempt to modify a file in some way forbidden except to its owner or super-user. It is also returned for attempts by ordinary users to do things allowed only to the super-user.

2 ENOENT No such file or directory

This error occurs when a file name is specified and the file should exist but does not, or when one of the directories in a path name does not exist.

3 ESRCH No such process

The process whose number was given to signal and ptrace does not exist, or is already dead.

4 EINTR Interrupted system call

An asynchronous signal, such as interrupt or quit, that the user has elected to catch, occurred during a system call. If execution is resumed after processing the signal, it will appear as if the interrupted system call returned this error condition.

5 EIO I/O error

Some physical input-output error occurred during a **read** or **write**. This error may in some cases occur on a call following the one to which it actually applies.

6 ENXIO No such device or address

Input-output on a special file refers to a subdevice which does not exist, or beyond the limits of the device. It may also occur when, for example, a tape drive is not dialed in or no disk pack is loaded on a drive.

7 E2BIG Arg list too long

An argument list longer than 5120 or 10240 bytes is presented to **exec**. The length is system dependent.

8 ENOEXEC Exec format error

A request is made to execute a file which, although it has the appropriate permissions, is not an a.out file.

9 EBADF Bad file number

Either a file descriptor refers to no open file, or a read (resp. write) request is made to a file which is open only for writing

(resp. reading).
10 ECHILD No children
> Wait and the process has no living or unwaited-for children.

11 EAGAIN No more processes
> In a fork, the system's process table is full or the user is not allowed to create any more processes.

12 ENOMEM Not enough core
> During an exec or break, a program asks for more memory (core) than the system is able to supply. This is not a temporary condition; the maximum memory size is a system parameter. The error may also occur if the arrangement of text, data, and stack segments requires too many segmentation registers.

13 EACCES Permission denied
> An attempt was made to access a file in a way forbidden by the protection system.

14 EFAULT Bad address
> The system encountered a hardware fault in attempting to access the arguments of a system call.

15 ENOTBLK Block device required
> A plain file was mentioned where a block device was required, e.g. in mount.

16 EBUSY Mount device busy
> An attempt to mount a device that was already mounted or an attempt was made to dismount a device on which there is an active file directory (open file, current directory, mounted-on file, active text segment).

17 EEXIST File exists
> An existing file was mentioned in an inappropriate context, e.g. link.

18 EXDEV Cross-device link
> A link to a file on another device was attempted.

19 ENODEV No such device
> An attempt was made to apply an inappropriate system call to a device; e.g. read a write-only device.

20 ENOTDIR Not a directory
> A non-directory was specified where a directory is required, for example in a path name or as an argument to chdir.

21 EISDIR Is a directory
> An attempt to write on a directory.

22 EINVAL Invalid argument
> Some invalid argument: dismounting a non-mounted device, mentioning an unknown signal in signal, reading or writing a file for which lseek has generated a negative pointer. Also set by math functions.

23 ENFILE File table overflow
> The system's table of open files is full, and temporarily no more files can be opened.

24 EMFILE Too many open files

Customary configuration limit is 20 per process.

25 ENOTTY Not a terminal

The file mentioned in **stty** or **gtty** is not a terminal or one of the other devices to which these calls apply.

26 ETXTBSY Text file busy

An attempt to execute a shared-text program which is currently open for writing (or reading!). Also an attempt to open for writing a shared-text program that is being executed.

27 EFBIG File too large

The size of a file exceeded the maximum imposed by the system (about 10^9 bytes).

28 ENOSPC No space left on device

During a **write** to an ordinary file, there is no free space left on the device.

29 ESPIPE Illegal seek

An **lseek** was issued to a pipe. This error should also be issued for other non-seekable devices.

30 EROFS Read-only file system

An attempt to modify a file or directory was made on a device mounted read-only.

31 EMLINK Too many links

An attempt to make more than 32767 links to a file.

32 EPIPE Broken pipe

A write on a pipe for which there is no process to read the data. This condition normally generates a signal; the error is returned if the signal is ignored.

33 EDOM Math argument

The argument of a function in the mathematical library (3M) is out of the domain of the function.

34 ERANGE Result too large

The value of a function in the mathematical library (3M) is unrepresentable within machine precision.

---

exec l, exec v — execute a file   EXEC (2)

```
execl(name, arg0, arg1, ..., argn, 0)
char *name, *arg0, *arg1, ..., *argn;

execv(name, argv)
char *name, *argv[];

extern char **environ;
```

exec in all its forms overlays the calling process with the named file, then transfers to the entry point of the core image of the file. There can be no return from a successful exec; the calling core image is lost.

Files remain open across **exec** unless explicit arrangement has been made. Ignored/held signals remain ignored/held across these calls, but signals that are caught (see **signal**(2)) are reset to their default values.

Each user has a *real-user-id* and *real-group-id* and an *effective-user-id* and *effective-group-id*. The real-id identifies the person using the system; the effective-id determines his access privileges. exec changes the effective user-id and group-id to the owner of the executed file if the file has the *set-user-id* or *set-group-id* modes. The real user-id is not affected.

The name argument is a pointer to the name of the file to be executed. The pointers arg[0], arg[1], ..., address null-terminated strings. Conventionally arg[0] is the name of the file.

From C, two interfaces are available. execl is useful when a known file with known arguments is being called; the arguments to execl are the character strings constituting the file and the arguments; the first argument is, conventionally, the same as the file name (or its last component). A zero argument must end the argument list.

The execv version is useful when the number of arguments is unknown in advance; the arguments to execv are the name of the file to be executed and a vector of strings containing the arguments. The last argument string must be followed by a zero pointer.

argc is conventionally at least one and the first member of the array points to a string containing the name of the file.

argv is directly usable in another execv because argv[argc] is 0.

envp is a pointer to an array of strings that constitute the environment of the process. Each string consists of a name, an =, and a null-terminated string value. The array of pointers is terminated by a null pointer.

The C run-time start-off routine places a copy of envp in the global cell environ, which is used by execv and execl to pass the environment to any subprograms executed by the current program. The exec routines use lower-level routines as follows to pass an environment explicitly:

```
execve(file, argv, environ);
execle(file, arg0, arg1, ..., argn, 0, environ);
```

execlp and execvp are called with the same arguments as execl and execv, but duplicate the shell's actions in searching for an executable file in a list of directories. The directory list is obtained from the environment.

To aid execution of command files of various programs, if the first two characters of the executable file are #! then exec attempts to read a pathname from the executable file and use that program as the command interpreter for the command file.

A single parameter may be passed the interpreter, specified after the name of the interpreter; its length and the length of the name of the interpreter combined must not exceed 32 characters. The space or tab following the #! is mandatory, and the pathname must be explicit (no paths are searched).

exit — terminate process   EXIT(2)

exit(status)
int status;

_exit(status)
int status;

exit is the normal means of terminating a process. exit closes all the process's files and notifies the parent process when it executes a **wait**. The low-order 8 bits of **status** are available to the parent process.

This call can never return.

The C function **exit** may cause cleanup actions before the final exit. The function _exit circumvents all cleanup, and should be used to terminate a child process after a **fork**(2) to avoid flushing buffered output twice.

---

fork — spawn new process   FORK(2)

fork()

fork is the only way a new process is created. With **fork**, the new process's core image is a copy of that of the caller of **fork**. The only distinction is that the value returned in the old (parent) process contains the process-id of the new (child) process, while the value returned in the child is 0. Process-id's range from 1 to 30,000. This process-id is returned by **wait**(2).

Files open before the fork are shared, and have a common read-write pointer. In particular, this is the way that standard input and output files are passed and also how pipes are set up.

---

getuid, getgid, geteuid, getegid — get user and group identity   GETUID(2)
getpid — get process identification

getuid()
geteuid()
getgid()
getegid()
getpid()

getuid returns the real user-id of the current process, **geteuid** the effective user-id. The real user-id identifies the person who is logged in, in contradistinction to the effective user-id, that determines the access permission at the moment. It is thus useful to programs using the *set user-id* mode, to find out who invoked them.

getgid returns the real group-id, **getegid** the effective group-id.

getpid returns the process-id of the current process. Most often it is used to generate uniquely-named temporary files.

---

ioctl, stty, gtty — control device   IOCTL(2)

```
#include <sgtty.h>
ioctl(fildes, request, argp)
struct sgttyb *argp;
```

```
stty(fildes, argp)
struct sgttyb *argp;
```

```
gtty(fildes, argp)
struct sgttyb *argp;
```

ioctl performs a variety of functions on character special files (devices). For certain status setting and status inquiries about terminal devices, the functions stty and gtty are equivalent to

```
ioctl(fildes, TIOCSETP, argp)
ioctl(fildes, TIOCGETP, argp)
```

respectively.

Several ioctl(2) calls apply to terminals. Most of them use the following structure, defined in <sgtty.h>:

```
struct sgttyb {
        char    sg_ispeed;
        char    sg_ospeed;
        char    sg_erase;
        char    sg_kill;
        int     sg_flags;
};
```

The sg_ispeed and sg_ospeed fields describe the input and output speeds of the device according to the following table, which corresponds to the DEC DH-11 interface. If other hardware is used, impossible speed changes are ignored. Symbolic values in the table are as defined in <sgtty.h>.

B0	0	(hang up dataphone)
B50	1	50 baud
B75	2	75 baud
B110	3	110 baud
B134	4	134.5 baud
B150	5	150 baud
B200	6	200 baud
B300	7	300 baud
B600	8	600 baud
B1200	9	1200 baud
B1800	10	1800 baud
B2400	11	2400 baud
B4800	12	4800 baud
B9600	13	9600 baud
EXTA	14	External A
EXTB	15	External B

In the current configuration, only 110, 150, 300 and 1200 baud are really supported on dial-up lines. Code conversion and line control required for IBM 2741's (134.5 baud) must be implemented by the user's program. The half-duplex line discipline required for the 202 dataset (1200 baud) is not supplied; full-duplex 212 datasets work fine.

The **sg_erase** and **sg_kill** fields of the argument structure specify the erase and kill characters respectively. (Defaults are # and @.)

The **sg_flags** field of the argument structure contains several bits that determine the system's treatment of the terminal:

ALLDELAY	0177400	Delay algorithm selection
BSDELAY	0100000	Select backspace delays (not implemented):
BS0	0	
BS1	0100000	
VTDELAY	0040000	Select form-feed and vertical-tab delays:
FF0	0	
FF1	0100000	
CRDELAY	0030000	Select carriage-return delays:
CR0	0	
CR1	0010000	
CR2	0020000	
CR3	0030000	
TBDELAY	0006000	Select tab delays:
TAB0	0	
TAB1	0001000	
TAB2	0004000	
XTABS	0006000	
NLDELAY	0001400	Select newline delays:
NL0	0	
NL1	0000400	
NL2	0001000	
NL3	0001400	
EVENP	0000200	Even parity allowed on input (most terminals)
ODDP	0000100	Odd parity allowed on input
RAW	0000040	Raw mode: wake up on all characters, 8-bit interface
CRMOD	0000020	Map CR into LF; echo LF or CR as CR-LF
ECHO	0000010	Echo (full duplex)
LCASE	0000004	Map upper case to lower on input
CBREAK	0000002	Return each character as soon as typed
TANDEM	0000001	Automatic flow control

The delay bits specify how long transmission stops to allow for mechanical or other movement when certain characters are sent to the terminal. In all cases a value of 0 indicates no delay.

Backspace delays are currently ignored but might be used for Terminet 300's.

If a form-feed/vertical tab delay is specified, it lasts for about 2 seconds.

Carriage-return delay type 1 lasts about .08 seconds and is suitable for the Terminet 300. Delay type 2 lasts about .16 seconds and is suitable for the VT05 and the TI 700. Delay type 3 is unimplemented and is 0.

New-line delay type 1 is dependent on the current column and is tuned for Teletype model 37's. Type 2 is useful for the VT05 and is about .10 seconds. Type 3 is unimplemented and is 0.

Tab delay type 1 is dependent on the amount of movement and is tuned to the Teletype model 37. Type 3, called XTABS, is not a delay at all but causes tabs to be replaced by the appropriate number of spaces on output.

Characters with the wrong parity, as determined by bits 200 and 100, are ignored.

In raw mode, every character is passed immediately to the program without waiting until a full line has been typed. No erase or kill processing is done; the end-of-file indicator (EOT), the interrupt character (DEL) and the quit character (FS) are not treated specially. There are no delays and no echoing, and no replacement of one character for another; characters are a full 8 bits for both input and output (parity is up to the program).

Mode 020 causes input carriage returns to be turned into newlines; input of either CR or LF causes LF-CR both to be echoed (for terminals with a newline function).

CBREAK is a sort of half-cooked (rare?) mode. Programs can read each character as soon as typed, instead of waiting for a full line, but quit and interrupt work, and output delays, case-translation, CRMOD, XTABS, ECHO, and parity work normally. On the other hand there is no erase or kill, and no special treatment of \ or EOT.

TANDEM mode causes the system to produce a stop character (default DC3) whenever the input queue is in danger of overflowing, and a start character (default DC1) when the input queue has drained sufficiently. It is useful for flow control when the 'terminal' is actually another machine that obeys the conventions.

Several ioctl calls have the form:

```
#include  <sgtty.h>

ioctl(fildes, code, arg)
struct sgttyb *arg;
```

The applicable codes are:

TIOCGETP

> Fetch the parameters associated with the terminal, and store in the pointed-to structure.

TIOCSETP

> Set the parameters according to the pointed-to structure. The interface delays until output is quiescent, then throws away any unread characters, before changing the modes.

TIOCSETN

> Switching out of RAW or CBREAK mode may cause some garbage input.

With the following codes the arg is ignored.

TIOCEXCL

> Set 'exclusive-use' mode: no further opens are permitted until the file has been closed.

TIOCNXCL

Turn off 'exclusive-use' mode.

TIOCHPCL

When the file is closed for the last time, hang up the terminal. This is useful when the line is associated with an ACU used to place outgoing calls.

TIOCFLUSH

All characters waiting in input or output queues are flushed.

The following codes affect characters that are special to the terminal interface. The argument is a pointer to the following structure, defined in <sgtty.h>:

```
struct tchars {
        char      t_intrc;            /* interrupt */
        char      t_quitc;            /* quit */
        char      t_startc;           /* start output */
        char      t_stopc;            /* stop output */
        char      t_eofc;             /* end-of-file */
        char      t_brkc;             /* input delimiter (like nl) */
};
```

The default values for these characters are system dependent. A character value of -1 eliminates the effect of that character. The t_brkc character, by default -1, acts like a newline in that it terminates a 'line,' is echoed, and is passed to the program. The 'stop' and 'start' characters may be the same, to produce a toggle effect. It is probably counterproductive to make other special characters (including erase an kill) identical.

The calls are:

TIOCSETC

Change the various special characters to those given in the structure.

TIOCSETP

Set the special characters to those given in the structure.

---

kill — send signal to a process   KILL(2)

kill(pid, sig)

kill sends the signal **sig** to the process specified by the process number **pid**. The sending and receiving processes must have the same effective userid, otherwise this call is restricted to the super-user.

If the process number is 0, the signal is sent to all other processes in the sender's process group.

Processes may send signals to themselves.

---

link — link to a file   LINK(2)

link(name1, name2)
char *name1, *name2;

A link to name1 is created; the link has the name name2. Either name may be an arbitrary path name, subject to the restriction that both files are on the same physical file system.

---

lseek — move read/write pointer   LSEEK(2)

long lseek(fildes, offset, whence)
long offset;

The file descriptor refers to a file open for reading or writing. The read (respectively write) pointer for the file is set depending on whence as shown below.

The returned value is the resulting pointer location. Seeking far beyond the end of a file, then writing, creates a gap that occupies no physical space and reads as zeros.

0   The pointer is set to offset bytes.
1   The pointer is set to its current location plus offset.
2   The pointer is set to the size of the file plus offset.

---

nice — set process priority   NICE(2)

nice(incr)

The scheduling priority of the process is augmented by incr. Positive priorities get less service than normal. Priority 10 is recommended to users who wish to execute long-running programs.

Negative increments are ignored except on behalf of the super-user. The priority is limited to the range −20 (most urgent) to 20 (least).

The priority of a process is passed to a child process by fork(2). For a privileged process to return to normal priority from an unknown state, nice should be called successively with arguments −40 (goes to priority −20 because of truncation), 20 (to get to 0), then 0 (to maintain compatibility with previous versions of this call).

---

open — open for reading or writing   OPEN(2)

open(name, mode)
char *name;

open opens the file name for reading (if mode is 0), writing (if mode is 1) or for both reading and writing (if mode is 2). name is the address of a string representing a path name, terminated by a null character.

The file is positioned at the beginning (byte 0). The returned file descriptor may be used to subsequent calls for other input-output functions on the file.

---

pause — stop until signal   PAUSE(2)

pause()

   pause never returns normally. It is used to give up control while waiting for a signal from **kill**(2) or **alarm**(2).

---

pipe — create an inter-process channel   PIPE(2)

pipe(fildes)
int fildes[2];

   The **pipe** system call creates an input-output mechanism called a pipe. The file descriptors returned can be used in read and write operations. When the pipe is written using the descriptor **fildes**[1] up to 4096 bytes of data are buffered before the writing process is suspended. The data may be read from **fildes**[0].

   It is assumed that after the pipe has been created, two (or more) cooperating processes (created by subsequent **fork** calls) will pass data through the pipe with **read** and **write** calls.

   Read calls on an empty pipe (no buffered data) with only one end (all write file descriptors closed) returns an end-of-file.

---

profil — execution time profile   PROFIL(2)

profil(buff, bufsiz, offset, scale)
char *buff;
int bufsiz, offset, scale;

   buff points to an area of memory whose length, in bytes, is given by **bufsiz**. After this call, the user's program counter (pc) is examined each clock tick (1/60 seconds); **offset** is subtracted from it, and the result multiplied by **scale**. If the resulting number corresponds to a word inside **buff**, that word is incremented.

   The scale is interpreted as an unsigned, fixed-point fraction with binary point at the left: 0177777(8) gives a 1-1 mapping of pc's to words in **buff**; 077777(8) maps each pair of instruction words together. 02(8) maps all instructions onto the beginning of **buff** (producing a non-interrupting core clock).

   Profiling is turned off by giving a **scale** of 0 or 1. It is rendered ineffective by giving a **bufsiz** of 0. Profiling is also turned off after an **exec** call, but remains on in both child and parent after a **fork**. Profiling may be turned off if an update in **buff** would cause a memory fault.

---

read — read from file   READ(2)

```
read(fildes, buffer, nbytes)
char *buffer;
```

fildes corresponds to an open file and buffer is the location of nbytes contiguous memory into which the input will be placed. It is not guaranteed that all nbytes bytes will be read; for example if the file refers to a typewriter at most one line will be returned. In any event the number of characters read is returned.

If the returned value is 0, then end-of-file has been reached.

---

setuid, setgid — set user-id and group-id   SETUID(2)

```
setuid(uid)
setgid(gid)
```

The user-id (group-id) of the current process is set to the argument. Both the effective-id and the real-id are set. These calls are only permitted to the super-user or if the argument is the real-id or effective-id.

---

signal — catch or ignore signals   SIGNAL(2)

```
#include <signal.h>
(*signal(sig, func))()
void (*func)();
```

A signal is generated by some abnormal event, initiated either by user at a terminal (quit, interrupt), by a program error (bus error, etc.), or by request of another program (kill). Normally all signals cause termination of the receiving process, but a signal call allows them either to be ignored or to cause an interrupt to a specified location. The signals are listed in section 6.6.1.

If func is SIG_DFL, the default action for signal sig is reinstated; this default is termination, sometimes with a core image. If func is SIG_IGN the signal is ignored. Otherwise when the signal occurs func will be called with the signal number as argument. A return from the function will continue the process at the point it was interrupted.

Except for signals 4 and 5, a signal is reset to SIG_DFL after being caught. Thus if it is desired to catch every such signal, the catching routine must issue another signal call.

If a caught signal occurs during certain system calls, the call terminates prematurely. In particular this can occur during an ioctl, read, or write(2) on a slow device (like a terminal; but not a file); and during pause or wait(2). When such a signal occurs, the saved user status is arranged in such a way that when return from the signal-catching takes place, it will appear that the system call returned an error status. The user's program may then, if it wishes, re-execute the call.

The value of signal is the previous (or initial) value of func for the particular signal.

After a fork(2) the child inherits all signals. exec(2) resets all caught signals to default action.

---

stat, fstat — get file status   STAT(2)

```
#include <sys/types.h>
#include <sys/stat.h>

stat(name, buf)
char *name;
struct stat *buf;

fstat(fildes, buf)
struct stat *buf;
```

stat obtains detailed information about a named file. fstat obtains the same information about an open file associated with a valid file descriptor.

name points to a null-terminated string naming a file; buf is the address of a buffer into which information is placed concerning the file. It is unnecessary to have any permissions at all with respect to the file, but all directories leading to the file must be searchable. The layout of the structure pointed to by buf is defined in <sys/stat.h> and is explained in chapter 6.

The include file <sys/types.h> is also required to provide the necessary type declarations. ino_t, off_t, and time_t, name various width integer values; dev_t encodes major and minor device numbers.

When fildes is associated with a pipe, fstat reports an ordinary file with an i-node number, restricted permissions, and a not necessarily meaningful length.

st_atime is the time the file was last read. For reasons of efficiency, it is not set when a directory is searched, although this would be more logical. st_mtime is the time the file was last written or created. It is not set by changes of owner, group, link count, or mode. st_ctime is set both by writing and changing the i-node.

---

time, ftime — get date and time   TIME(2)

```
long time(0)

long time(tloc)
long *tloc;

#include <sys/types.h>
#include <sys/timeb.h>
ftime(tp)
struct timeb *tp;
```

time returns the time since 00:00:00 GMT, Jan. 1, 1970, measured in seconds. If tloc is non-null, the return value is also stored in *tloc.

The ftime entry fills in a structure pointed to by its argument, as defined by <sys/timeb.h>:

The structure contains the time since the epoch in seconds, up to 1000 milliseconds of more-precise interval, the local time zone (measured in minutes of time westward from Greenwich), and a flag that, if non-zero, indicates that Daylight Saving Time applies locally during the appropriate part of the year.

---

times — get process times   TIMES(2)

```
#include <sys/types.h>
#include <sys/times.h>

times(buffer)
struct tms *buffer;
```

    times returns time-accounting information for the current process and for the terminated child processes of the current process. All times are in 1/HZ seconds, where HZ is either 50 or 60 depending on your locality.

    The children times are the sum of the children's process times and their children's times.

---

umask — set file creation mode mask   UMASK(2)

```
umask(complmode)
```

    umask sets a mask used whenever a file is created by creat(2) or mkdir(1). The actual mode (see chmod(2)) of the newly-created file is the logical AND of the given mode and the complement of the argument. Only the low-order 9 bits of the mask (the protection bits) participate. The mask shows the bits to be turned off when files are created. The previous value of the mask is returned by the call.

---

unlink — remove directory entry   UNLINK(2)

```
unlink(name)
char *name;
```

    name points to a null-terminated string. unlink removes the entry for the file pointed to by **name** from its directory. If this entry was the last link to the file, the contents of the file are freed and the file is destroyed. If, however, the file was open in any process, the actual destruction is delayed until it is closed, even though the directory entry has disappeared.

---

wait — wait for process to terminate   WAIT(2)

```
wait(status)
int *status;

wait(0)
```

    wait causes its caller to delay until a signal is received or one of its child processes terminates. If any child has died since the last wait, return is immediate; if there are no children, return is immediate with the error bit set (resp. with a value of −1 returned). The normal return yields the process-id of the terminated child. In the case of several children several **wait** calls are needed to learn of all the deaths.

If **(int) status** is non-zero, the high byte of the word pointed to receives the low byte of the argument of **exit** when the child terminated. The low byte receives the termination status of the process.

If the parent process terminates without waiting on its children, the initialization process (process-id 1) inherits the children.

---

write — write on a file   **WRITE (2)**

write(fildes, buffer, nbytes)
char *buffer;

A file descriptor is a word returned from a successful **open, creat, dup,** or **pipe**(2) call. **buffer** is the address of **nbytes** contiguous memory that are written on the output file. The number of characters actually written is returned. It should be regarded as an error if this is not the same as requested.

Writes which are multiples of a block and begin on a block boundary in the file are more efficient than any others.

Appendix 3
C Subroutines

---

ctime, localtime, gmtime, asctime — convert date and time   CTIME(3)
timezone — name of the time zone

```
char *ctime(clock)
long *clock;
```

```
#include <time.h>
```

```
struct tm *localtime(clock)
long *clock;
```

```
struct tm *gmtime(clock)
long *clock;
```

```
char *asctime(tm)
struct tm *tm;
```

```
char *timezone(zone, dst)
```

ctime converts a time pointed to by clock such as returned by time(2) into an ASCII string and returns a pointer to a 26-character string in the following form. All the fields have constant width.

```
Sun Sep 16 01:03:52 1973\n\0
```

localtime and gmtime return pointers to structures containing the broken-down time. localtime corrects for the time zone and possible Daylight Saving Time; gmtime converts directly to GMT, which is the time UNIX uses. asctime converts a broken-down time to ASCII and returns a pointer to a 26-character string.

The structure declaration from the include file is:

```
struct tm {  /* see ctime(3) */
        int     tm_sec;
        int     tm_min;
        int     tm_hour;
        int     tm_mday;
        int     tm_mon;
        int     tm_year;
        int     tm_wday;
        int     tm_yday;
        int     tm_isdst;
};
```

These quantities give the time on a 24-hour clock, day of month (1-31), month of year (0-11), day of week (Sunday = 0), year − 1900, day of year (0-365), and a flag that is non-zero if Daylight Saving Time is in effect.

When local time is called for, the program consults the system to determine the time zone and whether the standard USA Daylight Saving Time adjustment is appropriate. The program knows about the peculiarities of this conversion in 1974 and 1975; if necessary, a table for these years can be extended.

timezone returns the name of the time zone associated with its first argument, which is measured in minutes westward from Greenwich. If the second argument is 0, the standard name is used, otherwise the Daylight Saving version. If the required name does not appear in a table built into the routine, the difference from GMT is produced; e.g. in Afghanistan timezone(−(60*4+30), 0) is appropriate because it is 4:30 ahead of GMT and the string GMT+4:30 is produced.

---

fclose, fflush − close or flush a stream   FCLOSE(3S)

#include <stdio.h>

fclose(stream)
FILE *stream;

fflush(stream)
FILE *stream;

fclose causes any buffers for the named stream to be emptied, and the file to be closed. Buffers allocated by the standard input-output system are freed. fclose is performed automatically upon calling exit(2).

fflush causes any buffered data for the named output stream to be written to that file. The stream remains open.

These routines return EOF if stream is not associated with an output file, or if buffered data cannot be transferred to that file.

---

feof, ferror, clearerr, fileno − stream status inquiries   FERROR(3S)

#include <stdio.h>

feof(stream)
FILE *stream;

ferror(stream)
FILE *stream

clearerr(stream)
FILE *stream

fileno(stream)
FILE *stream;

feof returns non-zero when end-of-file is read on the named input stream, otherwise zero.

298   The UNIX System   FERROR (3S)

ferror returns non-zero when an error has occurred reading or writing
the named stream, otherwise zero. Unless cleared by clearerr, the error indication lasts until the stream is closed.

clrerr resets the error indication on the named stream.

fileno returns the integer file descriptor associated with the stream.

These functions are implemented as macros and cannot be redeclared.

---

fopen, freopen, fdopen — open a stream   FOPEN (3S)

#include <stdio.h>

FILE *fopen(filename, type)
char *filename, *type;

FILE *freopen(filename, type, stream)
char *filename, *type;
FILE *stream;

FILE *fdopen(fildes, type)
char *type;

fopen opens the file named by filename and associates a stream with it.
fopen returns a pointer used to identify the stream in subsequent operations.
type is a character string having one of the following values.

r   Open for reading.
w   Create for writing.
a   Open for writing at the end of file, or create for writing.

fopen and freopen return the pointer NULL if filename cannot be accessed.

In addition, each type may be followed by a + to have the file opened
for reading and writing. r+p positions the stream at the beginning of the file,
w+ creates or truncates it, and a+ positions it at the end. Both reads and
writes may be used on read/write streams, with the limitation that an fseek,
rewind, or reading an end-of-file must be used between a read and a write or
vice-versa.

freopen substitutes the named file in place of the open stream. It returns
the original value of stream. The original stream is closed.

freopen is typically used to attach the preopened constant names, stdin,
stdout, stderr, to specified files.

fdopen associates a stream with a file descriptor obtained from open,
dup, creat, or pipe(2). The type of the stream must agree with the mode of
the open file.

fread, fwrite — buffered binary input/output   FREAD(3S)

#include <stdio.h>

fread(ptr, sizeof(*ptr), nitems, stream)
FILE *stream;

fwrite(ptr, sizeof(*ptr), nitems, stream)
FILE *stream;

fread reads, into a block beginning at ptr, nitems of data of the type of
*ptr from the named input stream. It returns the number of items actually
read.

fread and fwrite return 0 upon end-of-file or error.

If stream is *stdin* and the standard output is line buffered, then any partial output line will be flushed before any call to read(2) to satisfy the fread.

fwrite appends at most nitems of data of the type of *ptr beginning at
ptr to the named output stream. It returns the number of items actually written.

fseek, ftell, rewind — reposition a stream   FSEEK(3S)

#include <stdio.h>

fseek(stream, offset, ptrname)
FILE *stream;
long offset;

long ftell(stream)
FILE *stream;

rewind(stream)

fseek sets the position of the next input or output operation on the
stream. The new position is at the signed distance offset bytes from the beginning, the current position, or the end of the file, according as ptrname has
the value 0, 1, or 2.

fseek undoes any effects of ungetc(3S).

ftell returns the current value of the offset relative to the beginning of
the file associated with the named stream. It is measured in bytes and is the
only foolproof way to obtain an offset for fseek.

rewind(stream) is equivalent to fseek(stream, 0L, 0).

fseek returns −1 for improper seeks.

---

getc, getchar, fgetc, getw — get character or word from streamGETC(3S)

#include <stdio.h>

int getc(stream)
FILE *stream;

int getchar()

int fgetc(stream)
FILE *stream;

int getw(stream)
FILE *stream;

getc returns the next character from the named input stream.

getchar() is identical to getc(stdin).

fgetc behaves like getc, but is a genuine function, not a macro.

getw returns the next word (32-bit integer on a VAX 11) from the named input stream. It returns the constant EOF upon end-of-file or error, but since that is an integer value, feof and ferror(3) should be used to check the success of getw. No special alignment in the file is assumed by getw.

These functions return the integer constant EOF at end-of-file or upon read error.

A stop with message, *Reading bad file,* means an attempt has been made to read from a stream that has not been opened for reading by fopen.

---

getenv — value for environment name   GETENV(3)

extern char **environ;

char *getenv(name)
char *name;

getenv searches the environment list for a string of the form name = value and returns value if such a string is present, otherwise 0.

The external variable environ is an array of strings called the environment and is made available by exec(2) when a process begins. By convention these strings have the form name = value.

Further names may be placed in the environment by the export command and name=value arguments in sh(1). Arguments may also be placed in the environment at the point of an exec(2).

---

gets, fgets — get a string from a stream   GETS(3S)

#include <stdio.h>

char *gets(s)
char *s;

char *fgets(s, n, stream)
char *s;

FILE *stream;

gets reads a string into s from the standard input stream *stdin*. The string is terminated by a newline, which is replaced in s by a null character. gets returns its argument.

fgets reads n—1 characters, or up to a newline character, whichever comes first, from the stream into the string s. The last character read into s is followed by a null character. fgets returns its first argument.

gets and fgets return the constant pointer NULL upon end of file or error.

---

malloc, free, realloc, calloc — main memory allocator   MALLOC(3)

```
char *malloc(size)
unsigned size;

free(ptr)
char *ptr;

char *realloc(ptr, size)
char *ptr;
unsigned size;

char *calloc(nelem, elsize)
unsigned nelem, elsize;
```

and free provide a simple general-purpose memory allocation package. malloc returns a pointer to a block of at least size bytes beginning on a word boundary.

The argument to free is a pointer to a block previously allocated by malloc this space is made available for further allocation, but its contents are left undisturbed.

Needless to say, grave disorder will result if the space assigned by malloc is overrun or if some random number is handed to free

malloc allocates the first block of contiguous free space that is large enough found in a circular search from the last block allocated or freed, coalescing adjacent free blocks as it searches. It calls sbrk (see break(2)) to get more memory from the system when there is no suitable space already free.

realloc changes the size of the block pointed to by ptr to size bytes and returns a pointer to the (possibly moved) block. The contents will be unchanged up to the lesser of the new and old sizes.

realloc also works if ptr points to a block freed since the last call of malloc, realloc or calloc thus sequences of free, malloc and realloc can exploit the search strategy of malloc to do storage compaction.

calloc allocates space for an array of nelem elements of size elsize. The space is initialized to zeros.

Each of the allocation routines returns a pointer to space suitably aligned for storage of any type of object.

malloc, realloc and calloc return a null pointer (0) if there is no available memory or if the arena has been detectably corrupted by storing outside the bounds of a block.

When **realloc** returns 0, the block pointed to by **ptr** may be destroyed.

---

mktemp — make a unique file name   MKTEMP(3)

```
char *mktemp(template)
char *template;
```

   mktemp replaces **template** by a unique file name, and returns the address of the template. The template should be a file name with six trailing X's, that will be replaced with the current process-id and a unique letter.

---

monitor — prepare execution profile   MONITOR(3)

```
monitor(lowpc, highpc, buffer, bufsize, nfunc)
int (*lowpc)(), (*highpc)();
short buffer[];
```

   An executable program created by **cc −p** automatically includes calls for **monitor** with default parameters; **monitor** need not be called explicitly except to gain fine control over profiling.

   monitor is an interface to **profil**(2). **lowpc** and **highpc** are the addresses of two functions; **buffer** is the address of a (user supplied) array of **bufsize** short integers. **monitor** arranges to record a histogram of periodically sampled values of the program counter, and of counts of calls of certain functions, in the buffer. The lowest address sampled is that of **lowpc** and the highest is just below **highpc**. At most **nfunc** call counts can be kept; only calls of functions compiled with the profiling option −p of **cc**(1) are recorded. For the results to be significant, especially where there are small, heavily used routines, it is suggested that the buffer be no more than a few times smaller than the range of locations sampled.

---

perror, sys_errlist, sys_nerr — system error messages   PERROR(3)

```
perror(s)
char *s;

extern int sys_nerr;
extern char *sys_errlist[];
```

   perror produces a short error message on the standard error file describing the last error encountered during a call to the system from a C program. First the argument string **s** is printed, then a :, then the message and a newline. Most usefully, the argument string is the name of the program that incurred the error. The error number is taken from the external variable **errno** which is set when errors occur but not cleared when non-erroneous calls are made.

   To simplify variant formatting of messages, the vector of message strings **sys_errlist** is provided; **errno** can be used as an index in this table to get the message string without the newline. **sys_nerr** is the number of messages provided for in the table; it should be checked because new error codes may be added to the system before they are added to the table.

---

popen, pclose — initiate input-output to/from a process   POPEN(3S)

#include <stdio.h>

FILE *popen(command, type)
char *command, *type;

pclose(stream)
FILE *stream;

The arguments to popen are pointers to null-terminated strings containing respectively a shell command line and an input-output mode, either r for reading or w for writing. It creates a pipe between the calling process and the command to be executed. The value returned is a stream pointer that can be used (as appropriate) to write to the standard input of the command or read from its standard output.

A stream opened by popen should be closed by pclose, that waits for the associated process to terminate and returns the exit status of the command.

Because open files are shared, a type r command may be used as an input filter, and a type w as an output filter.

popen returns NULL if files or processes cannot be created, or the shell cannot be accessed.

pclose returns −1 if stream is not obtained via popen.

---

printf, fprintf, sprintf — formatted output conversion   PRINTF(3S)

#include <stdio.h>

printf(format [, arg] ...)
char *format;

fprintf(stream, format [, arg] ...)
FILE *stream;
char *format;

sprintf(s, format [, arg] ...)
char *s, format;

printf places output on the standard output stream stdout. fprintf places output on the named output stream. sprintf places output in the string s, followed by the null character.

Each of these functions converts, formats, and prints its second and subsequent arguments under control of the first argument. The first argument is a character string that contains two types of objects: plain characters, that are simply copied to the output stream, and conversion specifications, each of which causes conversion and printing of the next successive arg printf.

Each conversion specification is introduced by the character % followed by one of the following.

•   An optional minus sign − specifies left adjustment of the converted value in the indicated field.

- An optional digit string specifies a field width; if the converted value has fewer characters than the field width it will be blank-padded on the left (or right, if the left adjustment indicator has been given) to make up the field width; if the field width begins with a zero, zero-padding will be used instead of blank-padding.
- An optional period . serves to separate the field width from the next digit string.
- An optional digit string, precision, specifies the number of digits to appear after the decimal point, for e- and f-conversion, or the maximum number of characters to be printed from a string.
- The letter l specifies that a following d, o, x, or u corresponds to a long integer arg. (A capitalized conversion code accomplishes the same thing.)
- A character that indicates the type of conversion to be applied.

A field width or precision may be * instead of a digit string. In this case an integer arg supplies the field width or precision.

The conversion characters and their meanings are as follows. In no case does a non-existent or small field width cause truncation of a field; padding takes place only if the specified field width exceeds the actual width. Characters generated by printf are printed by putc(3).

dox   The integer arg is converted to decimal, octal, or hexadecimal notation respectively.

f   The float or double arg is converted to decimal notation in the style [−]ddd.ddd where the number of d's after the decimal point is equal to the precision specification for the argument. If the precision is missing, 6 digits are given; if the precision is explicitly 0, no digits and no decimal point are printed.

e   The float or double arg is converted in the style [−]d.ddd e ± dd where there is one digit before the decimal point and the number after is equal to the precision specification for the argument; when the precision is missing, 6 digits are produced.

g   The float or double arg is printed in style d, in style f, or in style e, whichever gives full precision in minimum space.

c   The character arg is printed.

s   arg is taken to be a string (char pointer) and characters from the string are printed until a null character or until the number of characters indicated by the precision specification is reached; however if the precision is 0, or missing, all characters up to a null are printed.

u   The unsigned integer arg is converted to decimal and printed (the result will be in the range 0 through MAXUINT, where MAXUINT equals 4294967295 on a VAX 11 and 65535 on a PDP 11).

%   Print a %; no argument is converted.

putc, putchar, fputc, putw — put character or word on a stream PUTC(3S)

#include <stdio.h>

int putc(c, stream)
char c;
FILE *stream;

putchar(c)

fputc(c, stream)
FILE *stream;

putw(w, stream)
FILE *stream;

putc appends the character c to the named output stream. It returns the character written.

putchar(c) is defined as putc(c, stdout).

fputc behaves like putc, but is a genuine function rather than a macro.

putw appends an int sized word w to the output stream. It returns the word written. putw neither assumes nor causes special alignment in the file.

The standard stream stdout is normally buffered if and only if the output does not refer to a terminal; this default may be changed by setbuf(3S). The standard stream stderr is by default unbuffered unconditionally, but use of freopen will cause it to become buffered; setbuf, again, will set the state to whatever is desired. When an output stream is unbuffered information appears on the destination file or terminal as soon as written; when it is buffered characters are saved up and written as a block. fflush may be used to force the block out before it has been filled.

These functions return the constant EOF upon error. Since this is an integer, ferror(3) should be used to detect putw errors.

---

puts, fputs — put a string on a stream   PUTS(3S)

#include <stdio.h>

puts(s)
char *s;

fputs(s, stream)
char *s;
FILE *stream;

puts copies the null-terminated string s to the standard output stream, stdout, and appends a newline.

fputs copies the null-terminated string s to the named output stream.

Neither routine copies the terminal null character.

scanf, fscanf, sscanf — formatted input conversion   SCANF(3S)

#include <stdio.h>

scanf(format [, pointer] ...)
char *format;

fscanf(stream, format [, pointer] ...)
FILE *stream;
char *format;

sscanf(s, format [, pointer] ...)
char *s, *format;

scanf reads from the standard input stream stdin. fscanf reads from the named input stream. sscanf reads from the character string s. Each function reads characters, interprets them according to a format, and stores the results in its arguments. Each expects as arguments a control string format, described below, and a set of pointer arguments indicating where the converted input should be stored.

The control string may contain conversion specifications, that are used to direct interpretation of input sequences. The control string may contain:

- spaces, tabs, or newlines, that match optional white space in the input.
- An ordinary character (not %) that must match the next character of the input stream.
- Conversion specifications, consisting of the character %, an optional assignment suppressing character *, an optional numerical maximum field width, and a conversion character.

A conversion specification directs the conversion of the next input field; the result is placed in the variable pointed to by the corresponding argument, unless assignment suppression was indicated by *. An input field is defined as a string of non-blank characters; it extends to the next inappropriate character or until the field width, if specified, is exhausted.

The conversion character indicates the interpretation of the input field; the corresponding pointer argument must usually be of a restricted type. The following conversion characters are legal:

%   A single % is expected in the input at this point; no assignment is done.

d   A decimal integer is expected; the corresponding argument should be an integer pointer.

o   An octal integer is expected; the corresponding argument should be an integer pointer.

x   A hexadecimal integer is expected; the corresponding argument should be an integer pointer.

s   A character string is expected; the corresponding argument should be a character pointer pointing to an array of characters large enough to accept the string and a terminating null character, that

will be added. The input field is terminated by a **space** or a
newline.

c   A character is expected; the corresponding argument should be a
character pointer. The normal skipping over space characters is
suppressed in this case; to read the next non-blank character, try
%1s. If a field width is given, the corresponding argument should
refer to a character array, and the indicated number of characters
is read.

e   A floating point number is expected; the next field is converted
f   accordingly and stored through the corresponding argument, that
should be a pointer to a **float**. The input format for floating point
numbers is an optionally signed string of digits possibly containing
a decimal point, followed by an optional exponent field consisting
of an **E** or **e** followed by an optionally signed integer.

[Introduce a string not to be delimited by space characters. The
left bracket is followed by a set of characters and a right bracket;
the characters between the brackets define a set of characters
making up the string. If the first character is not ^, the input
field is all characters until the first character not in the set
between the brackets; if the first character after the left bracket is
^, the input field is all characters until the first character that is
in the remaining set of characters between the brackets. The
corresponding argument must point to a character array.

The conversion characters *d, o* and *x* may be capitalized or preceded by *l*
to indicate that a pointer to **long** rather than to **int** is in the argument list.
Similarly, the conversion characters *e* or *f* may be capitalized or preceded by
the letter *l* to indicate a pointer to **double** rather than to **float**. The conversion
characters *d, o* and *x* may be preceded by *h* to indicate a pointer to **short**
rather than to **int**.

The **scanf** functions return the number of successfully matched and assigned input items. This can be used to decide how many input items were
found. The constant **EOF** is returned upon end of input; note that this is different from 0, that means that no conversion was done; if conversion was intended, it was frustrated by an inappropriate character in the input.

The **scanf** functions return **EOF** on end of input, and a short count for
missing or illegal data items.

---

setbuf — assign buffering to a stream   SETBUF (3S)

#include <stdio.h>

```
setbuf(stream, buf)
FILE *stream;
char *buf;
```

setbuf is used after a stream has been opened but before it is read or
written. It causes the character array **buf** to be used instead of an automatically allocated buffer. If **buf** is the constant pointer **NULL**, input-output will
be completely unbuffered.

A manifest constant **BUFSIZ** tells how big an array is needed:

char buf[BUFSIZ];

A buffer is normally obtained from malloc(3) upon the first getc or putc(3) on the file, except that the standard output is line buffered when directed to a terminal. Other output streams directed to terminals, and the standard error stream stderr are normally not buffered. If the standard output is line buffered, then it is flushed each time data is read from the standard input by read(2).

---

setjmp, longjmp — non-local goto   SETJMP(3)

#include <setjmp.h>

setjmp(env)
jmp_buf env;

longjmp(env, val)
jmp_buf env;

These routines are useful for dealing with errors and interrupts encountered in a low-level subroutine of a program.

setjmp saves its stack environment in env for later use by longjmp. It returns value 0.

longjmp restores the environment saved by the last call of setjmp. It then returns in such a way that execution continues as if the call of setjmp had just returned the value val to the function that invoked setjmp, which must not itself have returned in the interim. All accessible data have values as of the time longjmp was called.

---

stdio — standard buffered input-output package   STDIO(3S)

#include <stdio.h>

FILE *stdin;
FILE *stdout;
FILE *stderr;

The standard input-output library is described in chapter 5.

---

strcat, strncat, strcmp, strncmp, strcpy, strncpy, strlen,   STRING(3)
index, rindex — string operations

char *strcat(s1, s2)
char *s1, *s2;

char *strncat(s1, s2, n)
char *s1, *s2;

strcmp(s1, s2)
char *s1, *s2;

strncmp(s1, s2, n)

```
char *s1, *s2;

char *strcpy(s1, s2)
char *s1, *s2;

char *strncpy(s1, s2, n)
char *s1, *s2;

strlen(s)
char *s;

char *index(s, c)
char *s, c;

char *rindex(s, c)
char *s, c;
```

These functions operate on null-terminated strings. They do not check for overflow of any receiving string.

strcat appends a copy of string s2 to the end of string s1. strncat copies at most n characters. Both return a pointer to the null-terminated result.

strcmp compares its arguments and returns an integer greater than, equal to, or less than 0, according as s1 is lexicographically greater than, equal to, or less than s2. strncmp makes the same comparison but with at most n characters.

strcpy copies string s2 to s1, stopping after the null character has been moved. strncpy copies exactly n characters, truncating or null-padding s2; the target may not be null-terminated if the length of s2 is n or more. Both return s1.

strlen returns the number of non-null characters in s.

index and rindex return pointers to the first and last occurrence respectively of character c in string s, or zero if c does not occur in the string.

---

ungetc — push character back into input stream   UNGETC(3S)

```
#include <stdio.h>

ungetc(c, stream)
FILE *stream;
```

ungetc pushes the character c back on an input stream. That character will be returned by the next getc call on that stream. ungetc returns c.

One character of pushback is guaranteed provided something has been read from the stream and the stream is buffered. Attempts to push EOF are rejected.

fseek(3) erases all memory of pushed back characters.

ungetc returns EOF if the character cannot be pushed back.

Appendix 4
adb Requests

Formatted printing

?*format* Print from *a.out* file according to *format*.
/*format* Print from *core* file according to *format*.
=*format*
              Print the value of *dot*.
?w expr Write expression into *a.out* file.
/w expr Write expression into *core* file.
?l expr Locate expression in *a.out* file.

Breakpoint and program control

:b   Set a breakpoint at *dot*.
:c   Continue running program.
:d   Delete breakpoint.
:k   Kill the program being debugged.
:r   Run *a.out* file under **adb** control.
:s   Run the program a single step at a time.

Printing

$b   Print current breakpoints.
$c   C stack trace.
$e   Print external variables.
$f   Print floating registers.
$m   Print **adb** segment maps.
$q   Exit from **adb**.
$r   Print the general registers.
$s   Specify offset for symbol match.
$v   Print **adb** variables.
$w   Set output line width.

Miscellaneous

!   Call *shell* to read rest of line.
>*name* Assign dot to variable or register *name*.

Format Summary

a   The value of dot.
b   One byte in octal.
c   One byte as a character.
d   One word in decimal.

f	Two words in floating point.
i	Machine instruction.
o	One word in octal.
n	Print a newline.
r	Print a space.
s	A null-terminated character string.
*n*t	Move to next *n*-space tab.
u	One word as unsigned integer.
x	Hexadecimal.
Y	Date.
^	Backup dot.
"..."	Print string.

Expression components

decimal integer	E.g. 256
octal integer	E.g. 0277
hexadecimal integer	E.g. #ff
symbols	E.g. flag _main main.argc
variables	E.g. <b
registers	E.g. <pc <r0
(expression)	Expression grouping.

Binary operators

These operators group from left to right and there is no operator precedence.

+	Add.
−	Subtract.
*	Multiply.
%	Integer division.
&	Bitwise and.
|	Bitwise or.
#	Round up to the next multiple.

Unary operators

~	Not - logical complement.
*	Contents of location in **core** file.
@	Contents of location in **a.out** file.
−	Integer negate.

Appendix 5

ed Requests

312

Addresses

.	The current line.
n	The *n*-th line.
$	The last line of the document.
'*x*	Addresses the line marked with an *x*.
/*e*/	The next line containing *e*.
?*e*?	The previous line containing *e*.
a+*n*	Addresses line ± *n*.
a±	a ± 1.

Appendix 6

sh Requests

Syntax

item:	*word*
	input-output
	name = *value*
simple-command: item	
	simple-command item
command:	*simple-command*
	(*command-list*)
	{ *command-list* }
	for *name* do *command-list* done
	for *name* in *word* ... do *command-list* done
	while *command-list* do *command-list* done
	until *command-list* do *command-list* done
	case *word* in *case-part* ... esac
	if *command-list* then *command-list else-part* fi
pipeline:	*command*
	pipeline | *command*
andor:	*pipeline*
	andor && *pipeline*
	andor || *pipeline*
command-list:	*andor*
	command-list ;
	command-list &
	command-list ; *andor*
	command-list & *andor*
input-output:	> *file*
	< *file*
	>> *word*
	<< *word*
file:	*word*
	& *digit*
	& −
case-part:	*pattern*) *command-list* ;;
pattern:	*word*

pattern | word

else-part: elif command-list then command-list else-part
                    else command-list
                    empty

empty:

word: a sequence of non-blank characters

name: a sequence of letters, digits or underscores
                    starting with a letter

digit: 0 1 2 3 4 5 6 7 8 9

Syntactic characters

|	Pipe symbol.
&&	'andf' symbol.
||	'orf' symbol.
;	Command separator.
;;	Case delimiter.
&	Background commands.
( )	Command grouping.
<	Input redirection.
<<	Input from a here document.
>	Output creation.
>>	Output append.

Patterns

*	Match any character(s) including none.
?	Match any single character.
[...]	Match any of the enclosed characters.

Substitution

${...}	Substitute shell variable.
`...`	Substitute command output.

Quoting conventions

\	Quote the next character.
'...'	Quote the enclosed characters except for '.
"..."	Quote the enclosed characters except for $ ` \ ".

Reserved words

if	then	else	elif	fi
case	in	esac		
for	while	until	do	done
{}				

Appendix 7
troff Requests

Request summary

In the following summary certain abbreviations are used as follows.

F	A font name (see the .ft request).
M	A numerical expression.
N	A numerical expression.
R	A one or two character register name.

.ad *c*	Adjust output lines with mode *c*.
.af *R c*	Assign format to register *R* (*c*=**1, i, I, a, A**).
.am *xx yy*	Append to a macro.
.as *xx string*	Append *string* to string *xx*.
.bd *F N*	Embolden font *F* by *N*−1 units.
.bd S *F N*	Embolden Special Font when current font is *F*.
.bp ±*N*	Eject current page; next page number *N*.
.br	Break.
.c2 *c*	Set nobreak control character to *c*.
.cc *c*	Set control character to *c*.
.ce *N*	Center following *N* input text lines.
.ch *xx N*	Change trap location.
.cs *F N M*	Constant character space (width) mode (font *F*).
.cu *N*	Continuous underline in nroff; like **ul** in troff.
.da *xx*	Divert and append to macro *xx*.
.de *xx yy*	Define or redefine macro *xx;* end at call of *yy*.
.di *xx*	Divert output to macro *xx*.
.ds *xx string*	Define a string *xx* containing *string*.
.dt *N xx*	Set the diversion trap.
.ec *c*	Set escape character.
.el *anything*	Else part of if-else.
.em *xx*	End macro is *xx*.
.eo	Turn off escape character mechanism.
.ev *N*	Environment switched (*push down*).
.ex	Exit from nroff/troff.
.fc *a b*	Set field delimiter *a* and pad character *b*.
.fi	Fill output lines.
.fl	Flush output buffer.
.fp *N F*	Font named *F* mounted on physical position 1≤*N*≤4.
.ft *F*	Change to font *F* = x, xx, or 1-4. Also \fx,\f(xx,\fN.
.hc *c*	Hyphenation indicator character *c*.
.hw *word1* ...	Exception words.
.hy *N*	Hyphenate; *N* = mode.

.ie *c anything* If portion of if-else; has same forms as **if**.
.if *N anything* If expression $N > 0$, accept *anything*.
.if *'string1'string2' anything*
        If *string1* identical to *string2*, accept *anything*.
.if *c anything* If condition *c* true, accept *anything* as input, for multi-line use \{*anything*\}.
.if *!N anything* If expression $N \leqslant 0$, accept *anything*.
.if *!'string1'string2' anything*
        If *string1* not identical to *string2*, accept *anything*.
.if *!c anything* If condition *c* false, accept *anything*.
.ig *yy*   Ignore text till call of *yy*.
.in $\pm N$ Indent.
.it *N xx*   Set an input-line count trap.
.lc *c*   Leader repetition character.
.lg *N*   Ligature mode on if $N>0$.
.ll $\pm N$ Set line length.
.ls *N*   Output $N-1$ *V*s after each text output line.
.lt $\pm N$ Length of title.
.mc *c N*   Set margin character *c* and separation *N*.
.mk *R*   Mark current vertical place in register *R*.
.na   No output line adjusting.
.ne *N*   Need *N* vertical space (V = vertical spacing).
.nf   No filling or adjusting of output lines.
.nh   No hyphenation.
.nm $\pm N\ M\ S\ I$ Number mode on or off, set parameters.
.nn *N*   Do not number next *N* lines.
.nr *R* $\pm N\ M$ Define and set number register *R*; auto-increment by *M*.
.ns   Turn no-space mode on.
.nx *filename* Next file.
.os   Output saved vertical distance.
.pc *c*   Page number character.
.pi *program* Pipe output to *program* (nroff only).
.pl $\pm N$ Page length.
.pm *t*   Print macro names and sizes; if *t* present, print only total of sizes.
.pn $\pm N$ Next page number *N*.
.po $\pm N$ Page offset.
.ps $\pm N$ Point size; also \s$\pm N$.
.rd *prompt* Read insertion.
.rm *xx*   Remove request, macro, or string.
.rn *xx yy*   Rename request, macro, or string *xx* to *yy*.
.rr *R*   Remove register *R*.
.rs   Restore spacing; turn no-space mode off.
.rt $\pm N$ Return *(upward only)* to marked vertical place.
.so *filename* Switch source file *(push down)*.
.sp *N*   Space vertical distance *N in either direction*.
.ss *N*   Space-character size set to *N*/36 em.
.sv *N*   Save vertical distance *N*.
.ta *Nt* ...   Tab settings; *left* type, unless *t* =**R**(right), **C**(centered).
.tc *c*   Tab repetition character.
.ti $\pm N$ Temporary indent.

.tl 'left'center'right'
: Three part title.

.tm *string*
: Print *string* on terminal (UNIX standard message output).

.tr *abcd*....
: Translate *a* to *b*, *c* to *d*, ... on output.

.uf *F*
: Underline font set to *F* (to be switched to by **ul**).

.ul *N*
: Underline (italicize in troff) *N* input lines.

.vs *N*
: Vertical base line spacing (*V*).

.wh *N* xx
: Set location trap; negative is from page bottom.

Escape Sequences, functions and characters

\\
: \ (to prevent or delay the interpretation of \).

\e
: Printable version of the *current* escape character.

\´
: ´ (acute accent); equivalent to \\(**aa**.

\`
: ` (grave accent); equivalent to \\(**ga**.

\-
: − Minus sign in the *current* font.

\.
: Period (dot) (see **de**).

\(space)
: Unpaddable space-size space character.

\0
: Digit width space.

\|
: 1/6 em narrow space character (zero width in nroff).

\^
: 1/12 em half-narrow space character (zero width in nroff).

\&
: Non-printing, zero width character.

\!
: Transparent line indicator.

\"
: Beginning of comment.

\$*N*
: Interpolate argument $1 \leqslant N \leqslant 9$.

\%
: Default optional hyphenation character.

\(*xx*
: Character named *xx*.

*x, *(xx
: Interpolate string *x* or *xx*.

\a
: Non-interpreted leader character.

\b'*abc*...'
: Bracket building function.

\c
: Interrupt text processing.

\d
: Forward (down) 1/2 em vertical motion (1/2 line in nroff).

\f*x*,\f(*xx*,\f*N*
: Change to font named *x* or *xx*, or position *N*.

\h'*N*'
: Local horizontal motion; move right *N* (*negative left*).

\k*x*
: Mark horizontal *input* place in register *x*.

\l'*Nc*'
: Horizontal line drawing function (optionally with *c*).

\L'*Nc*'
: Vertical line drawing function (optionally with *c*).

\n*x*,\n(*xx*
: Interpolate number register *x* or *xx*.

\o'*abc*...'
: Overstrike characters *a*, *b*, *c*, ...

\p
: Break and spread output line.

\r
: Reverse 1 em vertical motion (reverse line in nroff).

\s*N*,\s±*N*
: Point-size change function.

\t
: Non-interpreted horizontal tab.

\u
: Reverse (up) 1/2 em vertical motion (1/2 line in nroff).

\v'*N*'
: Local vertical motion; move down *N* (*negative up*).

\w'*string*'
: Interpolate width of *string*.

\x'*N*'
: Extra line-space function (*negative before, positive after*).

\z*c*
: Print *c* with zero width (without spacing).

\{
: Begin conditional input.

\}
: End conditional input.

\(newline)
: Concealed (ignored) newline.

X
: *X*, any character *not* listed above.

Predefined General Number Registers

%	Current page number.
ct	Character type (set by *width* function).
dl	Width (maximum) of last completed diversion.
dn	Height (vertical size) of last completed diversion.
dw	Current day of the week (1-7).
dy	Current day of the month (1-31).
hp	Current horizontal place on *input* line.
ln	Output line number.
mo	Current month (1-12).
nl	Vertical position of last printed text base-line.
sb	Depth of string below base line (generated by *width* function).
st	Height of string above base line (generated by *width* function).
yr	Last two digits of current year.

Predefined Read-Only Number Registers

.$	Number of arguments available at the current macro level.
.A	Set to 1 in troff, if −a option used; always 1 in nroff.
.H	Available horizontal resolution in basic units.
.T	Set to 1 in nroff, if −T option used; always 0 in troff.
.V	Available vertical resolution in basic units.
.a	Post-line extra line-space most recently utilized using \x'N'.
.c	Number of *lines* read from current input file.
.d	Current vertical place in current diversion; equal to **nl**, if no diversion.
.f	Current font as physical quadrant (1-4).
.h	Text base-line high-water mark on current page or diversion.
.i	Current indent.
.l	Current line length.
.n	Length of text portion on previous output line.
.o	Current page offset.
.p	Current page length.
.s	Current point size.
.t	Distance to the next trap.
.u	Equal to 1 in fill mode and 0 in nofill mode.
.v	Current vertical line spacing.
.w	Width of previous character.
.x	Reserved version-dependent register.
.y	Reserved version-dependent register.
.z	Name of current diversion.

Special characters

Char	Code	Char	Code	Char	Code
'	'	ν	\(*n	~	\(ap
'	`	ξ	\(*c	≠	\(!=
—	\(em	ο	\(*o	→	\(->
-	–	π	\(*p	←	\(<-
-	\(hy	ρ	\(*r	↑	\(ua
-	\-	σ	\(*s	↓	\(da
•	\(bu	ς	\(ts	×	\(mu
□	\(sq	τ	\(*t	÷	\(di
_	\(ru	υ	\(*u	±	\(+-
¼	\(14	φ	\(*f	∪	\(cu
½	\(12	χ	\(*x	∩	\(ca
¾	\(34	ψ	\(*q	⊂	\(sb
fi	\(fi	ω	\(*w	⊃	\(sp
fl	\(fl	Α	\(*A	⊆	\(ib
ff	\(ff	Β	\(*B	⊇	\(ip
ffi	\(Fi	Γ	\(*G	∞	\(if
ffl	\(Fl	Δ	\(*D	∂	\(pd
°	\(de	Ε	\(*E	∇	\(gr
†	\(dg	Ζ	\(*Z	¬	\(no
'	\(fm	Η	\(*Y	∫	\(is
¢	\(ct	Θ	\(*H	∝	\(pt
®	\(rg	Ι	\(*I	∅	\(es
©	\(co	Κ	\(*K	∈	\(mo
+	\(pl	Λ	\(*L	|	\(br
−	\(mi	Μ	\(*M	‡	\(dd
=	\(eq	Ν	\(*N	☞	\(rh
*	\(**	Ξ	\(*C		\(lh
§	\(sc	Ο	\(*O	Ⓐ	\(bs
'	\(aa	Π	\(*P	|	\(or
`	\(ga	Ρ	\(*R	○	\(ci
	\(ul	Σ	\(*S	⌈	\(lt
⁄	\(sl	Τ	\(*T	⌊	\(lb
α	\(*a	Υ	\(*U	⌉	\(rt
β	\(*b	Φ	\(*F	⌋	\(rb
γ	\(*g	Χ	\(*X	{	\(lk
δ	\(*d	Ψ	\(*Q	}	\(rk
ε	\(*e	Ω	\(*W	|	\(bv
ζ	\(*z	√	\(sr	⌊	\(lf
η	\(*y		\(rn	⌋	\(rf
θ	\(*h	≥	\(>=	⌈	\(lc
ι	\(*i	≤	\(<=	⌉	\(rc
κ	\(*k	≡	\(==		
λ	\(*l	≃	\(~=		
μ	\(*m				

Appendix 8
vi Requests

Simple requests

^D	Scroll the window forwards.
^U	Scroll the window backwards.
^F	Move forward a page.
^B	Move backward a page.
return	Move the cursor down.
—	Move the cursor up.
space	Move the cursor right.
backspace	Move the cursor left.
dd	Delete the current line.
i	Insert text before the current character.
o	Insert text after the current line.
p	Put back deleted or yanked text.
x	Delete the current character.
Y	Yank lines into a buffer.
:w *file*	Write out the changes to *file*.
:q	Quit. :q! bypasses checking.
del	Abandon the current request.

Screen and cursor control

H	Move cursor to the home (first) line of the screen.
L	Move cursor to the last line of the screen.
M	Move cursor to the middle of the screen.
hjkl	Move the cursor left, down, up or right respectively.
wbe	Move the cursor forward, back, or to the end of a word.
/.../	Search forwards for the pattern ....
?...?	Search backwards for the pattern ....
z.	Center the screen at the current line.
z cr	Redraw the screen at the current line; cr denotes return.
z *n*.	Use an *n* line window centered on the screen.
%	Move to the next or previous balanced (,), {, or }.
^E	Display one more line at the bottom of the screen.
^L	Redraw the screen.
^Y	Display one more line at the top of the screen.
0	Move the cursor to the start of the line.

Editing requests

A...	Append to the end of the current line (ends with **esc**).
C...	Change the rest of the line (ends with **esc**).
D	Delete the rest of the line.
I...	Insert at the beginning of the current line (ends with **esc**).
J	Join the current line and the next line.
X	Delete the character before the cursor.
cw...	Change the current word (ends with **esc**).
r*x*	Replace the current character with *x*.
~	Change the case (upper/lower) of the current character.
&	Repeat the last :s request.

Using ed requests

ed requests may be used from vi by preceding them with a :.

:sh	Execute a shell.
:!cmd	Execute **cmd** and return to vi.
:r *file*	Read *file*.
:s...	Substitute one string for another.
:g...	Globally search for a string.

Objects

Objects are specified as follows:

c	A single character.
w	The next alphanumeric word.
W	The next non-blank word.
H	The home line (top) of the screen. 3H is 3 lines from the top of the screen.
L	The last line on the screen. 3L is 3 lines from the bottom of the screen.
/.../	The next line containing the pattern ....
)	The end of the current sentence. A sentence ends with a blank line, or one of the characters . ! ? followed by a blank line or two spaces.
(	The start of the current sentence.
}	The end of the current paragraph. A paragraph is defined as ending with a blank line or one of the nroff requests .bp, .IP, .LP, .PP, .QP, .LI, or .P.
{	The start of the current paragraph.
]]	The end of the current section; defined as ending with one of the nroff macros .NH, .SH, .HU, or .H
[[	The start of the current section.

The following requests take one of the objects listed above:

c*x*...	Change up to and including *x* with material terminated by an **esc**.
d*x*	Delete up to and including *x*.

y*x*	Yank the object *x* for use by a subsequent p or P request.
>*x*	Indent by 8 spaces up to and including the line containing *x*.
<*x*	Remove an indent of 8 spaces up to and including the line containing *x*.
!*x cmd*	The text of the object specified is passed as the standard input to cmd. The command is executed and its standard output replaces the object text.

Counts

A number preceding a request is a repeat count with the following exceptions.

new window size	[[ ]] : / ?
scroll amount	^D ^U
line or column number	z G	

Setting options

Each option has a name and is set by one of the forms

    :set *option-namo*
    :set *option-name=value*

and is unset by

    :set no *option-name*

The options are described below with the abbreviation, if any, in parentheses.

autoindent(ai)	Supply program indentation automatically.
autowrite(aw)	Automatic write before :n and !.
ignorecase(ic)	Ignore upper/lower case when searching.
list	Tabs print as ^I.
number(nu)	Lines are displayed prefixed by numbers.
paragraphs(para)	The names of nroff macros that start paragraphs for the } and { requests. Initially set to IPLPPPQPbpP LI.
redraw(re)	Simulate a smart terminal.
sections(sect)	The name of macros that start sections for the [[and]] requests. Initially set to NHSHH HU.
term	The name of the terminal type being used.

Appendix 9
A Macro Library

```
. .                    \" The macro library described in chapter 7.
. .
. .                    \" The first few requests set registers and traps
. .                    \" for general use.  Later requests are grouped by
. .                    \" function and are described in section 7.1.4.
. .                    \" ================================
. .
. .                    \" default ligatures
.lg 0
. .                    \" double spacing for nroff or drafts
.if n .ls 2
. .                    \" vertical line spacing — publisher's style
.ps 10
.vs 12p
. .                    \" line and title lengths
.ll 4.65i
.lt 4.65i
. .                    \" rs register for current indentation
.nr rs 0
.in \n(rs
. .                    \" pd register for inter—paragraph vertical gap
.if n .nr pd 1
.if t .nr pd .4
. .                    \" register hl for half line spacing
.if n .nr hl 1v
.if t .nr hl .5v
. .                    \" register sd for section heading line spacing flag
.nr sd 1
. .                    \" ip register for indented paragraphs
.nr ip 2
. .                    \" fn register for figure numbering
.nr fn 0 1
. .                    \" set traps for page top and bottom
. .                    \" =======================
. .
. .                    \" top of page trap
.wh 0 aa
. .                    \" end of page trap
.if n .wh −5 zz
.if t .wh 9i zz
```

```
..              \" top of page macro
.de aa
.ev 1
.lt 7i
.tl '--"--'
.ll 4.65i
.lt 4.65i
'sp 5
.ps 8
.ft R
.if e .tl '%\h'2m'The UNIX System''\\*(sh'
.if o .tl '\\*(sh''\\*(ct\h'2m'%'
.ev
'sp
.mk
..
..              \" end of page macro
.de zz
'sp
.tl "\\*(pn"
\\.ds pn
'bp
..
..              \" set end of file macro
.em ee
..              \" end of file macro
.de ee
.af % 1
.tm LAST \\n%
..
..              \" two column output for index
.de 2c
.ie \\n(sw \{
.nr sw 0
.in 0
.bp
.ns \}
.el \{
.nr sw 1
.rt
.in |3i \}
..
..
..              \" The requests seen by a user of the library follow
..              \" ===============================
..
.de CH          \" chapter heading     .CH 1 "Introduction"
.}H "Chapter \\$1" "\\$2"
\\.ds sh \\$1
```

```
. .
.de AH          \" appendix heading      .AH 1 "Commands"
.}H "Appendix \\$1" "\\$2"
. .
.de }H          \" internal macro for chapter and appendix headings
.sp 7
\\.ds cf \\$1
\\.ds ct \\$2
\\.ds pn \\n%
.ft H
.ps 24
.sp 24p
.ce 2
\\$1
.sp 2
\\$2
.sp 4
.ft
.ps
.mk
. .
.de SH          \" section heading       .SH 1.1 "History"
.if n .sp 2
\\.ds sh \\$1
.if t .sp 15p
.ne 2
.ps +2
.ft HB
.in \\n(rs
\\$1\\ \\ \\$2
.ps −2
.ft R
.if n .sp
.if t .sp 6p
.NS
. .
.de SS          \" sub section    .SS 6.2.1 "Command names"
.sp \\n(sd
\\.ds sh \\$1
.ne 3
.ft HB
.in \\n(rs
\\$1\\ \\ \\$2
.ft R
.sp 3p
.NS
. .
.de MS          \" minor section .MS "Use of backslash"
.sp \\n(sd
```

```
.ne 2
.ft HI
.in \\n(rs
\\$1
.ft R
.sp 3p
.NS
..
.de NS          \" turn off line space after heading
.it 1 on        \" turn on line spacing unless another heading
.nr sd 0
..
.de on
.nr sd 1
..
.de LP          \" blocked paragraph start      .LP
.sp \\n(pd
.in \\n(rs
.ta 2m
..
.de PP          \" normal paragraph start       .PP
.LΡ
.ti +2m
..
..              \"                              .IP "(a)" 12
.de IP          \" indented paragraph with hanging text
.MP "\\fR\\$1\\fP" "\\$2"
..
.de BU          \" bulletted paragraph    .BU
.MP "\\fR\(bu\\fP" "4"
..
..              \"                              .MP "main()" 12
.de MP          \" indented para with hanging program text
.sp \\n(pd
.ie \\$2 .nr xi \\$2-\\n(ip
.el .nr xi 4
.in \\n(rs+\\n(xi+\\n(ip
.ta \\n(xi
.ti -\\n(xi
.ft H
\&\\$1\t\c
\.if \\w´\\$1´u-\\n(xim .br
.ft R
..
.de XV
.nr hl +.1v
..
.de VX
.nr hl -.1v
```

```
. .
.de HL          \" half line spacing      .HL
.sp \\n(hlu
. .

. .
. .                \" Displays and blocked program text
. .                \" =====================
. .
.de DS          \" display start          .DS
'in +2m
'ta 4m 8m 12m 16m 20m 24m 28m 32m
.HL
'nf
'ne \\$1

. .
.de DE          \" end display            .DE
.HL
.fi
.in −2m
.ft R

. .
.de TS          \" tbl start              .TS
.HL
.DS

. .
.de TE          \" tbl end                .TE
.DE
.HL

. .
.de EX          \" start of example     .EX 24
.ft H
.fl
.ss 20
'DS \\$1

. .
.de XE          \" end example            .XE
.DE
.ss 12
.ft R

. .
.de RS          \" relative section start  .RS
.nr rs +2

. .
.de RE          \" relative section end   .RE
.nr rs −2

. .
.de RU          \" horizontal rule              .RU
.br
\l'4.65i−4'
```

```
. .
.de FX              \" figure in the text      .FX 24
'EX \\$1
'RU
. .
.de XF              \" end of figure in text   .XF
'RU
.XE
. .
.de FG              \" inclusion of figure      .FG lock.c 13
.FX \\$2
.so figs/\\$1
.XF
. .
.de FC              \" caption of a figure      .FC 6.3 "Create a lock file"
.ft B
.ce
Figure \\$1\ \ \\$2
 ft R
.sp
.NS
. .
.de CN              \" command text                    .CN "ls"
\&\fH\\$1\fR
. .
.de DN              \" definition in text              .DN "mode"
\&\fI\\$1\fR
. .
.de SN              \" symbol (character) name in text      .SN "NEWLINE"
\&\fH\\$1\fR
. .
.de HI              \" sub section heading font        .HI "heading"
\&\f(HI\\$1\fP
. .
.de IX              \" index macro
.tm \\$1 \\$2 \\$3 \\$4 \\$5 \\$6 \\$7    \\n%
. .
.de CX              \" commutative index
.IX "\\$1," "\\$2"
.IX "\\$2," "\\$1"
. .
. .                 \" String definitions
. .                 \" ==========
.if \n(mo-0 .ds MO January
.if \n(mo-1 .ds MO February
.if \n(mo-2 .ds MO March
.if \n(mo-3 .ds MO April
.if \n(mo-4 .ds MO May
.if \n(mo-5 .ds MO June
```

```
.if \n(mo-6 .ds MO July
.if \n(mo-7 .ds MO August
.if \n(mo-8 .ds MO September
.if \n(mo-9 .ds MO October
.if \n(mo-10 .ds MO November
.if \n(mo-11 .ds MO December
..                               \" D       .
.ds D \&.
..                               \" DD      ..
.ds DD .\|.
..                               \" ZZ      ...
.ds ZZ \&.\|.\|.
..                               \" ST      *
.ds ST \s+1\(**\s-1
..                               \" VT      |
.ds VT \|\(or\|
..                               \" AP      >>
.ds AP >\h'-.2m'>
..                               \" HE      <<
.ds HE <\h'-.2m'<
..                               \" TW      ~
.ds TW \v'.6m'\s+4~\s0\v'-.6m'
..                               \" CT      ^
.ds CT \v'.6m'\s+4^\s0\v'-.6m'
..                               \" AT      @
.ds AT \v'-.2m'@\v'.2m'
                                 \" T       circled T for tab
..

..
.ds T \|\h'.5n'\v'-.2n'\s7\zT\s0\s12\v'.2n'\h'-.5n'\(ci\|\s0
..

..                                 \" subscripts
.ds 0 \v'.25m'\s-40\s0\v'-.25m'
.ds 1 \v'.25m'\s-41\s0\v'-.25m'
.ds 2 \v'.25m'\s-42\s0\v'-.25m'
.ds 3 \v'.25m'\s-43\s0\v'-.25m'
.ds n \v'.25m'\s-4n\s0\v'-.25m'
```

Appendix 10

The ms Macro Library

This package of nroff and troff macro definitions provides a canned formatting facility for technical papers in various formats. When producing 2-column output on a terminal, filter the output through col(1).

The macro requests are defined below. Many nroff and troff requests are unsafe in conjunction with this package, however these requests may be used with impunity after the first .PP:

.bp	Begin new page.
.nf	
.br	Break output line here.
.sp n	Insert n spacing lines
.ls n	Line spacing. n=1 single, n=2 double space.
.na	No alignment of right margin.

Output of the eqn, neqn, refer, and tbl(1) preprocessors for equations and tables is acceptable as input.

Request summary

Request	Initial Value	Cause Break	Explanation
.1C	yes	yes	One column format on a new page.
.2C	no	yes	Two column format.
.AB	no	yes	Begin abstract.
.AE	-	yes	End abstract.
.AI	no	yes	Author's institution follows. Suppressed in TM.
.AT	no	yes	Print 'Attached' and turn off line filling.
.AU *x y*	no	yes	Author's name follows. x is location and extension, ignored except in TM.
.B *x*	no	no	Print *x* in boldface; if no argument switch to boldface.
.B1	no	yes	Begin text to be enclosed in a box.
.B2	no	yes	End text to be boxed, print it.
.BT	date	no	Bottom title, automatically invoked at foot of page. May be redefined.
.BX *x*	no	no	Print *x* in a box.
.CS *x...*	-	yes	Cover sheet info if TM format, suppressed otherwise. Arguments are number of text pages, other pages, total pages, figures, tables, references.
.CT	no	yes	Print 'Copies to' and enter no-fill mode.
.DA *x*	nroff	no	'Date line' at bottom of page is x. Default is today.
.DE	-	yes	End displayed text. Implies .KE.

331

.DS *x*	no	yes	Start of displayed text, to appear verbatim line-by-line. x=I for indented display (default), x=L for left-justified on the page, x=C for centered, x=B for make left-justified block, then center whole block. Implies .KS.
.EG	no	-	Print document in BTL format for 'Engineer's Notes.' Must be first.
.EN	-	yes	Space after equation produced by eqn or neqn.
.EQ *x y*	-	yes	Precede equation; break out and add space. Equation number is y. The optional argument *x* may be I to indent equation (default), L to left-adjust the equation, or C to center the equation.
.FE	-	yes	End footnote.
.FS	no	no	Start footnote. The note will be moved to the bottom of the page.
.HO	-	no	'Bell Laboratories, Holmdel, New Jersey 07733'.
.I *x*	no	no	Italicize *x*; if *x* missing, italic text follows.
.IH	no	no	'Bell Laboratories, Naperville, Illinois 60540'
.IM	no	no	Print document in BTL format for an internal memorandum. Must be first.
.IP *x y*	no	yes	Start indented paragraph, with hanging tag x. Indentation is y ens (default 5).
.KE	-	yes	End keep. Put kept text on next page if not enough room.
.KF	no	yes	Start floating keep. If the kept text must be moved to the next page, float later text back to this page.
.KS	no	yes	Start keeping following text.
.LG	no	no	Make letters larger.
.LP	yes	yes	Start left-blocked paragraph.
.MF	-	-	Print document in BTL format for 'Memorandum for File.' Must be first.
.MH	-	no	'Bell Laboratories, Murray Hill, New Jersey 07974'.
.MR	-	-	Print document in BTL format for 'Memorandum for Record.' Must be first.
.ND *date*	troff	no	Use date supplied (if any) only in special BTL format positions; omit from page footer.
.NH *n*	-	yes	Same as .SH, with section number supplied automatically. Numbers are multilevel, like 1.2.3, where n tells what level is wanted (default is 1).
.NL	yes	no	Make letters normal size.
.OK	-	yes	'Other keywords' for TM cover sheet follow.
.PP	no	yes	Begin paragraph. First line indented.
.PT	pg #	-	Page title, automatically invoked at top of page. May be redefined.
.PY	-	no	'Bell Laboratories, Piscataway, New Jersey 08854'
.QE	-	yes	End quoted (indented and shorter) material.
.QP	-	yes	Begin single paragraph which is indented and shorter.
.QS	-	yes	Begin quoted (indented and shorter) material.

.R	yes	no	Roman text follows.
.RE	-	yes	End relative indent level.
.RP	no	-	Cover sheet and first page for released paper. Must precede other requests.
.RS	-	yes	Start level of relative indentation. Following .IP's are measured from current indentation.
.SG x	no	yes	Insert signature(s) of author(s), ignored except in TM. x is the reference line (initials of author and typist).
.SH	-	yes	Section head follows, font automatically bold.
.SM	no	no	Make letters smaller.
.TA x...	5...	no	Set tabs in ens. Default is 5 10 15 ...
.TE	-	yes	End table.
.TH	-	yes	End heading section of table.
.TL	no	yes	Title follows.
.TM x...	no	-	Print document in BTL technical memorandum format. Arguments are TM number, (quoted list of) case number(s), and file number. Must precede other requests.
.TR x	-	-	Print in BTL technical report format; report number is x. Must be first.
.TS x	-	yes	Begin table, if x is H table has repeated heading.
.UL x	-	no	Underline argument (even in troff).
.UX	-	no	'UNIX'; first time used, add footnote 'UNIX is a trademark of Bell Laboratories.'
.WH	-	no	'Bell Laboratories, Whippany, New Jersey 07981'.

Appendix 11
The ASCII Character Set

Octal values							
000 nul	001 soh	002 stx	003 etx	004 eot	005 enq	006 ack	007 bel
010 bs	011 ht	012 nl	013 vt	014 np	015 cr	016 so	017 si
020 dle	021 dc1	022 dc2	023 dc3	024 dc4	025 nak	026 syn	027 etb
030 can	031 em	032 sub	033 esc	034 fs	035 gs	036 rs	037 us
040 sp	041 !	042 "	043 #	044 $	045 %	046 &	047 ´
050 (	051)	052 *	053 +	054 ,	055 −	056 .	057 /
060 0	061 1	062 2	063 3	064 4	065 5	066 6	067 7
070 8	071 9	072 :	073 ;	074 <	075 =	076 >	077 ?
100 @	101 A	102 B	103 C	104 D	105 E	106 F	107 G
110 H	111 I	112 J	113 K	114 L	115 M	116 N	117 O
120 P	121 Q	122 R	123 S	124 T	125 U	126 V	127 W
130 X	131 Y	132 Z	133 [	134	135]	136 ^	137 _
140 `	141 a	142 b	143 c	144 d	145 e	146 f	147 g
150 h	151 i	152 j	153 k	154 l	155 m	156 n	157 o
160 p	161 q	162 r	163 s	164 t	165 u	166 v	167 w
170 x	171 y	172 z	173 {	174 |	175 }	176 ~	177 del

Hexadecimal							
00 nul	01 soh	02 stx	03 etx	04 eot	05 enq	06 ack	07 bel
08 bs	09 ht	0a nl	0b vt	0c np	0d cr	0e so	0f si
10 dle	11 dc1	12 dc2	13 dc3	14 dc4	15 nak	16 syn	17 etb
18 can	19 em	1a sub	1b esc	1c fs	1d gs	1e rs	1f us
20 sp	21 !	22 "	23 #	24 $	25 %	26 &	27 ´
28 (	29)	2a *	2b +	2c ,	2d −	2e .	2f /
30 0	31 1	32 2	33 3	34 4	35 5	36 6	37 7
38 8	39 9	3a :	3b ;	3c <	3d =	3e >	3f ?
40 @	41 A	42 B	43 C	44 D	45 E	46 F	47 G
48 H	49 I	4a J	4b K	4c L	4d M	4e N	4f O
50 P	51 Q	52 R	53 S	54 T	55 U	56 V	57 W
58 X	59 Y	5a Z	5b [	5c	5d]	5e ^	5f _
60 `	61 a	62 b	63 c	64 d	65 e	66 f	67 g
68 h	69 i	6a j	6b k	6c l	6d m	6e n	6f o
70 p	71 q	72 r	73 s	74 t	75 u	76 v	77 w
78 x	79 y	7a z	7b {	7c |	7d }	7e ~	7f del

Bibliography

Aho, A. V., Ullman, J. D. 1977. *Principles of Compiler Design.* Addison Wesley: Reading, Mass.

Book, R. V. (Ed.). 1980. *Formal Language Theory. Perspectives and Open Problems.* 325-44. Academic Press: New York.

Bourne, S. R. 1978. "UNIX Time-Sharing System: The UNIX Shell". *Bell Sys. Tech. J.* **57(6)** 1971-90.

Crisman, P. A. (Ed.). 1965. *The Compatible Time-Sharing System.* M.I.T. Press: Cambridge, Mass.

Deutsch, L. P., Lampson, B. W. 1965. *SDS$_n$ 930 time-sharing system preliminary reference manual.* Doc. 30.10.10, Project GENIE$_n$. Univ. Cal. at Berkeley.

Deutsch, L. P., Lampson, B. W. 1967. "An online editor," *Comm. Assoc. Comp. Mach.* **10(12)**, 793-9, 803.

Dolotta, T. A., Mashey, J. R. 1976. "An Introduction to the Programmer's Workbench," *Proc. 2nd Int. Conf. on Software Engineering.* 164-8.

Dolotta, T. A., Haight, R. C., Mashey, J. R. 1978. "UNIX Time-Sharing System: The Programmer's Workbench," *Bell Sys. Tech. J.* **57(6)** 2177-2200.

Feiertag, R. J., Organick, E. I. 1971. "The Multics input-output system" *Proc. Third Symposium on Operating Systems Principles.* 35-41.

Hartley, D. F. (Ed.). 1968. *The Cambridge Multiple Access System — Users Reference Manual.* University Mathematical Laboratory: Cambridge, England.

Johnson, S. C. 1975. "Yacc — Yet Another Compiler-Compiler. Comp. Sci. Tech. Rep. No. 32." Bell Laboratories: Murray Hill, New Jersey.

Johnson, S. C. 1978. "Lint, a C Program Checker. Comp. Sci. Tech. Rep. No. 65." Bell Laboratories: Murray Hill, New Jersey.

Johnson, S. C., Ritchie, D. M. 1978. "UNIX Time-Sharing System: Portability of C Programs and the UNIX System," *Bell Sys. Tech. J.* **57(6)** 2021-2048.

Kernighan, B. W., Cherry, L. L. 1977. "A System for Typesetting Mathematics," *Comm. Assoc. Comp. Mach.* **18** 151-7

Kernighan,B. W., Ritchie, D. M. 1978. *The C Programming Language.* Prentice-Hall: Englewood Cliffs, New Jersey.

Kernighan, B. W., Lesk, M. E., Ossanna, J. F. 1978. "UNIX Time-Sharing System: Document Preparation," *Bell Sys. Tech. J.* **57(6)** 2115-35.

Lesk, M. E. 1975. "Lex — A Lexical Analyzer Generator. Comp. Sci. Tech. Rep. No. 39." Bell Laboratories: Murray Hill, New Jersey.

Lesk, M. E. 1977. "Typing Documents on UNIX and GCOS: The —ms Macros for Troff." Bell Laboratories: Murray Hill, New Jersey.

Lycklama, H., 1978. "UNIX Time-Sharing System: UNIX on a Microprocessor," *Bell Sys. Tech. J.* **57(6)** 2087-2101.

McMahon, L. E., Cherry, L. L., Morris, R. 1978. "UNIX Time-Sharing System: Statistical Text Processing," *Bell Sys. Tech. J.* **57(6)** 2137-54.

Ossanna, J. F. 1976. "NROFF/TROFF User's Manual. Comp. Sci. Tech. Rep. No. 54." Bell Laboratories: Murray Hill, New Jersey.

Richards, M. 1969. "BCPL: A Tool for Compiler Writing and Systems Programming," *Proc. AFIPS SJCC.* **34**

Ritchie, D. M., Johnson, S. C., Lesk, M. E., Kernighan, B. W. 1978. "UNIX Time-Sharing System: The C Programming Language," *Bell Sys. Tech. J..* **57(6)**, 1991-2019

Ritchie, D. M. 1978. "UNIX Time-Sharing System: A Retrospective," *Bell Sys. Tech. J.* **57(6)** 1947-69.

Ritchie, D. M., Thompson, K. 1978. "The UNIX Time-Sharing System," *Bell Sys. Tech. J.* **57(6)** 1905-29.

Ritchie, D. M. 1980. *The Evolution of the Unix Time-sharing System.* Language Design and Programming Methodology: Lecture Notes in Computer Science 79, 25-35, Springer-Verlag: New York.

Thompson, K. 1975. *The UNIX Command Language. Structured Programming—Infotech State of the Art Report* 375-384. Nicholson House, Maidenhead, Berkshire, England: Infotech International Ltd.

Thompson, K., Ritchie, D. M. 1975. *UNIX Programmer's Manual. Sixth Edition.* Bell Laboratories: Murray Hill, New Jersey.

Thompson, K. 1978. "UNIX Time-Sharing System: UNIX Implementation," *Bell Sys. Tech. J.* **57(6)** 1931-46.

Thompson, K., Ritchie, D. M. 1978. *UNIX Programmer's Manual. Seventh Edition.* Bell Laboratories: Murray Hill, New Jersey.

Index

337